FEB 92

Ambiguous Lives

Ambiguous Lives

Free Women of Color
in Rural Georgia,
1789–1879

Adele Logan Alexander

The University of Arkansas Press
Fayetteville 1991

95 94 93 92 91   5 4 3 2 1

*This book was designed by Ch. H. Russell
using the Bembo and Zephyr Script typefaces.*

The paper used in this publication meets the minimum requirements of the
American National Standard for Permanence of Paper for Printed Library
Materials Z39.48-1984. ∞

Library of Congress Cataloging-in-Publication Data

Alexander, Adele Logan, 1938–
    Ambiguous lives: free women of color in rural Georgia, 1789–1879/Adele
Logan Alexander.
            p.   cm.
    Includes bibliographical references and index.
    ISBN 1-55728-214-5 (alk. paper).
    1. Afro-American women—Georgia—History.
    2. Afro-American women—Georgia—Hancock County—History.
    3. Georgia—History—1775–1865—Biography.
    4. Georgia—History—1865– —Biography.
    5. Hunt family.
    6. Hancock County (Ga.)—Biography.
    I. Title.
    E185.93.G4A45   1991
    975.8´00496073022—dc20
    [B]   91-10151
                                                                                                              CIP

Frontispiece:
Amanda America Dickson. *Courtesy of Virginia Kent Anderson Leslie.*
Louisa Horton. *Courtesy of Arthur Silvers.*
Adella Hunt Logan. *Courtesy of Herndon Home, Atlanta, Ga.*

For my family, with abiding love:
Clifford, Elizabeth, and Mark Alexander,
and Wenonah Bond Logan.

Contents

Illustrations

Charts

Maps

Plates

Acknowledgments

More than a study about women of color, more even than a work about the elusive nature of freedom, this is the story of a Southern family. My thanks go first, therefore, to members of the Logan family who bound me irrevocably to Adella Hunt Logan by bestowing her name on me. They also offered tantalizing shreds of information about the Hunts and the Sayres from further back in my childhood than I can clearly remember. Much later I found other members of the extended Hunt family whom I had never known before, and they have shared their own recollections and records. Special thanks go to the wise and caring senior members of this group: the late Mamie McLendon Thomas and Katherine Neal Hunt. In addition, Rowena Hunt Bracken, Diane Milam Exum, George Gardiner, Edith Ingram Grant, Charity, Charles, Katie Bell, and La Notre Hunt, Ann Ingram, Wanda Hunt McLean, Houser Miller, Arthur Silvers, Linda Snead, Romie Turner, and so many others have my enduring appreciation.

Virginia Shadran and the staff at the Georgia Department of Archives and History helped me through the rich resources of those state archives. Dovie Patrick in Special Collections at Atlanta University's Woodruff Library answered endless questions and provided valuable documentation from that institution's records. Herman Mason assisted me at the Fulton County public library and introduced me to unexpected materials on African-American genealogy in Georgia. Donnie Bellamy offered information from both his own research and the records of Fort Valley State College, Daniel Williams helped me at Tuskegee Institute, and Carole Merritt gave wise counsel and unearthed previously unknown photographs from the collection at the Herndon Home in Atlanta.

Early in my research, the late James Bonner, Middle Georgia's most eminent historian, provided an invaluable framework of reference for this work. John Rozier and Forrest Shivers shared decades of accumulated wisdom and research about the history of Hancock County; Lois W. Lane offered more help than I ever expected concerning people of color in Milledgeville; Bolton Lunceford gave me her refreshing insights during a difficult research trip. Kent Leslie contributed to this work in many significant ways. She shared information about the remarkable Dickson family, took photographs, and was an enthusiastic and informed companion during my travels throughout Middle Georgia.

Rosalyn Terborg-Penn must take at least some credit or blame for enticing me into African-American women's history in the first place, and I always feel her supportive presence over my shoulder. My thanks also go to Arnold Taylor, who raised questions that had never occurred to me and that moved some parts of this work down new and worthwhile avenues. Eileen Boris and Asunción Lavrin both read this study in its earliest forms, and their keen observations and critical comments helped so much when my objective perspective had all but disappeared. Edna Medford read through the manuscript with care as it neared completion and showed me inconsistencies, redundancies, and other problems that my own eye had missed. But Joseph P. Reidy, more than all others, helped at every step. He saw many drafts as the work evolved into a thesis at Howard University, and then agreed to begin all over when I started the final manuscript. He provided me with access to the extensive files of the Freedmen and Southern Society Research Project at the University of Maryland. His knowledge of the period and the region, and his sensitivity to the central questions of race and gender have kept this work on track and saved me from numerous theoretical and factual pitfalls. My gratitude to him is immeasurable. For the remaining problems and shortcomings, I alone am responsible.

Willard Gatewood, whose work about people of African descent is so thoroughgoing and insightful, read the original thesis. He urged me to consider the University of Arkansas Press and encouraged them, in turn, to consider me. I greatly appreciate that guidance. At the press itself I had the support of Miller Williams and the valuable editorial assistance of the sharp-eyed and perceptive Sandra Frierson.

As for the members of my family who have tolerated me so cheerfully during this period, I have nothing but thanks for their devotion. In particular, I appreciate my mother, Wenonah Bond Logan, who contributed so much with her interest and observations. My son Mark boosted my spirits with timely suggestions, praise, and encouragement, and his Amy, who recently joined our family, has brought joy to our lives. Elizabeth has not only offered a daughter's incomparable moral support but supplemented it with the intellectual stimulation and insights provided by her own academic and creative achievements and interests. Finally, and ever important, there is my husband, my dear friend Clifford, from whom all good things flow. His enthusiastic readings, love, support, advice, and unflagging good spirits have carried me through.

Ambiguous Lives

Prologue: Heredity

Her soul was beautiful, wherefore she kept it veiled
in lightly-laced humility and fear, out of which
peered anxiously and anon the white and blue and
pale gold of her face—beautiful as daybreak or as
the laughter of a child.

W. E. B. Du Bois
"The Princess of the Hither Isles"
Darkwater: Voices from Within the Veil, *1920*

Shortly after eight o'clock in the evening on Wednesday, May 26, 1897, Adella Hunt Logan, an intense woman in her mid-thirties whose rigid posture and "ivory cast" skin inevitably drew attention to her presence, rose from one of the bare wooden pews and approached the podium to address a large gathering in Atlanta University's Ware Memorial Chapel. The new dark-panelled hall, illuminated by gas-lit chandeliers, had been named for the late Edmund Asa Ware, the school's first president and one of Logan's mentors. She taught at Tuskegee Institute in Alabama but had attended Atlanta University nearly two decades earlier. In repose, Logan's face showed a near classic beauty, but an unfashionable ardor often glinted in her eyes. Elegant yet conservative in dress, the broad hands and blunt fingers that clasped the sheaf of papers she carried belied her otherwise fragile stature. As always, she had twisted and piled her long hair into a heavy coronet atop her head, but stubborn tendrils sprang loose and softened her austere demeanor.[1]

The conference had been challenging. Earlier that day, Logan and others had listened attentively to lectures on health and welfare concerns in the African-American community and engaged in "animated discussion" about the problems of high infant mortality and the importance of early childhood education. Participants had assembled in Atlanta from around the nation to attend the university's Conference for the Study of Problems Concerning Negro City Life. Under the stewardship of W. E. B. Du Bois, reports from these conferences would soon become renowned as valued sociological surveys on various aspects of "Negro life" in the United States. The women and men who attended the 1897 conference included African-American teachers, ministers, physicians, lawyers, and other professionals from Fisk, Lincoln, Howard, and Meharry as well as Atlanta University and its associated schools.[2]

She spoke that evening about prenatal and hereditary influences. "How rarely in the every day ordering of our lives," she asked, "do we give any attention to that silent but powerful thing known as heredity?" "To be sure, the grandfather sowed wild oats," she continued, "and it is charged that a great-great-grandmother was born out of wedlock, but that was generations ago . . . it may be so far back indeed, that no living person remembers having heard of the peculiarity." Logan did not attribute her illustrative examples to personal history, but the subject engaged her emotions more thoroughly than abstract intellectual discussion would have evoked. "In respect to time, the force of heredity cannot be checked by a generation," she stated, "we are today reaping what was sown, not by our fathers alone, but by their fathers and grandfathers . . . 'unto the third and fourth generation of them' was the decree thundered down from Mt. Sinai by the voice of Almighty God!"[3]

Why would Logan choose to talk about heredity, and why did the topic so rouse her passions? Did her intensity betray a personal identification? Could the example of "the boy [who] takes his large nose from his grandmother, the small mouth from his father," refer to her own family's physiognomy? Did her grandfathers "sow wild oats," or was her great-great-grandmother "born out of wedlock"? Were these fictive illustrations, or did they reveal her "family skeleton[s] in the closet"?[4]

In truth, she pulled those examples straight from her own family. Adella's African-American and Cherokee grandmother was the genetic donor of the "large nose," and her Anglo-American father the source of the "small mouth." At least one of her grandfathers did "sow wild oats," and children born out of wedlock may have been more the rule than the exception among her antecedents and for many others. Her family closets contained their share of skeletons, yet her oratory also reflected the broader applicability of her thesis. She believed that heredity and family background directed people's lives and controlled their destinies. Neither the members of her attentive audience at Atlanta University nor anyone else, she argued, could extricate themselves from their past to "purify and change the blood that coursed in their veins," even if they wanted or tried to do so. They remained captives of history.[5]

Logan's lecture, delivered to a gathering of distinguished African-American leaders—often described by Du Bois as the "talented tenth"—at the end of the nineteenth century, provides a window through which to view her life and the lives of others much like her. Her exhortations about heredity show one way leading back into the shadowy past of those Americans whose antecedents were both black and white. On another occasion Logan stated, "I was not born a slave, nor in a log cabin."[6] That firm assertion reflected the fact that she belonged to a group that included some of the children and grandchildren of biracial unions in the antebellum South who never were slaves. Several generations of Adella Hunt Logan's family—the Hunts of Hancock County—traversed those obscure paths in rural Georgia, and others attending the conference at Atlanta University had similar origins.

In 1897 those well-educated delegates comprised a representative portion of the African-American privileged class. Following emancipation, educational opportunities for people of color increased, but, nonetheless, all too few could acquire the academic grounding they needed to compete successfully in a hostile world. Segregation denied them access to most institutions, and for many women and men of color, financial strictures also prohibited extended time in the classroom. A handful of more fortunate African-Americans, including Adella Hunt Logan and most of her brothers and sisters, did manage to attend college. While many people of color remained mired in grinding poverty little removed from their economic condition under slavery, a few others, though rarely affluent, became more financially secure. Even during the antebellum years members of this more privileged class sometimes had interacted with whites as well as blacks. They had no more inborn talent, intelligence, or ability than others of their race, but they had greater social and economic opportunities and made the best of them. After the Civil War, they often served as educators, business men and women, physicians, and legal practitioners, and they also dealt with the white-controlled power structure as best they could to benefit the African-American community in its entirety.

The Hunts knew well how to interact with white people because for many decades they had lived with Anglo-Americans, many of whom were members of their own family. The preponderance of those antecedents was so great in the Hunt family that Adella and her brothers and sisters were people of color who looked indisputably white. But in spite of opportunities and perhaps even temptations to do otherwise, she and all of her siblings, save one, elected to remain and work among African-Americans in the rural South. Logan and her forebears lived through harsh times, and their mixed racial heritage brought them some advantages but also frequently created serious conflicts and complications.

Adella Hunt Logan, her brothers and sisters, and their parents and grandparents before them had never been slaves in the plantation-dominated Georgia black belt, where free people of color were a very small and anomalous minority. With few exceptions, slaves were black and all blacks were enslaved in that region. In the years after emancipation, she matured into a fiercely independent person who worked to ameliorate the debilitating social and physical conditions in which most rural black people lived. She also developed a finely honed sense of political awareness and struggled to achieve political rights for African-American women in a place and at a time when most people considered them unworthy and unprepared for equality, both because they were not white and because they were not men. Logan herself only provides a point of departure from which to examine a whole group of women of color and their families who shared similar backgrounds and experiences. Observing her and others who preceded and surrounded her reveals the complex and often unfamiliar contours of their lives.

Stating flatly that most writings in American history have dealt with powerful white men and neglected the poor, the powerless, the nonwhite, and women is simplistic, but nonetheless true. For the most part, insightful studies about the people who have been outsiders to power are a product of the fairly recent past. But if nonwhites and most women have been overlooked far too often, how much more true has this been for women of color? What Du Bois sometimes called these "voices from within the veil" have been heard only infrequently and indistinctly.[7] With some notable exceptions, the women who appear in historical literature are white, and African-Americans most often have been portrayed as black, impoverished, male, and—before emancipation—enslaved. Little has been written about women of color, about African-Americans who were neither truly "black" nor poor, and especially about people of color who were both female and free. The challenge is to move beyond a nonarticulated image of people of color—to break apart that undifferentiated mass, and then to reconstruct a more accurate, vivid, and finely focused picture of the past.

Historians often write about the "heroes" whose stories are most easily accessible and study groups that can be neatly categorized. By and large, the slave population of the South, though hardly monolithic, was at least fairly well defined by law, economics, social custom, and race. Free people of color, on the other hand, have frustrated scholars. They are elusive—hard to find, identify, and define. Information about them has been difficult to obtain because of legal, economic, and social marginality, some illiteracy, and the frequent need to conceal or camouflage all traces of their lives. To ensure their own security and survival, free women and men of color often operated circuitously and through indirection.

Although such people as the Hunts of Hancock County, Georgia, were not slaves, doubts still remain as to the extent of their freedom, its source, and even its legitimacy. These so-called "free" men and women of color frequently dwelt in an ill-defined penumbra between bondage and freedom. Subject always to prevailing racism, most were neither affluent nor impoverished, neither helpless nor empowered. Some of the children of interracial unions were not clearly identifiable as either black or white. Lacking careful study, free people of color might appear to be more easily definable by what they were not than by what they were. They led complex and ambiguous lives, subject to dislocation and frequent metamorphoses.

Free men and women of color in most of the rural plantation South rarely formed a large enough mass for their behavior to be statistically analyzed and determined. Theirs was an atypical splinter group—a small intermediary caste within a social, economic, and legal system deliberately structured to include only the polar extremes of those who were black and enslaved, or white and free. This subcaste of the African-American community was admittedly small, but it was far more than an insignificant aberration. Free people of color—especially women, who so often are neglected—are worthy of serious attention. Broader generalizations and lessons about our society can be drawn from their lives and experiences to extricate them from their seemingly isolated eddies and sweep them into the main currents of American life. The rationale for this exploration and scrutiny is at least threefold.

First, though members of this small and amorphous substratum in American society cannot be easily categorized, they never existed in a vacuum. Rather than sharing nothing with and absorbing nothing from others, free men and women of color incorporated many elements from the people around them and reflected them in many ways. Although plantation masters and their slaves were mutually interdependent on many levels and the family was the basic unit of social organization for both blacks and whites, their lives resembled one another's in few ways. Similarly, the social, productive, and religious lives of slave women differed in almost every respect from those of their white mistresses. The expressive culture of slavery and that of the white South had some similarities, but far more areas of distinct difference. On the other hand, free and multiracial families like the Hunts occupied a social, genetic, political, and cultural middle ground. They drew their allegiances, their characteristics, their strengths, and their weaknesses from both black and white: from those held in bondage, and from women and men of the slaveholding class. Adding further complexity to their heritage, like a number of other families from the Southern frontier, the Hunts had Native American antecedents as well.

Second, people who have lived outside the larger, more identifiable and clearly stratified segments of American society are important in and of themselves because they illustrate the country's endless diversity. An uncomplicated social structure constituted only of black and white, rich and poor, free and slave can be more easily defined and understood. However, the richness of texture, the gradations and subtleties of shade and color, the intricacies of experience that constitute the tangled skein of history should not be sacrificed for the sake of facile categorization.

The noted sociologist, philosopher, and historian W. E. B. Du Bois, who knew the Hunts well, effectively gave another compound reason that justifies interest in the small segment of society whom they represented. If everyone in Adella Hunt Logan's generation of the Hunt family looked white, Du Bois queried, if only one of their many antecedents was "black," and if life in the nineteenth-century South routinely heaped pain and humiliation on people of color, as it surely did, why then did the Hunts and other similar "voluntary Negroes" choose to remain a part of the African-American community? He asked rhetorically why Adella's younger brother Henry never decided to become the white man that his skin color and features so obviously declared him, when "thousands of men and women like him have done so." Du Bois articulated a cogent response for those who wondered why Henry Hunt "chose to be a Negro, because after all there was involved so evidently the element of deliberate choice." Du Bois understood the ludicrous social and political ramifications of race as well as any American of his time. "From long teaching and deeply planted conviction," he explained with obvious distaste, "the overwhelming opinion of white Americans is that the fact of one black ancestor in eight or sixteen makes [a] tremendous difference of identity, of treatment and opportunity . . . before such a paradox the whole natural resentment of a normal man arises in protest."[8]

As paradoxical as that might be, and however much the resentment of any "normal man" should justifiably "arise in protest," Du Bois spoke honestly. Yet, even as he pinpointed and exposed the prevailing prejudices of white Americans, he had little doubt that the choice was clear for the Hunts. They and others chose to remain and identify with the darker race for two predominant reasons: responsibility and love, both providing secure anchors in a hostile world. Du Bois understood Henry Hunt and other similar men and women. He knew that "to take a stand in America as anything but a Negro would have made him supremely unhappy, because here was an opportunity for battle, and battle on the highest plane." The Hunt family and some other more advantaged people of color had a sense of mission—a dedication to work with and for those who most needed their support. Equally important, Du Bois also recognized and respected the indissolubility of kinship ties and the allegiance of heredity—so significant to Adella—which bound such families together. "After all," he concluded, "life is primarily family and friends [and] one cannot lightly cast off this enveloping and intriguing bond of love and affection and seek to create a new place in a strange world."[9]

The Hunts and similar families who had been free long before emancipation emerged from the centuries when slavery dominated the American South with a little education, some opportunities, and a few other material advantages. Their lives provide a fertile but scarcely cultivated ground for study. Many theories can be postulated, but nothing can supplant Du Bois's clear-headed vision. He recognized and appreciated both their sense of responsibility to the African-American community in its entirety and the importance of the strong and enduring bonds of kinship.

The Hunts' story remains rooted in nineteenth-century rural Georgia, and location is a formative factor that cannot be ignored. These people were different from other Americans who shared their status in society, even their Southern contemporaries. In the North, the border states, and the port cities of the Deep South, free men and women of color often comprised a significant and distinct community. By the outbreak of the Civil War, they outnumbered slaves in Delaware and the District of Columbia, and New Orleans was the home of a number of French-speaking mulatto, quadroon, and octoroon women who sometimes lived in relationships of contractual concubinage with affluent white men. In the plantation belt, however, neither the size of the free community nor the lives of its women replicated the circumstances that prevailed elsewhere. As to time and chronology, women of color living on the late eighteenth-century frontier differed from the independent farmers, domestic servants, and the antebellum mistresses of rural Georgia's "big houses" a generation later. They, in turn, hardly resembled the dedicated young scholars of the Reconstruction years. Although these women resided in the same circumscribed locale, their lives evolved from one decade to the next.

Free people of color in the plantation belt have been studied little, but historical work about related subjects cuts across many fields. This book owes a great deal to earlier scholarship about Southern women—both black and white, slave and free—about free people of color in other regions of the country, and about the African-American family, to theories and ideologies of race, and to community studies about Middle Georgia.[10] But as helpful as it has been, that body of work barely addresses the experiences of free women of color and their families in the rural South.

This study weaves together a broad range of materials to reclaim and reconstruct the lives of those women. Personal recollections, shreds of material culture, and private papers and photographs in the possession of family and friends have been used in conjunction with slave narratives, travel accounts, and published diaries. That evidence has been reinforced by such documentation from county courthouses as registers of free persons of color, wills, land transfers, and trial accounts. Similarly, church records and newspaper accounts have supplemented census data. Information about education has been gathered from Atlanta University and Freedmen's Bureau records. Proceedings from Georgia's Supreme Court and its legislative bodies, local store ledgers, and diverse public correspondence have also been woven in. While little architectural evidence from the antebellum years survives in Middle Georgia, the imposing mansion called Pomegranate Hall remains intact in Sparta, Georgia, and stands as mute testimony to the lives of a whole generation of women in the Hunt family.[11]

One of the knottiest problems encountered while developing this study has been finding and using the most appropriate possible terminology. Racial categorizations are often demeaning, fallacious, and futile. This book does not pretend to be in any way a study in physical anthropology, but racial determinations have social, legal, and even economic implications that far outweigh their insignificant biological importance, and these societal ramifications should be acknowledged.[12] In the United States today, most people with any recognizable trace of African ancestry are usually called either "Afro-" or "African-American," or "black." Those terms suffice well enough in a contemporary frame of reference. "Negro" and "colored" have fallen into disuse and now sound outdated at best and even condescending or offensive. When those terms are included here, they reflect specific dated usage. The unqualified use of either "black" or "African-American," however, would be both inaccurate and misleading in this context. Some historians and theoreticians might argue otherwise, because regardless of skin color Americans of African descent all have suffered from the devastating impact of racism. But, at least in part, the lives of the people portrayed here were different in certain legal and social respects from other Americans of African descent, because in the period before emancipation they lived in a society where, although they were certainly not "white," neither were they "black." In most cases, therefore, they are more appropriately called "people of color," "mulattoes," "nonwhite," or some such terms, reflecting their often ambiguous racial status. The children of unions between white and nonwhite parents are sometimes designated "biracial" or "multiracial." Few plantation slaves who labored in the fields of Middle Georgia had any recognizable white ancestry. Slaves, therefore, are generally described as "black" or "African-American," unless specific information indicates otherwise, and slaveholders are referred to as either "white" or "Anglo-American." The nonwhite population of Middle Georgia dominated the region numerically, and therefore it cannot properly be called a "minority," but in the period following emancipation when social structure and institutions in the South changed so dramatically, the lighter skinned and the darker skinned, the formerly free and the formerly slave, all became part of a more inclusive "African-American" community. This terminology is, and will continue to be, the source of disagreements, and some readers may dispute these decisions. Nonetheless, the terms have been deliberately selected to fit the particular situation and to reflect the evolving historical context as accurately as possible.

This is a story about the changing significance of race as well as the importance of gender. It is also about personal freedom and the way that condition has been compromised over the years. Certain aspects of this story have broader applicability, but it nonetheless remains a tale deeply rooted in Middle Georgia, where it transpires. But all of the threads that weave the story together are tied to the Hunts—especially the women. Almost a century passed between the end of the Revolutionary era, when the first members of that family arrived in the state, and the late nineteenth century, when many left. This study follows the Hunts and other similar families through those years, during which they all changed so much.

Du Bois always struggled with the paradox of "two-ness," the ambivalence that he believed all Americans of African ancestry experienced.[13] On one hand they were Americans, having, at least in some part, the confidence, superiority, and virtues that their national identity was supposed to impart. On the other, they were Negroes, bound to kin, taking pride in their heritage, yet somehow different, often demeaned, their voices heard only from "within the veil." For free women of color, an ever-present "two-ness," a divided identity, dominated their lives in many ways. They were female—part of "humankind" but not "mankind"—living in a male-dominated society. They were free in name, but rarely in fact. They were people of color whom the vagaries of life often separated from the enslaved majority of their race.

In 1897 Adella Hunt Logan delivered her impassioned address to a gathering of influential African-Americans at Atlanta University. She argued that the family was a powerful formative and nurturing factor in the pervasive presence of that "two-ness." Hereditary influences, she believed, were central to all human experience and could be traced back through many generations. Nonetheless, she also knew that their precise significance was difficult to assess, "for the reason that [they] may be the result of complex causes and combined forces."[14] Those "complex causes" and "combined forces" swirled around her, and rarely were they more complex or intricately combined than in the ambiguous lives of her own family and other free people of color who shared similar experiences in the antebellum South, many of whom then became an integral part of a new African-American privileged class.

HUNT AND SAYRE FAMILIES

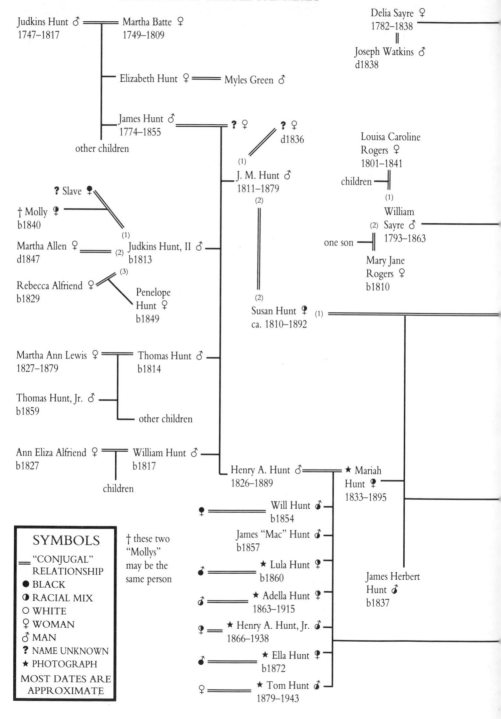

SYMBOLS

— "CONJUGAL" RELATIONSHIP
● BLACK
◑ RACIAL MIX
○ WHITE
♀ WOMAN
♂ MAN
? NAME UNKNOWN
★ PHOTOGRAPH

MOST DATES ARE APPROXIMATE

† these two "Mollys" may be the same person

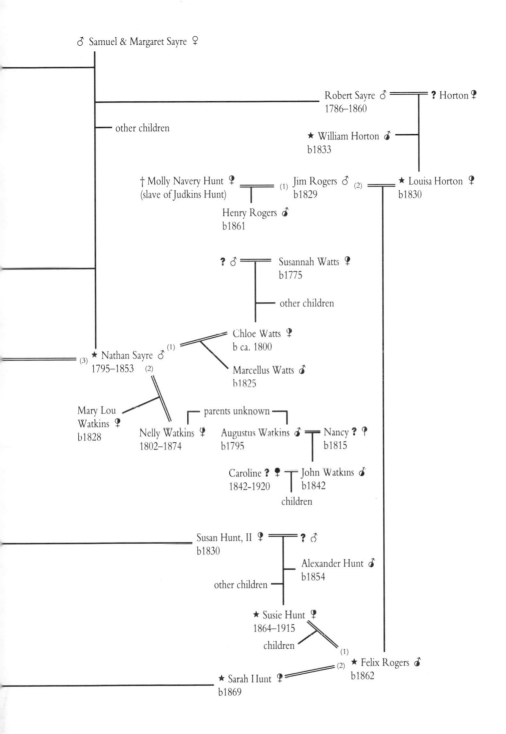

♂ Samuel & Margaret Sayre ♀

other children

Robert Sayre ♂
1786–1860

? Horton ♀

★ William Horton ♂
b1833

† Molly Navery Hunt ♀
(slave of Judkins Hunt)

(1) Jim Rogers ♂
b1829

(2) ★ Louisa Horton ♀
b1830

Henry Rogers ♂
b1861

? ♂

Susannah Watts ♀
b1775

other children

★ Nathan Sayre ♂ (1)
1795–1853

Chloe Watts ♀
b ca. 1800

Marcellus Watts ♂
b1825

(2)

Mary Lou
Watkins ♀
b1828

parents unknown

Nelly Watkins ♀
1802–1874

Augustus Watkins ♂
b1795

Nancy ? ♀
b1815

Caroline ? ♀
1842-1920

John Watkins ♂
b1842

children

Susan Hunt, II ♀
b1830

? ♂

Alexander Hunt ♂
b1854

other children

★ Susie Hunt ♀
1864–1915

children

(1)

(2) ★ Felix Rogers ♂
b1862

★ Sarah Hunt ♀
b1869

NINETEENTH-CENTURY MIDDLE GEORGIA

10 MILES TO CHEROKEE CORNERS
15 MILES TO ATHENS
60 MILES TO ATLANTA
30 MILES TO AUGUSTA
20 MILES TO MACON
95 MILES TO SAVANNAH

ATHENS
ATLANTA · AUGUSTA
MIDDLE GEORGIA
MACON
SAVANNAH
GEORGIA

GREENE
TALIAFERRO
PUTNAM
HANCOCK
WARREN
GLASCOCK
BALDWIN
WASHINGTON

Scull Shoals
Mercer College
Penfield
Woodville
Liberty Hall
CRAWFORDVILLE
Union Point
GREENSBORO
Barnett
White Plains
Camak
Cracker's Neck
Powelton
WARRENTON
Springfield
Mt. Zion
Mayfield
Turnwold Plantation
Culverton
Crooked Creek
Jewell's Mills
GIBSON
EATONTON
Union Chapel
Dixie
SPARTA
Shoals of Ogeechee
Waller's Ferry
Island Creek
Devereux
Dickson Lands
Sheffield's Ferry
Linton
MILLEDGEVILE
Pittsburgh
Oglethorpe University
Scottsboro
SANDERSVILLE
Davisboro
Hebron
Tennile
Harrison

APPALACHEE RIVER
GEORGIA RAILROAD
LITTLE RIVER
WILLIAMS CREEK
OCONEE RIVER
BIG BRIER CREEK
RAILROAD
MACON & AUGUSTA
OGEECHEE RIVER
RIVER
EATONTON
CEDAR CREEK
BRANCH
TOWN CREEK
GUM CREEK
OCONEE RIVER
CENTRAL RAILROAD

N

5 4 3 2 1 0   5   10 MILES

★ ANTEBELLUM STATE CAPITAL
◎ COUNTY SEATS
● SMALLER COMMUNITIES
--- SHERMAN'S MARCHES, NOVEMBER, 1864
■ SCHOOLS

1

Pioneers on
the Georgia Frontier

This is . . . the ancient land of the Cherokees—
that brave Indian nation which strove so long for its
fatherland, until Fate and the United States government drove them beyond the Mississippi . . .
This is the land of the Creek Indians; and a hard
time the Georgians had to seize it . . . Waist deep
they fought beneath the tall trees, until the war-cry
was hushed and the Indians glided back into the
west. Small wonder the wood is red. . . . Then
came the black slaves. Day after day the clank of
chained feet marching from Virginia and Carolina
to Georgia was heard in those rich swamp lands.

W. E. B. Du Bois
The Souls of Black Folk, 1903

In 1787 Martha Batte Hunt and her husband, Capt. Judkins Hunt,
two of Adella Hunt Logan's great-grandparents, departed from
Brunswick County, Virginia, leading their "family" of twenty-nine—
including twelve white and seventeen black members—down the
rough wagon trail that led through the southern Appalachian wilderness. The Hunts joined a burgeoning stream of pioneers who
migrated to the Lower South during the final years of the eighteenth
century. Seeking more abundant, inexpensive, and fertile land, they

piled their belongings onto wagons, crammed them into rolling hogsheads, and traveled west from Lawrenceville, Virginia, to pick up the "great Philadelphia wagon road," which they followed southward from Danville through the North Carolina towns of Salem and Charlotte, to Camden, South Carolina, and then on to Augusta, Georgia. Three older sons—barely past boyhood—departed from the family caravan as it passed through North Carolina, but the rest continued the trek south. The road was arduous enough through the rugged terrain in the Carolinas, but, after leaving Augusta, the route southwestward further deteriorated into little more than a narrow, muddy, and rutted trading path cleared by the local Creek and Cherokee Indians.[1]

In Judkins Hunt's youth, his father had "bound him to a Joyner," and during the struggle for independence, the strapping six-foot-two-inch Judkins became captain of a company of revolutionary soldiers. By the time of the family's exodus southward, he was a farmer and slaveholder who owned more than five hundred acres of land in Greensville and Brunswick counties.[2] Generations earlier, Judkins's ancestor Ralph Hunt, also looking for new lands and opportunities, had embarked from England for the New World. In 1652 he settled in Newtown, Long Island. Ralph Hunt was one of many colonial Englishmen who took up arms in the 1660s to challenge the authority of the Dutch who controlled New Amsterdam. In his later years he became a surveyor and a "guide and counselor in all matters of importance in the community," and he was elected a town magistrate. During the late seventeenth and early eighteenth century, Ralph Hunt's descendants migrated from Long Island toward the south and west—to New Jersey, Pennsylvania, and eventually Virginia.[3]

By 1787 Martha Batte Hunt's family had lived in Virginia for almost a century and a half, and her antecedents claimed a more exalted social status than the Hunts. The first Batte to sail the Atlantic from England, Capt. Henry Batte, Lord of the Manor of Okewell Hall, arrived in the Virginia colony about 1646. There he married Mary Lound, and their family lived in Henrico and Charles City counties, where Henry Batte served in the colonial House of Burgesses. At the time of her departure from Virginia, Captain Batte's great-granddaughter Martha was thirty-eight years old. For eighteen years she had been married to the forty-year-old Judkins Hunt, and she was the mother of ten surviving children.[4]

Because they were only considered "chattel," no records survive to document the origins, ages, family relationships, descriptions, or occupations of the seventeen slaves who, having no choice in the matter, accompanied the white Hunts from Virginia to Georgia. Four of them bore the names Moses, Jude, Jesse, and Anakee, but nothing more is known about them.[5]

Hauling farm equipment and household furnishings down the rugged road through the wilderness, accompanied by a cavalcade of cattle, pigs, mules, and poultry, Ralph Hunt and Henry Batte's descendents, Martha and Judkins, plus four daughters, three sons, and the slaves, finally completed the almost five hundred–mile journey from Virginia to Georgia. Even under optimal conditions, avoiding accidents and the almost inevitable wagon breakdowns, the trek would have taken two months. The Hunts settled on the Georgia frontier in Washington County along the east bank of Fort Creek in an area that in 1793 was partitioned off to form a new county named Hancock.[6]

The Hunt family hacked a clearing from the wilderness and built a substantial log cabin situated beside a crude wagon road and near an all-important source of running water. No trace of the house remains, but remnants of a sluice gate built alongside Fort Creek's white-water rapids, where the sandy-banked stream still tumbles across granite outcroppings, may be part of the mill first used by Judkins Hunt.[7]

Massive hewn oak logs, "twelve or fourteen inches in diameter" formed the body of the Hunts' "wonderful cabin," which featured "portholes around each story for defense against marauding hostile Indians." The house included "four rooms with a passage between and a cellar or store room below." The "passage between"—a characteristic of early Southern domestic architecture that ventilated the house by drawing in cool breezes during the oppressive summers—was known as a "dogtrot." Martha and Judkins adorned the walls of their home "with the skins of animals, two rifles supported on horns, bunches of turkey tails, tobacco, a flint rock and a bunch of punk."[8]

Most women on the Southern frontier knew how to use firearms to ward off wild animals, kill deer, 'possum, and birds for food, and even shoot at Indians. Martha Hunt and her four daughters may have hunted, repulsed the local Creeks, cleared the land, and cultivated it alongside the white men and slaves, and they always labored diligently in and around the house. Their home included a "loom, a spinning wheel, a flax wheel, seven hundred pounds of soap, much honey [and] lard" stored in Martha's cellar. Georgia's pioneer women carded flax, cotton, and wool, spun the fiber into thread, wove cloth on handmade looms, and dyed it with colors drawn from bark, roots, and berries. They made all of the family's clothing, household linens, curtains, and rugs. Like other early Hancock County settlers, the Hunts cooked over an open fireplace fitted with both a crane to hang iron pots and kettles and a spit for roasting meat and fowl. Black and white female members of the Hunt household also preserved fruits and vegetables, spun, wove, quilted, made soap and candles from suet, gardened, kept bees, raised poultry, and cured meat.[9]

Much like the Hunts, other settlers known as "Chesapikers" came to Georgia at the end of the eighteenth and the beginning of the nineteenth century from the more populous states of Maryland and Virginia. For more than a hundred and fifty years, the fertile, low-lying delta lands along Georgia's coast had been heavily populated and dominated by sizable plantations largely devoted to the cultivation of long-fibered Sea Island cotton and rice. The port of Savannah, renowned for its fashionable society and elegant mansions, was the state's largest city and a jewel of the South, but inland Georgia remained untamed frontier territory into the nineteenth century.

That part of the state where the Hunt family settled, and which officially became Hancock County in 1793, straddled the fall line. Its climate was variable but generally mild, typified by hot summers and few cold winter days. The county's northern half was six hundred feet above sea level, and that altitude brought with it conditions more conducive to good health than those that prevailed in lower lying areas. Shaped like an irregular hexagon, Hancock County stretches roughly twenty-five to thirty miles across in any direction, and today seven counties abut it. Circling counterclockwise around Hancock, Warren and Taliaferro are located on its northeast, Greene and then Putnam to the north and northwest, Baldwin on the southwest, Washington directly south, and finally Glascock to the east.[10] These counties constitute the heart of a region often called Middle Georgia. In 1804 Baldwin County's largest town, Milledgeville, became the "permanent seat of Government of this State."[11] The area's two major rivers—the Ogeechee to the east, which flowed all the way to the Atlantic, and the Oconee, which formed Hancock's western boundary and then became a tributary of the great Altamaha—both featured turbulent falls and shoals where the waters surged across boulder-strewn rapids on their way southeastward to the sea. In the early nineteenth century, when white settlers first began to populate the region, the streams were replete with fish, and wild game filled both the pine, scrub oak, walnut, and maple forests of the upland heights and the bay, gum, and poplar thickets of the swampier lowlands. Above the fall line, rich black earth and red Georgia clay characterized much of the hilly northern portion of the eight-county region, but the land flattened out below the rapids, and the soil became a sandy loam. Some iron was discovered in Hancock County, as well as a little gold, chalcedony, and quartz. Judkins Hunt's land yielded both "lydian stone and brown jasper," but Georgia granite, often used for gravestones as well as building con-struction, was the region's most prevalent mineral.[12]

Commercial short-fiber cotton production did not flourish in Middle Georgia until Eli Whitney, a resourceful young tutor from Massachusetts, visited the state and perceived the need for a device that would efficiently separate the lint from the seeds and thereby increase the profitability of the inland cotton. Whitney may have appropriated the idea for a cotton gin from a black plantation hand or his white hostess, but in 1793 he alone patented the mechanism, which quickly changed the face of the nineteenth-century South.[13] The manufacture of the first gins and the rapid adoption of Whitney's new cotton processors throughout the state stimulated both staple agricultural production and an increase in both the white and the black population.

Through the end of the eighteenth century and before the rise of the inland plantation economy, however, much of Middle Georgia remained the land of the Creeks. Their ancestral homelands con-verged with those of the Cherokees at a point known as Cherokee Corners on the Oconee River just north of Greene County. As land-hungry white settlers moved westward across the state clearing forests, planting crops, and building new settlements, they encoun-tered and confronted these indigenous Americans who vigorously resisted that unwelcome intrusion.

Fort Creek, the stream beside which the Hunts built their cabin, was a tributary of the larger Shoulderbone Creek. In 1786 one of many treaties between the United States and the Creek nation had been signed there, by the site of some ancient Indian burial grounds. The Treaty of Shoulderbone Creek was supposed to bring an end to the skirmishes between the settlers and the Indians, but, like many other such pacts, it failed.[14]

Absalom Chappell, a nineteenth-century gazetteer of Georgia lore and history, whose grandfather's plantation was also located near Fort Creek, believed that the Creeks were "by far the most numerous, powerful and warlike of all the Indian tribes in North America." He recalled that the settlers "built what was dignified as a fort, a strong wooden stockade or block house, entrenched, loop-holed, and sur-mounted with lookouts at the angles" alongside the waterway. That fortification was one of several block houses in Hancock County where whites retreated during Indian raids. The frontier strongholds were large compounds where "enough ground was enclosed to allow room for huts or tents for the surrounding families when they should take refuge therein." Middle Georgia's new residents cared little that they were interlopers on the Indians' ancestral grounds. They were eager for land, and most of them chose to remember only that "there had been massacres of white women and children, burning of homes, stealing of livestock and other property, so the settlers looked upon every Indian as an enemy to be destroyed."[15]

Pioneers from Hancock repeated the tale of "Happy Jack," a stagecoach driver who in 1815 was attacked by a war party consist-ing, he claimed, of "four hundred Indians." Reportedly, they took Jack completely by surprise when "he heard the war whoop [and] reached for his rifle but got only his bugle." The raiders killed the passengers and stole both his horses and the stage. Settlers in a nearby county told a story about the Indians who tomahawked a Mr. and Mrs. Bentley and their female slave. In 1828 Georgia's legislature responded to these incidents by banning the Creeks from the state, arguing that "many inconveniences and injuries result to the citizens of this State . . . from the unlimited intercourse of the Indians of said nation," including stealing, destroying property, and generally "dis-turbing the peace." Settlers generally found the Cherokees less antag-onistic than the Creeks, but though the frequency of hostile encounters between the new farmers and both Indian nations fluctu-ated over the years, they did not cease entirely until the Indians were coerced into ceding all of their Georgia lands to the United States and forced westward.[16]

Hancock County's newly arrived white farmers acted in accordance with what they believed was an undisputed right to clear, occupy, and work the land, even when they encountered outraged resistance from the indigenous people. Local legend claims that "because of the courage and heroism of these pioneer settlers, their principal town which had long been a trading post, was named Sparta in memory of the ancient city of the Peloponesus." In 1805 the state legislature chartered Sparta as the county seat. Most settlers lived on scattered farms, but a few other such small communities as Linton, Devereux, and Powelton sprang up at roughly the same time, and a village called Mount Zion was settled near Fort Creek about seven miles northwest of Sparta.[17]

Absalom Chappell articulated the views held by most pioneers in Middle Georgia. Progress, he argued, required "the white man with the axe and the plow, the banner and the saw, and . . . the array and habitments of civilization, superseding the Indian in his hunting knife and his bows and arrows." Chappell believed that the "superior" Anglo-American culture operating hand-in-hand with its preeminent power would and should dominate the area's indigenous people, "putting an end to the reign of Pan and the Satyrs." "No metamorphosis the world ever saw, or fiction ever forged," he wrote, "was more beautiful, picturesque and lovely than the change that was wrought, and wrought too with magical suddenness and on a largeness of scale that made the wonderful blend with the beautiful." Adhering to that philosophy, white settlers may have felt almost obligated to accomplish that mission and dominate, if not annihilate, the "heathen" culture wherever they encountered it.[18]

In spite of those prevailing attitudes toward the Native Americans, some white Southerners retained romantic illusions about life among the Indians. Because the Cherokees resisted the intrusion of the new white farmers with less ferocity than the Creeks, more than a few enthusiastic settlers on the Georgia frontier sang:

All I want in this cre-a-tion,
Is a pretty little girl and a big plan-ta-tion,
'Way up yonder in the Cherokee Nation.[19]

Many Anglo-Americans who came to Middle Georgia brought slaves with them, and complex relationships developed between those black people and the Indians. On occasion, slaves ran off to nearby Indian villages, where they sometimes adopted the dress of the Creeks, served as their interpreters, and enjoyed greater freedom and privileges than they did among the whites. In other instances, Indian raiding parties absconded with slaves as they might with any other valued property belonging to the white intruders. Moravian missionaries reported several slave abductions in Middle Georgia during the early years of the nineteenth century. White settlers, of course, became outraged when their human chattel was taken away, and they staged retaliatory counterraids on Native American villages. In 1803 the state legislature authorized "Indian agents" to go into the Creek nation to arrest "such slaves as may abscond, or be stolen" and return them to their owners. Although most Creeks were indigent by the standards of the white community, the missionaries observed that "many Indians owned Negro slaves." At the time of his death in 1793, Creek Chief Alexander McGillivray supposedly possessed three hundred slaves, but how many had been kidnapped, how many were presented to him as tribute, and how many the chief bought is not known. A number of affluent Cherokees also emulated their new white neighbors, and through both capture and purchase became owners of black slaves even before the turn of the century.[20]

Absalom Chappell expressed the opinions held by most nineteenth-century white Georgians about blacks as well as Native Americans. Virtually without exception, whites on the frontier and throughout the antebellum South believed themselves superior to both the indigenous people whom they dispossessed and to the Africans whom they enslaved and demeaned. In the early years when the settlers claimed and cleared Middle Georgia, Chappell gave credit to the work performed by the slaves—those "humble, laborious unpaid hands," as he described them, "by which most of the harsh heavy work was done." He found the "child of the Sun eminently submissive, cheerfully servile in his nature, and apt and docile in a high degree." The enslaved African was truly fortunate, Chappell argued, because "who shall say that Heaven in revealing the American continent did not design it as an asylum for him." Chappell had no doubt that with his experience in the American South, the black man had "exchanged a worse and a barbarous, for a better, a more civilized form of slavery, an exchange which was at once a blessing to him, to us, and to mankind." Slaves, he concluded, owed a heavy debt of gratitude to the white man "for a striking betterment of his condition, physical, moral religious, . . . [and] for all civilization and Christianity he has ever attained." Chappell and others of his race believed that the Africans belonged to an inferior race. Few whites had any knowledge, comprehension, or appreciation of the traditions and the heritage that the slaves brought with them. However, they thought that, unlike the "savage" Indians who were being crushed by the march of Anglo-American "progress," the "docile and servile" Africans should be Christianized and kept in bondage under the protective custody of the intellectually, morally, and culturally superior white man.[21]

Garnett Andrews, a noted lawyer, retained different childhood recollections about the slaves, however. In the early years of the nineteenth century during his youth in Middle Georgia, he recalled that "the country was full of 'outlandish' or 'new negroes' as they were called." Others referred to those slaves newly arrived from Africa as "salt-backs." Andrews remembered that "many professed to have been Princes and Princesses in their own country . . . [and] had marks of distinction on their flesh." Unlike Chappell, who believed that the Africans should be grateful for their opportunities in a "civilized" and Christian land, Andrews remembered the fierce desperation of those who "destroyed their lives," hoping that death would bring them freedom, and at least a spiritual "return to their own country."[22]

As reflected in its local paper, *The Missionary,* some people in Hancock County's Mount Zion community may also have held somewhat less intransigent views about slavery and people of African descent. That journal and its editorial board—the Reverends Benjamin Gildersleeve and Nathan Beman, and a planter named Joseph Bryan—did not openly oppose the institution of slavery during the early decades of the century. *The Missionary,* in fact, ran regular advertisements for local sales of slaves and posted rewards for runaways. Nonetheless, although the paper never advocated any social or legal equality among the races, its pages reflected an unexpected open-mindedness about nonwhite societies and individuals. One article also described the Christian "duty and benefit in educating slaves" although that stance clearly placed the newspaper in opposition to state law, and another praised both the character and effectiveness of certain African missionaries.[23]

The debate over the responsibility of masters to their slaves and all aspects of the relationships among the races continued. Both the little-known Judkins Hunt who lived at Mount Zion and Thomas Jefferson, the country's most influential intellectual leader in the late eighteenth and early nineteenth centuries, were native Virginians. Jefferson, whose reportedly intimate relationship with a slave woman of multiracial heritage has become the subject of extensive speculation, demeaned the physical, intellectual, and moral attributes of black people. Although he probably failed to live by the principles that he articulated, Jefferson declared his repugnance toward miscegenation between blacks and whites. On the other hand, he considered the country's indigenous people "noble savages" who, over time, might be successfully amalgamated—genetically, physically, and culturally—into the new American society. His private passion for the reputedly handsome Sally Hemings may have belied his publicly stated beliefs, but Jefferson argued that women of African descent were less physically attractive than either white or Indian women, and that their sexual preferences and practices were overtly bestial.[24]

As has been widely assumed about the long-lasting liaison between Jefferson and Hemings, some sexual unions between blacks and whites involved masters and their own slave women and subsequently resulted in the birth of children. On other occasions, however, conception occurred following a single encounter between virtual strangers. Around 1815, for example, a young slave named Mary attracted the attention of a libidinous male guest in the Hancock County home of Superior Court Judge Hugh Taylor. Taylor, responding as an amenable host, promptly agreed to his visitor's lecherous appeal, and dispatched the servant to the guest's bedchamber when the man retired. Shortly thereafter, the newly pregnant Mary was "married off" to a black house servant who was designated to serve as the baby's "nominal parent" in place of its biological white father, who left town immediately following that one sexual incident and, as a matter of course, assumed no responsibility for his actions.[25]

With the rise of the cotton kingdom in the Lower South, federal policy forcibly removed most Native Americans to lands west of the Mississippi before 1830. In that same period, Middle Georgia's slave population expanded dramatically. A few offspring of unions between Indians and either black or white newcomers remained behind as the Creeks and Cherokees departed, but the number of mulatto children, such as Mary's, resulting from sexual encounters between blacks and whites increased. In the Carolinas and Georgia as well, these people of mixed racial parentage were sometimes known as "mustee" or "mestizo," and in local usage, those terms often implied Native American ancestry as well. On other occasions they referred to themselves as "new people." "Mulatto," the word used more frequently, sprang from the same derivation as "mule," the sterile hybrid offspring of a mare and a male ass. Some whites thought (or perhaps hoped) that like the mule, mulattoes—who served as constant and visible reminders of the infidelities, weaknesses, and insensitivities as well as the brutality of white men—would also prove infertile, and would die out after several generations.[26]

Some people in Middle Georgia also called them "no-nations," implying that they were outsiders to both black and white society.[27] That term, however, more appropriately might be applied to the descendants of Cherokees and blacks, because the Cherokees often adopted the prejudices of their white neighbors and tried to avoid any identification with African-Americans, whom they considered their servants and their inferiors. Of all the indigenous American nations, the Cherokees may have developed the greatest aversion to people of African ancestry. The Cherokees withheld tribal membership from any child born to one of their own nation and a black person. In 1824 they outlawed intermarriages with blacks, and anyone violating that regulation could be both whipped and fined, although Indian women who established interracial alliances were generally punished less severely than men. Slave runaways and free people of color who came to their villages were neither given asylum, protected from white bounty hunters, nor otherwise made welcome. The Cherokees were never enslaved themselves, and they rigorously maintained the distance and the difference between their own free people and blacks.[28]

In spite of the prejudices and practices that were especially prevalent among the Cherokee, Christian missionaries in the region encountered a few children of black and Native American parentage whom they called "Indians of the Half Blood." Some African-American men—whether they had been captured or were runaways or former slaves—reportedly lived among the indigenous people, where some practiced polygamy. But whatever their own status or the nature of their conjugal relationships with Indian women, any children that black men had with those women would be born free. The child of any female slave remained a slave, but the child born to any free woman—black, red, or white—was also free. From colonial times, Georgia law clearly established that the status of every child "shall follow the condition of the mother." This perpetuated and ensured every master's ownership of all the offspring of his female slaves.[29]

One such person—the child of an Indian mother—was Mary Ann Battis, who was born in Baldwin County, Georgia, around 1810. Her father was thought to be black, and her mother was the daughter of a white man and a Creek woman. Battis was raised a Christian and apparently felt a strong kinship with the settlers' community because she remained at the Moravian mission near Milledgeville and chose not to go West when others in her tribe were forced out of Georgia.[30]

Rather than considering themselves "no-nations," estranged or isolated from the black, red, and white communities of their forebears, it seems probable that most of these multiracial children did their best to ignore the prejudices of both whites and Indians and incorporated different aspects of their heritage from all their progenitors. They were more than the recipients of scorn, pity, or largess from the economically and politically dominant white society, toleration or rejection from the Native Americans, and affection sometimes tempered with jealousy and hostility from the black community. In large part, they managed to shape and determine their own lives. They were people of color whose forebears bequeathed them a rich and diverse heritage. More often than not, they encountered complex kinship situations as well as difficult social, political, and legal conflicts in frontier Georgia. Because of, or perhaps in spite of, these adversities, they developed intricate relationships and ingenious means of survival, and they in turn influenced their families, associates, and the community around them.

Different circumstances in the lives of these people who had some Native American forebears conspired to keep them within the frontier communities of Middle Georgia when the Creeks and Cherokees were forced westward. In Baldwin County, Mary Ann Battis responded to the missionaries who had raised her and heeded the call of her own religious devotion. Another young woman, perhaps just a girl, became part of the Hunts' household in Mount Zion during the early years of the nineteenth century, more than likely as a servant.

She too might have first come from a nearby mission. Through reports in *The Missionary,* people in Hancock County's Mount Zion community could keep themselves informed about the work of the Christian missions to the Indians, including the Georgia Cherokees. In Hancock County she adopted the surname of the family for whom she worked and became known as Susan Hunt. She was later called a "free woman of color." Her mother was Cherokee and may have come from somewhere near Cherokee Corners, just north of Greene County. Her father was a mulatto—probably a slave. Susan's children, however, bore such a strong physical resemblance to their Native American antecedents, that years later local people called her daughter "Cherokee Mariah Lilly."[31]

The Cherokees seem to have been taller than their Creek neighbors to the south. Their women were described as "tall, slender, erect and of a delicate frame . . . and they move with a becoming grace and dignity." Visitors remarked that their skin had an "olive cast." But hair was the physical comparison mentioned most often between women of color in the Hunt family and their Native American relatives. Cherokee women rarely cut their hair, which often reached "down to the middle of their legs." They dressed it with bear grease, and wore it plaited or "clubbed" in one heavy braid, "ornamented with ribbons of various colors," and the Hunt women had much the same long, thick hair.[32]

In addition to that physical legacy, the Cherokee also provided a distinctive cultural heritage, which Susan would have brought with her to the Hunt's farm at Mount Zion. Although they gradually began using English, the traditional Cherokee language was a dialect of the southern Iroquois. In spite of the imposition and subsequent assimilation of many aspects of European culture and values, they placed little premium on personal wealth. Cherokee lands were individually controlled but communally owned by the whole village. In their dominantly matrilineal society, marriage gave Cherokee husbands no rights over their wives' property, and households typically consisted of a mother, her husband, their unmarried sons, daughters, and those daughters' children. Marriage, called "uniting the blankets," often lasted only for a short time, and divorce was easily obtained, frequently resulting in a kind of serial monogamy. Following any marital separation, adult children usually returned to their mothers' houses.[33]

By the beginning of the nineteenth century, Cherokees in the Carolinas and northern Georgia had interacted extensively with the white settlers and had adopted many European modes of dress, building construction, animal husbandry, and agriculture. "If adopting or imitating the manners and customs of the white people is to be termed civilization," one visitor commented, comparing them to other indigenous people of the southeastern United States, "perhaps the Cherokees have made the greatest advances." *The Missionary* echoed that sentiment, stating that "the Cherokees have made greater progress in civilization, than any of the other tribes of Indians." Most lived in porched wooden houses that included several rooms and were constructed of logs chinked with clay and overlaid with sapling roofs. To cover their doorways, however, they hung the traditional animal skins or blankets. Emulating the white settlers around them, they began using horses and raising cattle, and for the most part became sedentary agriculturalists. Women in the Cherokee villages wore printed cotton dresses or full, brightly colored skirts, leather belts, and lace-edged calico waistcoats. They adorned themselves with necklaces and bracelets made from Job's tears, shells, and trade beads. They worked the land alongside the men, cared for livestock, rode horseback, and helped to drive their cattle out to white settlements for sale. Other women's work included child care, wood gathering, clothing manufacture, and such household tasks as smoking and drying fresh meat, fish, and vegetables, cooking, and washing. They wove baskets from white oak splits and made household utensils from both gourds and oven-dried clay. Corn was boiled, baked in ashes, fermented, and ground for meal, gruel, and bread. It remained the most important staple of their diet, but they also raised beans, peas, pumpkins, squash, white potatoes, and tobacco. The Cherokee fished, trapped, and hunted birds, squirrel, deer, and rabbits. They shot and ate wild turkey, whittled the bones into tools, and used the feathers to decorate their mantles and fit their arrows.[34]

Their lore, certainly familiar to Susan Hunt, included tales about the bellicose and independent "War Woman," who fought alongside the Cherokee men, and "Pretty Woman," who held the power to determine the fate of the nation's prisoners of war. But another popular legend told of the young wife whose irate father-in-law sent her back in shame to her maternal family because she did not know how to cook.[35]

Cherokee women also adhered to tribal superstitions, followed traditional ritual practices, and had knowledge of herbal medicine. They used allspice, pimiento, and amaranth for menstrual problems. Tansy tied around the waist helped to prevent miscarriage and slippery elm bark, touch-me-not stems, cones from the prickly pine, and ginger all eased the discomforts of pregnancy. A pregnant women was warned against standing in a doorway, which supposedly delayed childbirth, or wearing a neckerchief because it might cause her umbilical cord to knot. Fennel, buckeye, and raspberry leaf tea or blackberry root syrup were prescribed to alleviate the pains and complications of childbirth, and "decoctions" of greenbrier root, sycamore, or hemlock aided in expelling the afterbirth. A Cherokee woman's grandmother and mother always delivered her babies, and the children had to be ritually doused, then bathed in running water every morning for two years. Women were considered impure during menstruation, pregnancy, and throughout childbirth, and they subsequently underwent traditional inundations to restore their cleanliness. They drank hop vine and skullcap root teas and applied milkweed ointment and sumac to soothe their breasts and promote the flow of milk during a prolonged four years of nursing. This extended nursing, reinforced by doses of an infusion made from the bruised and steeped roots of the squeeze weed, supposedly suppressed menstruation and prevented conception.[36]

In spite of the Indians' strong cultural heritage and their vigorous resistance, white settlers in Middle Georgia soon displaced both the Creeks and Cherokees and brought the region under their complete domination. Anglo-American men maintained all official records, became the registered owners of most property, published the newspapers, controlled the churches and schools, and successfully thwarted the attempts of anyone who might try to threaten their pervasive hegemony. Except that many slaveholders kept records of their human chattel for financial reasons, documenting the lives of people of color in Middle Georgia during the early decades of the nineteenth century was considered unimportant.

Understandably, neither the histories nor even the names of Susan Hunt's parents are known. Although her African-American father was probably a slave, her Native American mother ensured Susan's freedom and that of her children and would have familiarized Susan with the old Indian customs. Hunt family tradition, corroborated by limited documentation, confirms that Susan and her descendants were widely recognized as free people of color, but compiling substantive information to better understand their lives and those of others who shared that heritage has presented a formidable challenge.[37]

Although the free status of any woman presumably bestowed that same condition on her children, people of color in Georgia could also establish their freedom in other ways. In the early years of the nineteenth century, a few people of African descent who had first arrived in the colony by the middle of the eighteenth still remained in the state and remained free, because between 1733 and 1750 colonial Georgia had prohibited slavery. At least in theory, that guaranteed the freedom of any of these people who could trace their Georgia residency back to that period. Some men and women of color also came to the state from foreign countries or from other states where they had been free, while still others had managed to purchase their own freedom or had been manumitted by their owners by the turn of the century. The bloody uprising in Saint Domingue that overthrew the French colonial regime there terrified white Southerners, who largely attributed that revolution to the insurrectionary presence of free persons of color. "Most vigorous measures [must be] taken to defeat their infernal designs," one Augusta man wrote about free people of color, "may God preserve us from the fate of St. Domingo." Members of the legislature responded by prohibiting virtually all manumissions in the early years of the nineteenth century. Even when state laws were briefly eased a few years later, freedom remained almost impossible for people of African descent to obtain.[38]

These were the acknowledged though narrow paths to freedom for people of color in Georgia, and their numbers remained few. In 1790 under 400 free people of color in the state comprised less than 0.5 percent of its total population. In 1800 they had increased to just over 1,000, or about 0.6 percent. The number increased to 1,800 in 1810 and stayed about the same in 1820. In 1830 they again comprised 0.5 percent of the population, although the total count grew to almost 2,500 as the state's population as a whole expanded. Middle Georgia had its share, but no more, of free men and women of color. The region reported 10 in 1790, 47 in 1800, 146 in 1810, 212 by 1820, and 300 by 1830.[39]

In spite of the paucity of information about how they both

acquired and maintained their freedom, a few hazy images of free people of color in Middle Georgia can be reconstructed. That task, however, is difficult at least in part because until 1850 most census records only supplied the names of heads of households, who almost inevitably were white men. This prejudicial record-keeping subsumed and often obliterated the identities of slaves, free people of color (most of whom had to live with white guardians), and even white women and children. Therefore, few free people of color can be distinguished by name in the early nineteenth-century censuses.

Nevertheless, some people of color, identifiable by name, did appear in those records, the Bustles among them. In 1820 John Bustle of Washington County had three in his family; Priscilla Bustle headed a large household of ten, and Isaac, a family of four. In addition, Solomon and Nancy Bustle each lived nearby, but alone. Judging by their ages, those five probably were siblings. Ten years later, most of them had moved up to Hancock County, where a man listed as James Bustle (probably earlier reported as John), Priscilla, and Isaac resided in three separate dwellings close by one another, and their combined families totaled twenty-three men, women, and children. Their brother Solomon moved even further north to Warren County, where he lived with a white woman about his own age who may have been his "wife."[40]

As far back as 1811 in Warren County, five other siblings, "Rachel Ruff and Jack Ruff, minor persons of color, were bound out to David Mims," and "Fanny, Judith and Bethena Ruff . . . were bound out to Benjamin Wynne." At that time, Bethena Ruff was only a year and a half old, Jack was nine, Rachel eleven, Judith fourteen, and Fanny seventeen. The children's enforced servitude under the guardianship of Mims and Wynne was intended to continue until they turned eighteen. Fanny Ruff, at least, remained in Warren County, and by 1830 she lived there with her four children. Warren was also home to two branches of the Moss family.[41]

In 1829 Dilsey Ruff, a spinner and weaver, with her seven children appeared in neighboring Taliaferro, which had recently been carved out from portions of Warren and Greene counties. That year county officials reported that some of the Ruffs had dark skins, but called others "molatto." They also registered free people of color bearing the surnames Floyd, Grant, James, and Jones, for a countywide total of twenty-two. One of the women, Zancy Floyd, had been freed by a former master in North Carolina, and the Taliaferro County clerk described both Zancy and her spouse Allen James as "yellow complected." Their different surnames would seem to show that like slaves, free people of color could rarely if ever enter into legally sanctioned marriages. Allen James's mother, Sarah, who lived in the same county, had purchased her own freedom in North Carolina in 1796. Subsequently, all of Sarah James's children who had accompanied her to Middle Georgia also were free. In 1793 Nancy Grant, a woman with a "dark complexion," had been manumitted by Daniel Grant in nearby Wilkes County. Taliaferro's free men of color worked as farmers. The women were spinners (recorded as "spincers" and "spinsters"), weavers, laundresses, and "housekeepers," euphemistically implying that some men—perhaps white—were responsible for their keep.[42]

As early as 1796, the state legislature ruled that two men of color, "Reuben Going and John Going, of Greene County . . . are hereby authorized and enabled to take, hold, and enjoy property both real and personal." Their brother Thomas also gained his limited freedom through a private legislative act which nonetheless carefully ensured that:

> nothing herein contained shall extend or be construed to . . . entitle the said Thomas Going, to serve in the capacity of a juror . . . nor to render him a competent witness . . . where the personal rights or property of any white person are . . . concerned; nor to entitle [him] to vote at elections, nor to have or hold . . . any office of trust or emolument, civil or military, within this state.

Other members of the Going family turned up in nearby Taliaferro, Hancock, and Baldwin counties during the ensuing decades.[43]

In addition to the Goings, by 1820 Greene County, just west of Taliaferro, had become the home of free people of color named Anderson, Grant, King, Tate, Todd, and Lucas. Willie Lucas was unusual in that he headed a household of seven persons including his wife, a free "colored" woman, and their two children, but in addition three unidentified white females—one child, one young woman, and another over forty-five—also lived with them. In 1823 the state legislature passed a private bill stating that "the said negro, Chloe," a slave belonging to James Robinson also from Greene County, "is hereby liable to all the fines, penalties and privileges, now imposed upon, and allowed to, free people of color in this state." Neither county records nor the census provide any more information about the woman named Chloe. In 1830 that same county was also home to one of the region's more unusual and mysterious free women of color. Betsy Perry, an unmarried "colored" woman more than fifty-five years of age who shared her household with no other free relatives of any race, owned twenty-seven slaves: eight children, thirteen young adults, three older women, and the same number of older men. Beyond this acknowledgment of her ownership of slaves in the federal census, nothing at all is known about Betsy Perry.[44]

Even before 1830, church rolls in the region included a few free people of color as members. Keziah English was an original member of the Williams Creek Church in Warren County, founded in 1787, and James and Dennis Jones belonged to Putnam County's Crooked Creek Primitive Baptist congregation.[45]

The only known serious criminal act attributed to a free person of color during this period was an 1822 incident concerning Putnam County's John Brown. Claiborn Griffin, a white man, accused Brown, a free man of color, of attempted murder. Court accounts indicate that Brown had thrown a rock at Griffin. It missed and apparently did no harm. No witnesses either corroborated or contradicted Griffin's testimony. A judicial panel assembled to hear criminal complaints against both slaves and free persons of color found Brown guilty and sentenced him to be "hung by the neck until you are Dead, Dead, Dead." The severity of Brown's punishment would have served to remind free people of color in the region just how tenuous their lives and personal liberty really were.[46]

Brown's treatment also reflects patterns seen in slave trials. The courts considered crimes in which whites were victims far more serious than crimes against people of African descent. In Baldwin County in 1812, a slave convicted of the attempted rape of a white woman, who claimed no injury at all, was hanged under the provisions of a law passed in 1806, while a few years later a slave who murdered another black man was treated relatively leniently and only whipped and branded. In addition, any person even suspected of having "negro blood" could be endangered if he or she claimed to be free. In that same county in 1819, Milledgeville officials who found the olive cast of his skin somewhat "suspicious" arrested a fourteen-year-old boy who was just passing through town on the way to rejoin his parents.[47]

Beyond these scanty reports, little can be determined about the few free people of color who lived in Middle Georgia at the end of the eighteenth and the early years of the nineteenth century. Georgia legislators, however, always unduly concerned themselves with questions pertaining to that small group. Free people of color were misfits in a slave society. No matter how few their numbers, they constituted a disturbing third caste in a structure designed to accommodate only two. Whites throughout the South thought that the example set by people of color who lived outside of bondage encouraged runaways, planted the seeds for slave insurrection, and constantly created the potential for social disorder. They were usually described as lazy, unhappy scoundrels and reprobates. Because they were not white, they were automatically treated as inferiors. Journals, court cases, and legislative actions reflect the fact that whites in Georgia almost unanimously agreed that the lives of free people of color should be controlled and circumscribed in every possible way.

Even before 1800, the legislature had established that any woman or man of color—"negroe, Indian, mulattoe, or mestisoe"—was presumed to be a slave "unless the contrary can be made to appear." After 1801 free people of color were always supposed to have white guardians who would be held responsible for their behavior and would act on their behalf in all legal proceedings and transactions—as if they were perpetual minors. Free persons of color, the legislature also decreed, "shall be proceeded and tried by the justices and jury [as] . . . for the trial of slaves and in like manner." It reenforced that provision in 1807, when it perceived a need to "protect citizens [from] injury and inconvenience from the number of free negroes, mulattoes and mustizos, of vicious and loose habits" in Milledgeville and other major towns of the state, and further ensured that they would "be subject to the same police regulations and restrictions as slaves are."[48] A year earlier, the state had already amended the penal code to institute the death penalty for any "slave, free negro, Indian, mulatto or mustizo who attempts to . . . rape any white person." White men, on the other hand, could never be subject to execution or even any lesser punishment for the rape or attempted rape of a woman of color because those acts were not even acknowledged as crimes under the Georgia criminal code.[49]

In 1801 a new law permitted manumission only through act of the legislature. Shortly thereafter, however, that body amended the state constitution to deny itself the power to "pass laws for the emancipation of slaves, without the consent of each of their respective owners, previous to such emancipation." By that action, the state government established that an individual owner's property rights over his slave property should even supersede the authority of the state.[50]

In 1808 the legislature stated that "permitting . . . free negroes and persons of color to rove about the country in idleness and dissipation, has a dangerous tendency." To eliminate that "dangerous tendency," they decreed that if they lacked guardians, young "colored" males from the age of eight to twenty-one who were not slaves should be bound out to work for white people. The legislature also passed laws imposing a twenty-dollar head tax to discourage free men and women of color from coming into the state, and in 1818 it forbade any persons of color claiming free status from other states or countries from entering Georgia at all. In addition, any free men and women of color who had not registered with "the clerk of the inferior court of the county in which they reside" according to law—listing name, age, place of birth and residence, guardian, and occupation and remitting a required fee—were subject to arrest and could be sold as slaves. After that same date, they no longer had the right to acquire real property or hold slaves in certain local jurisdictions, with the proviso that the regulation would not invalidate any previously established ownership of such property.[51]

In the late 1820s the legislature eliminated many economic opportunities for free men and women of color in the town of Sparta by denying them the opportunity to operate "house[s] of public or private entertainment," or to sell "goods, wares, merchandise, spiritous liquors or provisions, or carry on any kind of traffic for the purpose of gain." In the final year of that decade, it specifically barred members of that caste from working in any business establishment involved with printing or the written word. Anyone involved in the supposedly subversive act of teaching either a free person of color or a slave to read could be fined, whipped, and jailed.[52]

It would seem reasonable to assume that because there were so few free people of color in the state that whites in Georgia would simply ignore them. But this was never so. The legislature asserted that the state's official policy was to discourage any increase in their numbers by denying them admission to the state and by thwarting manumission. Free people of color, they asserted, "constitute[d] a class of people, equally dangerous to the safety of free citizens of this state, and destructive to the comfort and happiness of the slave population thereof."[53] Although members of that group were viewed as less of a threat to the rigid caste system in the lower South during the early decades of the nineteenth century than they would be following the 1831 Nat Turner rebellion and in the years leading up to the Civil War, their lives nonetheless were always made difficult by law, by legal and economic strictures, and by social custom.[54]

For the "colored" Hunts, consistent oral tradition and other evidence corroborates their freedom, but they apparently had no official documentation to establish and confirm their status. Contrary to state-imposed requirements, they did not acquire legal guardians as the law demanded, and their names were never included on county registers of free persons of color. Until 1870 when they first appeared, categorized as "mulatto," Susan Hunt's kin were never listed at all in the censuses—not as slaves, not as free persons of color, not as Native Americans, nor even "passing" for white.[55] Susan Hunt's nonslave status had been established when her anonymous father had a child with a free Cherokee woman around 1810, about the same time that Mary Ann Battis was born to a black man and a Creek woman in Baldwin County, but very few Native Americans were included and recognized among Georgia's free people of color. Whatever first brought her there, or whatever the initial circumstances of her relationship with them, Susan remained with the white Hunts in Hancock County for many years. She lived in their home, adopted their name and established an intimate, complex, and changing relationship with them.[56]

Martha and Judkins, the first of the Anglo-American Hunts to settle in Hancock County, lived on a farm near the village of Mount Zion into the early decades of the nineteenth century. When Judkins Hunt died in 1817 he was buried next to Martha, who had predeceased him, in the family cemetery by Fort Creek. In his will he left but one slave to his son James. James had already taken over the original cabin, and he became the only one of Martha and Judkins's sons who remained in Hancock County. He had married prior to his father's death and already had several children himself. By the second decade of the nineteenth century, the family homestead had developed into a substantial plantation. Judge Garnett Andrews attested to its large and diversified work force of slaves at that time when he recalled from his own childhood days that James's son "aroused the envy of all the boys for wearing to school a pair of coarse boots made by Jack, his father's shoemaker."[57] James's father Judkins divided the body of his estate between two of his surviving daughters and one granddaughter. One daughter received a "negro woman named Dinah with all her increase," and another acquired "the following negroes, viz. Libun, Will, Claborn, Randol, Peg and Nan, with all the household furniture." Listed at $1,000, Libun was judged the most valuable of Judkins Hunt's slaves. The two women, Peg and Nan, were considered the least valuable at $200 and $250 respectively. Judkins Hunt also left one granddaughter a bay mare— inexplicably named "John."[58]

Judkins Hunt's will further stated that he had already given "their legacies of my estate" to his other daughters, and to two sons who had moved west to Jones County, Georgia. Indeed, on March 10, 1795, county records show that he had conveyed to six of his daughters and sons, three slaves each, with the same number going to his son-in-law, Myles Green. A year earlier, the Hancock County tax digest indicated that Judkins Hunt was the owner of twenty-seven slaves, which made him the county's third largest slaveholder. At one time the Hunt family in its entirety reportedly owned five hundred slaves, although that number cannot be substantiated.[59]

Although Judkins passed most of his slaves along to his children either during his lifetime or when he died, for one he reserved special treatment, which may suggest some ambivalence in his attitudes toward slavery. In his will, Judkins specified that he wanted a black man named Moses "to live where he pleases, as he is old and has been a faithful servant." Assuming that this vague phrase meant that one elderly slave who had been with him since childhood should be granted nominal freedom, it would hardly have qualified Judkins Hunt as an abolitionist; nonetheless, very few Georgia slaveholders chose to offer even that degree of freedom to any black person at all. During the early years of the nineteenth century most white Southerners shared commonly held sentiments about the importance, the validity, and the justice of slavery. They also knew that state law had erected rigid barriers against manumission, and therefore acted to liberate only a very few carefully chosen slaves who tended to be either their own offspring, favorite long-time retainers, or the least productive workers. Judkins Hunt's elderly bondsman Moses would have fallen into both of the two latter categories.[60]

In 1801 John Finley from neighboring Warren County willed most of his slaves to members of his white family, but also directed that "a negro woman named Judith" should be freed. John Browne, who lived in the same county, did not actually free any slaves when he wrote his will several years later, but rather stated that he wanted to bequeath four specifically named slaves "to a girl of color named Millie, whom I have legally emancipated agreeably to an Act passed in Virginia." He "earnestly entreat[ed]" his executors to "take good care of the above girl." Millie may have been his mistress or even his child, but in any case, she was clearly a favorite of John Browne's.[61]

Greene County's Thomas Cobb made an impassioned plea to the state's legislators through his 1830 will. "I deeply regret not having it in my power," he said, "to testify to the following servants of mine my gratitude for their faithful service, to wit, Milly, Winny, Frank and Charity, by immediately emancipating them." "I am aware of the policy of the laws at present in force in this State," he continued, and "I earnestly wish it were otherwise that I might set them at liberty." He directed his executors to "present this my dying request to the legislature." "In case the legislature shall refuse this request (which I cannot allow myself to believe they will)," he left one of these favorite slaves, in the care of his executors, "to see that she be not abused," and ordered that she should remain on his plantation in "a good and comfortable log or frame house . . . and that her employment be the same as that she has been accustomed to do." Nothing indicates that the legislature agreed to free Cobb's four slaves, and in this period, these few wills from Middle Georgia are almost unique in their intent.[62]

In 1801 state law denied a master the right to free his own slaves, and individual emancipation could be accomplished only when the slave owner petitioned the legislature for a private act of manumission. Those regulations were later modified to some degree, and the years between 1815 and 1818, when Judkins Hunt declared his apparent intent that Moses should be allowed to live as a free man, provided a keyhole of opportunity when Georgia law briefly became more lenient, and testamentary manumissions could be granted and not challenged. By the time that Thomas Cobb made out his will in

1830, however, rigid control over all manumissions had been fully reinstituted.

Journalistic commentary and reportage also reinforced the overall bias against free people of color in Georgia's early years. In 1796 the *Savannah Advertiser* wrote that emancipation was "not a prudent subject of discussion in Georgia." In 1807, not far from the core counties of Middle Georgia, an Augusta journal repeatedly listed several free men of color as debtors in the early years of the nineteenth century. In that same town in 1809, Flora Fishburne, a free woman of color, was condemned because she had "long harbored" her fugitive niece, a plantation runaway who had forged papers and tried to pass herself off as the wife of a local boatman. Acts of familial loyalty and affection such as Flora Fishburne's led to Georgia's first law that subjected free people of color to a year's incarceration for helping a slave to escape.[63]

Some years later, an editorial in Milledgeville's *Southern Recorder* chided Northerners for their hypocrisy concerning free people of color. When some Southern slaveholders reportedly wanted to send a few of "their negroes" North to freedom, the paper contended that white citizens in those states did not welcome "this kind of population," although they often complained bitterly that slaves in the South were treated "barbarously." Faced with the possibility that people of color might actually move there, the Milledgeville paper claimed that the Northerners' "kind feelings for the colored people . . . cooled very suddenly."[64]

For the most part, the white Hunts seem to have subscribed to the same attitudes about slavery and people of color advocated by most other white Southerners. They became part of the affluent planter class, they owned slaves, prospered from their labor, but there is no evidence that they abused them excessively.[65] Nonetheless, their convictions may not have been totally intransigent, as first indicated by Judkins Hunt's testamentary instructions that one slave should be allowed to live independently, and further demonstrated by their evolving relationship with Susan Hunt and her family of free people of color.

One of Judkins Hunt's sons-in-law, Myles Green, a Methodist minister to whom Judkins had bequeathed several slaves in 1795, dealt with his own concerns about African-Americans in a different way. He joined the Milledgeville Auxiliary Society for Colonizing the Free Persons of Color of the United States, established in 1819 as an affiliate of the American Colonization Society, which had been founded just a few years earlier.[66]

Middle Georgia had two affiliated chapters, one in Milledgeville and the second in Eatonton in neighboring Putnam County. These chapters subscribed to the parent society's publication, the *African Intelligencer,* and in 1822 local members included a number of prominent citizens who pledged up to twenty-five dollars per year to support the organization and its mission. Working with that group, Myles Green found himself among other clergymen, plus lawyers, judges, planters, educators, bank presidents, state legislators, and physicians. Even the state treasurer and a former governor belonged. Their unquestioned respectability and political influence allowed these men to win endorsement for their efforts from several important Georgia newspapers. Society members apparently convinced the legislature that their organization could make a positive contribution in helping to maintain an orderly society, because in 1821 a law was passed allowing free blacks to be turned over to the American Colonization Society for the purpose of transporting them to Africa.[67]

In Georgia, American Colonization Society members did not oppose slavery. Many, in fact, were major slaveholders. The continuing presence of free people of color, however, disturbed them, and emigration to a "territory on the coast of Africa" at the Society's expense was the "modest course" they advocated, supposedly to alleviate that situation. Africa, they argued, provided the ideal "asylum for persons of color who were then free . . . and for those who might become so by the proper means." From Mount Zion *The Missionary* also rhapsodized that "there is something delightful in the idea of the free black returning to the land of his ancestors, not merely to enjoy himself, but to be the bearer of civilization and religion to his benighted countrymen." The people of Africa, society members believed, inevitably would "feel a national sympathy for their returning brethren, which will ultimately secure them a favorable reception." The Middle Georgia auxiliary said that "several of the slave-holding states . . . have recognized and encouraged the plan of colonization," reflecting the "benevolence and humanity" of many white Southerners.[68]

Members of the Middle Georgia chapters of the society argued that their proposals would "promote the happiness of an unfortunate class of our fellow beings," because free people of color, they said, were subject to both "the suspicions of the whites and the hatred of the slaves." By facilitating colonization, they hoped to provide a solution to the "problem" of "a numerous body of free persons of color, who, deprived of many of the rights of freemen, and much of the protection of slaves, are a burden to themselves, a source of discontent to slaves, and a detriment to slave-holders." The state of Georgia, they correctly pointed out, encumbered these men and women with a "long list of civil incapacities . . . in the unequal ratio of taxation, [and] subjection to seizure and sale as slaves . . . for the venial offense, ignorantly or inadvertently committed, of failing to register themselves every year, with the clerks of the inferior courts." Colonization, they argued, "will give this degraded class of men a country and a home . . . it will place them on a theatre where they may, among themselves, enjoy that equality which they cannot hope to enjoy in this country." "Turn loose a person of color in the Southern country," they said, "and without adding to his happiness, you increase in the community an acknowledged nuisance; transport him to Africa, and you promote his happiness, make place for a more valuable white member of society, and add to the strength and security of the community." Society members saw free people of color as a troublesome group who occupied a shifting and comfortless middle ground, "midway between liberty and slavery, [who] know neither the restraints of vice, nor the incentives of virtue."[69]

They articulated the baseless, though widely held, concerns of many whites who were alarmed because "the last census shews the number of free persons of color in the United States and their rapid increase." There was no telling, they feared, "how large a portion of our population will, in the course of even a few years, consist of persons of that description." They also emphasized that the "advantages to the white population" inherent in their approach ensured that "every proprietor of slaves . . . [had] the right of disposing of his property as he pleases."[70]

In addition to those advantages that directly accrued to Anglo-Americans, society members further argued that colonization would also "ameliorate the condition of those that remain in slavery." They expressed concern about the "effects produced on our slaves, by the fascinating, but delusive appearance of happiness, exhibited in persons of their own complexion, roaming in idleness and vice among them." Removing free people of color from Georgia presumably would "render [the slaves] more industrious and attentive to our commands." Nonetheless, to ensure against any possible upsurge in the slaves' aspirations to return to Africa along with their free sisters and brothers, Colonization Society members insisted that those slaves must clearly be shown that "the only possible way, if indeed there were *any* way possible to accomplish it, would be to pursue an obedient, industrious, virtuous course." Thereby, "the desire to go to Africa might be turned to the greatest private and public advantage" and would serve as a "safe-guard against domestic insurrection."[71]

The society's "board of managers" reassured other white Middle Georgians that although many people misinterpreted their mission and "impugned" their motives, they were nonetheless firmly "opposed, not only to an incorporation, whether general or partial, of the colored people into the state; not only to any mixture of their blood with ours, but to all enlargement of persons of color in this country." Colonization Society members thus repudiated both social integration and miscegenation, and underscored their basic tenet that persons of color should be allowed to exercise the rights and privileges of citizenship only "*in the distant country of Africa.*" In conclusion, they urged others to join them in order to "participate in one of the greatest works of patriotism, humanity, and religion, which modern times have brought forth."[72]

In spite of this rhetoric, apparently the only manumitted slaves from Middle Georgia who went to Africa during the early decades of the nineteenth century were the people freed by Joel Early of Greensboro, who does not seem to have been a member of the society. Reportedly, a group from Early's plantation sailed for Liberia on the freighter *Montgomery* in April 1830. Readers in Mount Zion, however, read other reports in *The Missionary* such as that about "the brig Dewitt Clinton [that] sailed from New York . . . for Port au Prince, with one hundred and twenty free coloured men and women who are emigrating to Hayti."[73]

Involvement in Colonization Society efforts did not encourage its members to consider emancipation as an option for their own households, nor did it restrain them from owning and routinely buying and selling slaves. One Putnam County member, for example, sold a black woman to a local slave trader, and Judkins Hunt's son-in-law, Rev. Myles Green, served as witness to the transaction.[74] Society members rarely freed any of their own slaves, nor did they serve as legal guardians for free men and women of color or otherwise seek to help that "unfortunate" class for which they expressed such vocal but shallow compassion.[75] One member who to a limited degree contradicted that generality in the century's early decades was Milledgeville's Thompson Bird. On one hand, Bird did own and trade in slaves, but he also served as the legal guardian of a free spinner and weaver named Nancy, and several other free people of color. A relative, Williamson Bird, was guardian for a large group of free people of color in Taliaferro County.[76]

Although Anglo-Americans in Georgia could easily go along for years and never cross paths with one of them, most whites argued and probably convinced themselves that the state's few free people of color created serious societal problems. Journalistic comment, legislative actions, and Colonization Society discourse all substantiate that conclusion. In spite of the oppressive social environment and the restrictive laws that targeted and unfairly discriminated against the free people of color, whom most whites considered troublesome interlopers, a few individuals and families belonging to that anomalous intermediary caste managed to survive in Middle Georgia. The Ruffs, Mosses, Holts, Jameses, and Bustles lived and worked throughout Middle Georgia, and Susan Hunt remained on the white Hunts' plantation for a number of years.

After Judkins Hunt's death in 1817, his son James continued to farm at the homestead in Hancock County, not far from the village of Mount Zion, where a new family settled during the early 1820s. Those newcomers, the Sayres, hailed from New Jersey and arrived in Hancock County by way of Old Petersburg, Georgia, in the Broad River Valley some fifty miles to the northeast. Descended from Thomas Sayre, who had emigrated from Bedfordshire, England, in 1638, first settling in Lynn, Massachusetts, and then moving on to Southampton, Long Island, the Sayres who came to Georgia two centuries later were Northerners and staunch Presbyterians. The family's women were literate and devout. The men were well educated, ambitious, and sophisticated in their tastes. They were lawyers, merchants, and town folk, not farmers. Brothers Nathan, Robert, and William, William's wife, plus their sister Delia Sayre Watkins and her husband, all settled at Mount Zion, where they lived near the second generation of the Hunt family in Hancock County, the James Hunts, with whom their lives soon became inextricably intertwined.[77]

WOMEN OF COLOR
AND THE SAYRE BROTHERS

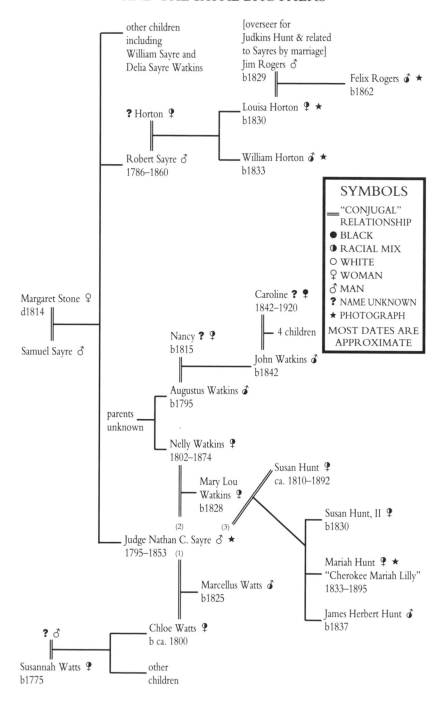

11

Pomegranate Hall

Many a man and woman in the South have lived
in wedlock as holy as Adam and Eve, and brought
forth their brown and golden children, but because
the darker woman was helpless, her chivalrous and
whiter mate could cast her off at his pleasure and
publicly sneer at the body he had privately
blasphemed.

W. E. B. Du Bois
"The Damnation of Women"
Darkwater: Voices from Within the Veil, 1920

By the beginning of the second quarter of the nineteenth century, the newly arrived Sayres had settled in the village of Mount Zion while the James Hunt family was comfortably established on their large nearby farm. Susan, a young free woman of color, lived near Mount Zion with them. One visitor described the area as a "pretty . . . circle of hills and fertile valleys."[1] Their local newspaper, *The Missionary,* though clearly not abolitionist in its policies, nonetheless advocated an unexpectedly open-minded attitude toward people of color—both blacks and Native Americans. The journal voiced editorial support for the American Colonization Society, and one of its publishers, Joseph Bryan, another transplanted Yankee like the Sayres, contributed generously to that organization. In addition, a family of free people of color lived with Bryan after 1830, and he served as their guardian for many years.[2]

On the Hunts' Mount Zion plantation and elsewhere throughout Middle Georgia, inland cotton production came to dominate the economy, and even as early as the 1830s overplanting that demanding crop had begun to devastate the land. Nonetheless, some fortunate, hardworking, and successful planters thrived. Productive land increasingly became concentrated in the hands of a few, and the major planters, including the Hunts, relied on a large force of slave labor to produce their crops. Thereafter, people of African descent always comprised more than half of the region's population.

If cotton production fueled the economy of the Lower South, a violent incident in the Upper South influenced the legislative and social course in all of the slaveholding states for many years. In August 1831 a black preacher named Nat Turner organized a rebellion among a group of his fellow slaves in Southampton County, Virginia, in the southernmost part of that state where many Middle Georgia settlers came from, the Hunts among them. Rumors persisted that free people of color had agitated the slaves and helped to organize the uprising. Nat Turner and his co-conspirators were not protesting the cruelty of one individual master, but rather they lashed out against the inherent injustice and the degrading nature of slavery itself. Before order was restored, as many as sixty white men, women, and children had died at the hands of the rebellious slaves. The event galvanized public opinion and struck fear in the hearts of whites. Though Turner himself hid in the nearby Dismal Swamp for a brief period, he was eventually captured and hanged, as were his cohorts. Law enforcement officials cracked down firmly on people of color, and legislatures throughout the South reacted swiftly. In that part of Virginia alone, well over one hundred blacks were either tried and executed or slain outright in bloody reprisals stimulated by the actions of Turner and his small band. White people considered Turner especially dangerous because he could read and write and because he invoked Biblical teachings, Christian beliefs, and messianic visions as inspiration for his actions. Newspapers throughout the country replayed the story. Whites responded to the episode and the subsequent furor not by examining their allegiance to the "peculiar institution," but by concluding that the root of the problem lay with people of African descent themselves.[3]

Fear and reaction spread like wildfire across the South in the wake of the Turner rebellion. Repression took several forms: more stringent controls over the slave population, further restrictions on the already circumscribed rights of free people of color, efforts to avoid social unrest by encouraging removal of that same group through colonization, and suppression of all antislavery discourse. The state of Georgia offered a five thousand–dollar reward for anyone who would bring the abolitionist William Lloyd Garrison to the South so that he might be tried for inciting revolution. Shortly after the Virginia uprising, the white citizens of Milledgeville rushed to arm themselves. Authorities routinely challenged every gathering of people of African descent and arrested at least nine Baldwin County slaves but had to release all but one when rumors of a local conspiracy proved ungrounded.[4]

Immediately following the Turner rebellion, the Georgia legislature passed laws denying slaves in Milledgeville the opportunity to hire out their own time or live apart from their masters. Clearly, they did not want slaves to behave like that presumably disruptive caste, the free people of color. New legislation also forbade both slaves and free people of color to sell most products and to operate public eating houses in Hancock County. Two years later, similar provisions pertaining to the town of Greensboro limited the personal and economic freedom of people of color there as well, and throughout the state they could no longer be employed by apothecaries or have any access to drugs. A bill applying to Warrenton required free people of color to pay a special four-dollar "Town Tax." Teaching people of color—slave or free—to read or write, or allowing them any access to a printing press became a misdemeanor punishable by fine and imprisonment, and free people of color could no longer "own, use or carry fire arms of any description whatsoever." Nat Turner had been a preacher, and in a direct response to fears stimulated by the power he supposedly wielded over his followers, the state of Georgia required the endorsement of three licensed and ordained ministers (understood to be white) before any person of color could preach. In 1835 the legislature further toughened the criminal code to severely punish free people of color who harbored runaway slaves, and suspended all constitutional limitations on search and seizure when any such activity was suspected. Officials could also keep them from registering in county court houses on the basis of an undefined "bad character." If men and women of color could not clearly document their free status and no one claimed them as slaves, they then could be fined and expelled from the state. Once having left, they forever lost their right to legitimately return to Georgia.[5]

By 1841 demands to further deny them access to learning or the written word resulted in legislation prohibiting either the sale or gifts of books, journals, paper, or ink to any people of color. Several years later the legislature denied them work as "mechanics and masons." In 1847 the state discouraged social interaction between the races by subjecting whites to fines of a thousand dollars and six months' imprisonment for gambling with any "negroes or free persons of color." After 1849, every free person of color in the state was automatically subjected to a head tax of five dollars, but at the same time "male citizens"—white men—were routinely taxed only twenty-five cents. That same year the legislature unilaterally resolved that the Congress of the United States should in no way atempt to interfere within the state of Georgia to limit the rights of slaveholders. Overall, during the 1830s and 1840s, Georgia's legislature consolidated the hegemony of the white planter class, inflicted severe economic inequities on free people of color, further denied them an education, limited civil liberties and freedom of expression, and generally tightened its legal controls over the activities of all persons of African descent.[6]

In 1843 one uncharacteristic piece of legislation countered those generalities, to a limited degree. It exonerated free people of color who had resided in Georgia since 1836 but had failed to register as required by law, but still required them to do so in the future, although children were not subjected to punishment for any such failure. People who did not comply with these laws concerning registry and guardianship were no longer forced to leave the state, but they still could be arrested and fined.[7]

Perhaps more important than any individual law passed in the 1840s was the 1848 state Supreme Court decision that defined free persons of color as residents but not citizens of the state. Always, the court decreed, they have been "regarded as our wards." "They have no political rights," it continued, "but they have personal rights." Throughout the antebellum years, people of color in Georgia retained their legal status as "wards," they never acquired any political rights, and the state laws continued to erode those limited personal rights.[8]

Notwithstanding the general alarm stimulated by the Turner rebellion resulting in an extended legislative and judicial response, most rural white folk enjoyed relatively peaceful lives in Middle

Georgia during these decades. They would have interacted with the small number of free people of color infrequently, if at all. Hancock County's Richard Malcolm Johnston, born and raised on his parent's plantation there, faithfully chronicled the lives of these white men and women, wrote about slaves as well, but never mentioned free people of color. As an adult, Johnston practiced law and taught at the Mount Zion Academy and another nearby school where he included some of the Hunt boys among his students. His reminiscences reflected his Middle Georgia childhood, when home, farm, church and school, and intricate relationships between generations, the races, and the sexes dominated every aspect of rural life.[9]

Johnston modelled the fictional village he called Dukesborough after Powelton, a small town viewed by some as "English in its rural simplicity."[10] He remembered the Hancock County of his youth as "a healthy, fertile region, undulating in small hills, vales and creeks and covered with dense forests of oak, hickory and kindred growth," where flowering trees blossomed "from St. Valentine's till past midsummer." Sowing, cultivating, and harvesting the crops marked the changing seasons.[11]

Johnston believed that although "patrician rule obtained for many years, as in all newly settled communities," rigid class distinctions relaxed over time. In his youth, "hospitality was regarded as an indispensable, even sacred duty, [and] leading citizens not infrequently sat at the board of their less gifted neighbors, and had the latter more often at their own." Other observers in Middle Georgia agreed that integrity was a better standard by which to judge an individual's worth than material wealth, and that in a "democratic society," neighborliness was a finer attribute than pride in an aristocratic heritage.[12]

This egalitarian spirit that reportedly characterized most social relationships in Middle Georgia nonetheless was clearly understood to include only the white population because the gulf between the races superseded all other class distinctions. White rural folk who owned neither land nor slaves and often survived only by participating in a barter economy were called "po' white trash," "piney woods men," or "crackers," and plantation house slaves, among others, sometimes regarded them with contempt. One isolated village in Greene County was even known as Cracker's Neck. But precarious financial standing and derisive designations notwithstanding, even the poorest and least esteemed white man knew he was free and independent, and believed himself superior to any person of color.

Richard Malcolm Johnston knew that plantation life often drew blacks and whites into close physical proximity with one another, and he believed that it encouraged both intimacy and loyalty. He nonetheless acknowledged that white people were rude and often cruel to their slaves, and clung to the belief that the "niggers" were little more than property. Judge Garnett Andrews painted a somewhat different picture of the relationships he observed between Middle Georgia's masters and slaves. He described one decadent and "obese old planter . . . lying on his sofa, having a negro woman scratching his head, two children picking his ears, two rubbing his hands and two his feet." Most whites in Middle Georgia considered African-Americans childlike, irresponsible, and irresistibly prone to steal and lie. The Nat Turner uprising, however, made them fear that people of color could be dangerous and deceitful as well.[13]

In at least certain respects, white men looked down on women as well as blacks. In some instances white women were idolized as unimpeachably pure and fragile goddesses—above either passion or suspicion—but they were also legally and socially subordinated to men in many ways. White men in Georgia rarely considered women their equals in matters concerning politics, economics, or the intellect. The proven capabilities of a few hardy and independent widows and other single women notwithstanding, most women occupied a distinctly separate domestic sphere that kept them removed from the economic arena and basically included only home, family, and church.

Marriage was widely understood to be a woman's ideal status, the goal to which all girls presumably aspired. "The young bride knew that with herself and her name she gave all else she possessed, and she let herself become absorbed into the one whom she believed that Heaven had sent for her one earthly guide and defender," said Johnston, who wrote about a number of presumably contented married couples. In that antebellum era, however, married women as a rule could not hold property in their own names, and any political role was unthinkable. In Georgia and throughout the South, marriage was virtually indissoluble. Women had great difficulty in obtaining divorces, even with apparently unquestioned cause, and generally they were granted only through individual legislative action. One white woman swore that her husband subjected her to constant abuse—even tossing a chamber pot filled with urine on her—and regularly forced the slave women on their plantation to have sexual relations with him; yet she had to appeal her case all the way to the state Supreme Court to obtain a divorce. The black women whom he had assaulted supported the wife's claims and testified readily in her behalf.[14]

Women of both races and all classes learned to tolerate abuse from men. Garnett Andrews described the boorish social and sexual behavior that characterized the conduct of many whites. One "parcel of dare devils" who went out "courting" in Middle Georgia "pinched their sweethearts' ears and cheeks until they squealed; slapped them with vigorous love-licks that made them grunt; hugged them with a bear's grip and kissed them with ravenous appetites." The minister of Mount Zion's Presbyterian church reportedly locked his wife in her bedroom when she disobeyed him, nailed the door shut after she tried to escape, and ultimately prevailed upon the church's elders to suspend her membership as punishment for her willfulness.[15]

In spite of the excesses of some overly zealous members of the clergy, churches attempted to moderate their parishioners' more blatant behavior. From their pulpits, many ministers denounced drinking, smoking, gambling, and fornication and occasionally even admonished members of their congregations for brutal treatment of slaves. Baptists and Methodists, who did not require an educated clergy, predominated in Middle Georgia, and, according to Johnston, "quite a number of men were members of some church, [and] the women were so almost without exception." Slaves often attended church with their masters and mistresses, generally standing at the rear or up in a gallery, while many others, sometimes surreptitiously, worshipped on their own. Sunday was usually recognized as a day of rest, but even during the week, church activities provided a focus for social as well as religious activities of many women—both black and white. Illiteracy was prevalent, but quite a few people who read nothing else could accurately quote both chapter and verse from the Bible.[16]

While not as numerous as the Baptists and Methodists, the Presbyterians also established churches in the region. Mount Zion's Presbyterian Church was incorporated in 1813 when its congregation raised the seven hundred dollars needed to construct a simple white frame building at a crossroads seven miles north of Sparta. The Sayres joined during the early 1830s and then transferred their membership to the new Sparta Presbyterian in the early 1840s. Members of the Hunt family attended a number of churches, but several, James Hunt's youngest son Henry included, joined Mount Zion Presbyterian. Although the church at Mount Zion remained important in that community's life, the associated academy became far better known.[17]

The Reverend Nathan S. S. Beman, yet another Yankee in Georgia, founded the Mount Zion academy shortly after he came to Hancock at the invitation of *The Missionary*'s editor, Joseph Bryan, and he became the church's minister as well in 1814. He was renowned for his disciplinary fervor as well as his rigorous curriculum. When he returned to the North in later years he became known as an avid abolitionist, but he publicly expressed no such views during his tenure in Middle Georgia. Because there was "no other classical school in all of the up country," Mount Zion's academy quickly acquired a unique reputation. By Richard Malcolm Johnston's accounts, "the rural people in general received no higher instruction in books than was to be obtained in what were known as Old Field schools." At those one room schoolhouses—usually just converted log outbuildings covered with clapboard—educational basics were taught haphazardly, "varying with the particular make-up of the schoolmasters."[18]

Some schools taught only boys, others only girls, but a few were coeducational. Middle Georgians had mixed sentiments concerning female education. Although many people expressed the conventional wisdom that a formal education was unnecessary and even harmful for girls, a few first-rate schools such as Sparta's Female Model School thrived in Middle Georgia by the 1830s. *The Missionary* argued that young women "should remember that a well improved mind is the jewel that will recommend her, is the accomplishment that will remain when the bloom of youth is faded away, is the ornament that far surpasses mere elegance of form or symmetry of features."[19]

At Mount Zion Academy Nathan Beman set a community standard for rigid discipline in the classroom. Most parents agreed that children should be regularly reprimanded with corporal punishment in school and at home as well, but Rebecca Latimer Felton, who grew up in a nearby county, expressed concern over the effect of physical correction. "In the homes where the lash was used, sons either despised the father or concluded it was the proper way to treat women," she argued. As for young women, "the daughters, afraid and disgusted, took chances hoping to do better in selecting kinder masters than their mothers had done."[20]

Johnston, Felton, and Andrews all documented the experiences of white people in Middle Georgia during the second quarter of the nineteenth century, touching on slave life as well, but said virtually nothing about the free men and women of color whom the legislature repressed and circumscribed at every turn. Most whites considered them irritating anomalies in a society designed to be strictly divided between free and slave, white and black, yet some members of this little-known intermediary group managed to survive in Middle Georgia.

Because they alone lived apart from any white guardians, the Bustles were Hancock's only free people of color whose names appeared in the 1830 census. Nonetheless, a list of free people of color in that county appearing in the Milledgeville *Southern Recorder* only four years later showed no Bustles at all. In those few intervening years the Bustles may have left the region. They never again showed up among the free people of color in any of the eight Middle Georgia counties prior to the Civil War. In 1870, however, a farmer and property holder named Eli Bustle turned up as one of the more successful people of color in Reconstruction Hancock County, suggesting that at least some members of the family may have "gone underground" rather than leaving.[21]

Replacing the Bustles, the free people of color from Hancock County listed in the *Southern Recorder* in 1834 included a seamstress named Eliza Shop and Frances Ashton, a washerwoman. Ashton apparently left the region soon thereafter because she appears in no other county records. Eliza Shop (sometimes spelled Shopp or Sharp) and her family, however, stayed around for many years. The *Southern Recorder* also listed a family of five Bellamys—Valentine, a Pennsylvania-born farmer whose age was given as seventy-seven, plus four children from three to seven years. During the 1840s and early 1850s Val Bellamy made two land transactions around the area known as Island Creek. In 1844 he bought 456 acres in that part of the county for four hundred dollars through his guardian, and then in 1853, sold 34 of those acres.[22]

By 1840 not a single family comprised of free people of color officially lived apart from white guardians in Hancock County. Nonetheless, the census did list forty-seven who resided with their guardians as prescribed by state law, but because they were not the heads of household, it did not provide their names.

Ten years later, in addition to three free people of color domiciled within the town of Sparta, another fifty-eight lived in the surrounding countryside. All of them worked on farms, with the exception of Lorraine Bryan and her five children including Cicero, a carpenter, who had once lived at Mount Zion under the guardianship of Joseph Bryan. The largest group was the combined Bellamy-Ross family—twenty-six persons in all—who farmed in the western reaches of the county. The families were linked through Mary Ross and Robert Bellamy, who lived together as man and wife and had one son born about 1851. Mary Ross later explained that she had "lived with a man but was never married to him according to law. The law did not allow us to marry then." The Rosses had apparently moved to Hancock in 1840. That year John Ross, the family's leader, purchased 314 acres of land "on the road from Buckhead to Waller's Ferry" for $75 through his guardian, Cinncinatus Jones. Ten years later he sold 100 of those acres to his brother, Currell, for $150. The families owned three farms quite close to one another. In addition to the Ross-Bellamy clan, the Ruffs, whose members resided in five separate households, continued to live in the northeast portion of the county near Warren and Taliaferro.[23]

In 1840 more than 70 free people of color lived in Warren County, but, as in several other counties, not one family is identifiable through the census alone. One white man there served as guardian for 22 free men, women, and children of color. A decade later, the number of free people of color in Warren had more than doubled to 156, more than ever lived in any other county in the eight-county region of Middle Georgia during the whole antebellum period. They included the Burnett, Moss, Ruff, Johnson, Jones, Loach, and Joiner families. The Burnetts lived in thirteen separate households, Mosses in eleven, Ruffs in eight, and Johnsons in three, and several residences included both Burnetts and Mosses. Howard Burnett, who owned a farm worth three hundred dollars, and Gideon Jones, a barber who had real estate valued at six hundred dollars, were the county's only notable "colored" property owners. With one exception, the free people of color in Warren had all been born in Georgia. Susan Loach, a black woman, came from Virginia. She presided over a three-generation household with a total of nine children, including her twins Sookey and Hannah, and one grandson. Susan Loach's sister lived nearby. According to the census, all of the Loaches—children included—were black and no adult males lived with the family, leading to the assumption that Susan's spouse and that of her oldest daughter both were slaves. Through the 1840s Warren County's free women of color worked as laundresses, seamstresses, spinners and weavers, and house servants. One white woman, Mercy Joiner, an unmarried domestic from South Carolina living in the southeast portion of the county, cared for three free mulatto children named John, Nancy, and Calvin, born in the mid-1840s. The children were never officially registered in the county courthouse, and they may have been her own offspring.[24]

By the 1830s, officials in Taliaferro, just west of Warren, made its free colored residents go to great lengths to prove the condition of their birth beyond all doubt. This compulsive concern, combined with the large numbers of children in some free families, suggests that local authorities may have feared that a slave might try to pass her baby off to a free woman of color to assure the child's freedom. It can only be guessed whether any actual incidents justified that belief. In 1847 Elizabeth Acree, a white midwife, swore that she had attended the birth of several such children. "I was with Zancy Floyd and Allen James, free persons of color," Acree stated, "when their children were born" during the 1830s. Another woman attested: "I, Rachel King (midwife) do hereby certify that I was with Martha Floyd a free Woman of Colour when her child Josephine was born of her body, that the said Josephine will be five years old the sixth day of March 1848." Two physicians, one of whom was Hancock County's E. W. Alfriend, a brother-in-law of the Hunt family, vowed that they too attended the births of several black children, "born of the body of a free mother."[25]

In 1840, of thirty-eight free persons of color in Taliaferro County, only one elderly man, Daniel Lee, can be identified by name through the census because he alone did not live in a household headed by a white man. In 1843, and almost every year thereafter, Jane Lesley, an elderly white woman who lived with Andrew and Catherine Adams, a free man and woman of color, went to the courthouse in Crawfordville to swear before county officials that a young man named William Lesley, described as "a bright yellow," was her son. William Lesley was a blacksmith who lived with the free Jones family, and his mother testified repeatedly that he was "not what is termed a free person of color, but he is termed a mustizo by the laws of said state." Jane Lesley never identified William's father, but he may have been the slave known as "Uncle Dave" who had to leave Alexander Stephens's Crawfordville plantation "because he got in trouble with a white woman." William Lesley had several sons of his own who also may have had a white mother—no woman of any race ever registered or claimed the boys—and William subsequently established their free status in Taliaferro as well. In 1850 another multi-branched extended family of color in that county included Grants, Floyds, Joneses, Jameses, and Ruffs.[26]

In 1845 Alexander Stephens, Taliaferro's leading politician, publicly denounced the "moral evil of slavery." Stephens was clearly not an abolitionist, but one of his former slaves distinctly remembered that a couple named Harry and Eliza were widely known as "Stephens's free niggers," and by 1860 Mary Stephens and her daughter Harriet, trusted house servants as well, were enumerated among Taliaferro's free people of color. They held real and personal property valued at fifteen hundred dollars and lived near Alexander Stephens's home, Liberty Hall, on Crawfordville's northern outskirts.[27]

By 1840 twenty-three free people of color lived in Greene County, and their number had more than doubled ten years later. Three units of the Ruff family spilled over from Hancock, Warren, and Taliaferro, and four households included people named Grant—also present in Taliaferro. Financially, the most successful family was that of Ned and Hannah Parks. Ned was a carpenter who owned real estate valued in 1850 at $150. By 1860, his estate had increased to $3,000, and his sons Ned, Jr. and Albert had also become carpenters. Ned, Sr., died in 1868, leaving a will—unusual for a black man—in which he bequeathed the property to his wife and children. His daughter Lucy Parks Hoffman acquired half of his cattle and other livestock, and his son Albert specifically received "all of my tools both Carpenter and Cabinet."[28]

As in most of the other Middle Georgia counties, no free people of color in Putnam County just southwest of Warren were identifiable by name in the 1840 census, but in 1850 the Roberts and

Cuthbert families resided there. Green Roberts was a shoemaker, and he and his wife Philice had five children. Their son John, John's wife Louisa, and their three children lived next door. A laundress named Elizabeth Cuthbert led a large three-generation family in Putnam including her grown daughter Matilda, a teenaged son, and Matilda's three young children. With one exception, they were described as mulattoes. No adult man lived with the Cuthberts, leading to speculation that the children's fathers may have been local white men. The thirty free people of color who lived in Putnam in 1840 decreased to only twenty-five ten years later.[29]

In 1832 Milledgeville's *Southern Recorder* listed seventeen free people of color from Baldwin County bearing the surnames Moss, Norman, Mercer, Smothers, and Taliaferro. A man named Joe Butler, "alias Joe Holt," who had been manumitted years earlier in the state of New Jersey, also appeared in the newspaper listing. But none of those names were recorded in the 1840 census, although it included a total of sixty-eight unnamed people of that description who lived with white guardians. According to Baldwin's Registry of Free Persons of Colour, however, only eight people registered in the county courthouse that same year. Four years later, county officials were keeping more nearly complete records, and they registered sixty-three free people of color. From the 1830s through the next two decades, free men of color in Baldwin worked as blacksmiths, barbers, bricklayers, carpenters, house servants, and farmers. One was a wagon maker and another a shoemaker. The women were cooks, laundresses, housemaids, seamstresses, and spinners. Most had been born in Baldwin and the nearby counties, but several came from Maryland, Virginia, and North Carolina. Census names and numbers always differed to some degree from the county registers, and by 1850 the official count had dropped to twenty-seven.[30]

Baldwin County's Foard family included Richard, a blacksmith, and his wife Elizabeth Bugg; George, a farmer; Harriet, a cook; and Henry, Baldwin's only free black shoemaker. The Foards, who came from nearby Jones County, were all in their twenties when they first registered in the courthouse in 1845. Henry Foard's life reflects the ties that often bound the community of slaves to that of the free blacks. A former Baldwin County slave named Ferebe Rogers recalled that her "daddy was an ole-time free nigger." Although she did not give his name, he must have been Henry Foard, whom she described as "a good shoemaker [who] could make as fine shoes and boots as you ever seen." Ferebe's mother was a slave, and therefore her white master claimed ownership of her thirteen children even though their father was a free man. "De ole-time free niggers had to tell how dey make dey livin', an if dey couldn't give satisfaction 'bout it, dey was put on de block and sold to de highest bidder," Ferebe Rogers said. "Most of 'em sold for 3 years for $50," she explained, but her own father "brought $100 when he was sold for three or four years." Henry Foard registered as a free person of color from 1845 through 1848, and in 1850 he lived with his brothers and sister. He apparently remained in Baldwin County long enough to father thirteen children, but after 1850 he disappeared from official records, perhaps, as his daughter Ferebe explained, because he was temporarily sold into slavery when he "couldn't give satisfaction" concerning the legitimacy of his occupation and was "sold to de highest bidder."[31]

The life of Baldwin County's Wilkes Flagg and his family contains many contradictions. Supposedly, the Virginia-born Flagg purchased his own freedom and that of his wife Lavinia Robinson and their son, Wilkes, Jr., from their owner, Williamson Fort, in the 1830s, although self-purchase was not recognized as a legal form of manumission in Georgia at the time, and the Flaggs do not appear as free people in either the 1840 or 1860 censuses. Although it seems questionable, some reports assert that he became pastor of an independent black Baptist church as early as 1845. By 1850 Wilkes Flagg owned a blacksmith shop and home valued at four hundred dollars on the south side of Milledgeville. The census that year described him as a forty-five-year-old mulatto. Wilkes Flagg was a handsome man with pale eyes and wavy hair. He dressed impeccably and catered official state dinners for several Governors. The white Fort family remembered him as "a remarkable man, copper colored, six feet high, weighed about 180 pounds, very dignified and with the manners of a Chesterfield." In spite of laws that clearly forbade educating any person of color, he had "been taught to read and write by the elder white children of the [Fort] family." The 1850 census described the thirty-eight-year-old Georgia-born Lavinia as a mulatto too, but in a photograph she appears dark-skinned and quite formidable. In 1846 a white man named S. P. Myrick announced in the local newspaper that "having purchased Wilkes, I shall carry on the Shop heretofore occupied by him." Myrick may have known that self-purchase was technically impermissible or invoked the law which decreed that free persons of color who left the state—Flagg traveled in the North—or failed to register in the county courthouse were subject to re-enslavement. Regardless of Myrick's claims, court trials, and the dubious circumstances under which the Robinson-Flaggs acquired their freedom, most people in Baldwin County seem to have considered them free.[32]

In 1834 the legislature decided to reward a young Virginia-born slave carpenter named Sam Marlor for his heroism in fighting a fire at the state house. The state appropriated sixteen hundred dollars to purchase him from his owner, Milledgeville's most renowned architect, John Marlor, and declared him free. Sam Marlor and his seven children registered in the county courthouse only once, in 1853, and the family never appeared in the census prior to the war. Nonetheless, county officials evidently accepted his children as free, although no evidence appears that Marlor had a nonslave wife, and he may have postponed their registration until she died.[33]

In addition to Marlor, the state legislature manumitted several other slaves during the 1830s. In 1833 it acted to free a woman named Mary and her daughter Cordelia. The case was unusual not only because the legislature manummitted so few people, but because Mary and Cordelia were acknowledged as the property of Lovewell C. Fluellin, a "free man of colour."[34]

In 1831 Eli Fenn, a middle-aged white man from Washington County, just south of Hancock, petitioned the Georgia legislature to free Sophia, a young woman of color who lived with him, and the legislature agreed that she should be "entitled to all the rights, immunities and privileges, as though she had been born free." Although the source of their freedom is unknown, the Chesters and Cooleys became that same county's largest free families of color during the 1840s. In 1843 the black Chesters, led by a woman named Elishia and including her nine children, went to court to remove themselves from the guardianship of Absolom Chester. They dutifully acquired a new guardian, who posted the required "bond of five hundred dollars for his faithful performance as said guardian." The Cooleys and some of the Chesters remained in the county, and by 1850 the Echols and Wiggins families had joined them.[35]

In June 1852 that same county's newspaper, the *Central Georgian,* featured an anecdote that reinforced white Georgians' views about the universality of black slavery, ridiculed free women of color, and questioned their opposition to slavery:

> A gentleman recently from Africa while at one of the civilized colonies on the coast, met a young colored woman whom he had known in Old Virginia, who had obtained her freedom for good conduct, and had emigrated to Liberia. "Where are you traveling to, Mary?" said the gentleman. "I'm going down to the village on the sea shore. I'm tired of seeing nigger, nigger! I want to see some white folks!"
> "But are you doing well here?"
> "O, very well. I have four slaves who make palm leaf hats."
> "Slaves, Mary! You emancipated, to have slaves in your own land?"
> "Oh, yes," said she with great simplicity, "must do as they do in Old Virginny."[36]

Middle Georgia was neither supportive of nor hospitable to members of this small and unwelcome group. Relatively little is known about them, and not much has been recorded about the opinions that most white people in the area held about their caste during the middle decades of the nineteenth century. Nonetheless, Garnett Andrews recalled one incident from his early days as a judge. "Have you got a free negro in your county whose crimes are recorded on his back," asked a white man who approached the bench, referring to laws requiring free persons of color to work under contract as punishment for debt or a misdemeanor, "that I may hire him to hate him?" "I never intended to marry," he continued bitterly, "but now I shall, that I may have children to hate his children."[37]

Few free persons of color lived in Middle Georgia during the fourth and fifth decades of the nineteenth century. Most white people seem to have either despised, scorned, or ignored them. In spite of the somewhat moderating editorial opinion expressed in the pages of their local newspaper, *The Missionary,* and by supporters of the American Colonization Society, those were the predominant attitudes that both the white Hunts and the Sayres encountered in rural Hancock County. Nonetheless, Susan Hunt, a free woman of color, would have a lasting impact on those families' collective lives.

Although the exact date of the Sayres' arrival in Hancock County cannot be determined, Nathan Sayre purchased his first land in Hancock in 1822, and in 1824 his name appeared on the ledger of a local store. In the spring of 1825 he served as secretary to the committee of leading local citizens that planned a gala ball celebrating the visit of the Marquis de Lafayette, and in June 1826 he addressed a meeting convened by a number of citizens "for the purpose of expressing their opinion and sentiments in relation to the [recent] treaty with the Indians." Mount Zion's Presbyterian church recorded Nathan's sister-in-law's membership in 1830, yet no Sayres appeared in the census that year in Hancock. Since there is little question that they did reside in the county by that time, their absence from the census must be explained by oversight, inaccuracy, or even temporary absence.[38]

Nathan Sayre probably moved into his new home, Pomegranate Hall, in Sparta, the county seat, during the early 1830s, although work on the house continued for several more years. Relatives visited him there later in that decade, yet in 1840 Nathan still officially lived near the Hunts at Mount Zion. Sparta and Mount Zion were only six or seven miles apart and probably Sayre, a busy lawyer who would have wanted easy access to the county courthouse, moved into town shortly after 1830 but retained his country house and property for some time thereafter.[39]

Nathan Sayre's public life as a state's attorney, legislator, and judge is well reported. His private life, however, is harder to reconstruct. Nonetheless, the censuses of 1840 and 1850, his will, and other documents provide a somewhat more complete picture of his personal life and behavior. Among his other slaves he owned two young mulattoes—one male and one female—born between 1825 and 1828 when Sayre was a vigorous young man. A slave named Chloe was the mother of Marcellus, one of those young mulattoes. Chloe's elderly mother was a slave named Susannah Watts, born in 1775. But for some reason, the 1830 census listed Susannah Watts as a free white woman who headed her own household in Sparta—one that included several younger free people of color. This one-time designation of Susannah Watts as both free and white, and her later confirmation as a slave exemplifies the shifting, questionable, and amorphous lines of both race and freedom. In addition to Susannah, Chloe, and Marcellus, Sayre's will mentioned a second group of mulatto slaves named Nelly, Augustus, and Mary Louise. Nelly and Augustus were brother and sister, and Mary Louise was Nelly's daughter. With little question, Marcellus and Mary Louise were fathered by Nathan Sayre. Since they were both mulattoes, their male parent most probably was a white man. Although an outsider could have fathered one such child in his household, more would be far less likely. Nathan Sayre had no overseer or other white employee in residence who would have been in continual intimate contact with his slaves. But the fact that seems to establish most clearly that they were Nathan's "family" was that his will provided for the emancipation of these six slaves.[40]

Nathan Sayre was a thirty-year-old bachelor when the first mulatto child was born in his household. Certainly his education, professional standing and wealth would have made him an extremely desirable potential husband for any white woman in Hancock, but at least among the upper classes and aspirants to that status, the "pure" Southern white lady was sexually unavailable. Any sort of sexual impropriety was considered inexcusable for an upper-class white woman, and even a suggestion of a dalliance of that nature would tarnish her reputation, since her chastity was supposed to yield only to marriage. A bachelor of Nathan Sayre's status in his community could hardly have "trifled with" a white woman whom he did not plan to marry. Slavery, however, provided both the domestic intimacy and the authoritarian environment that permitted and, at least for the man, often encouraged interracial sexual relations. The institution clearly allowed exploitation of black women by their masters. Nonetheless, in the minds of most white Southerners, their men remained blameless in any instances of "sexual debauchery." White ladies were expected to hold themselves above suspicion and deny any libidinous feelings, but the supposedly "debased" moral character of women of African descent was widely considered the major causative factor that encouraged promiscuity on the part of white men.[41]

Some questions arise as to the degree of coercion that was employed in such encounters, and the extent to which sexual license among white men was so widely tolerated and internalized that physical domination became essentially redundant. Hancock County's Lucius H. Holsey seems to have ruefully accepted that sort of behavior. His mother Louisa was a woman, "of pure African descent . . . fascinating appearance and comely parts." She was a slave who belonged to James Holsey, Lucius's white father. "Like many others of his day and time," he continued, James "never married, but mingled to some extent, with those females of the African race that were his slaves—his personal property." Similarly, long before his own brief marriage, David Dickson reportedly approached a thirteen-year-old slave named Julia Lewis in 1849, out on his Hancock County plantation one day, and "just rode up and swung her up on his horse and that was the end of that." Julia was described as strong-minded, small, and "copper colored," with beautiful teeth which she constantly polished with a sharp twig. Julia and David subsequently established a tenuous but long-standing relationship. They had only one child, resulting, it seems, from that first sexual encounter.[42]

The widespread toleration of white male sexual domination, however, does not adequately explain, nor by any means excuse, the behavior of masters with their female slaves. Some slave women from Middle Georgia recalled atrocious incidents of physical force and violence. Hancock County's Mollie Kinsey reported that when her sister was a young girl "they'd make her go out and lay on a table and two or three white men would have in'ercourse with her befo' they'd let her git up." Kinsey believed that those brutal attacks brought about her sister's premature death.[43]

Financial gain also motivated some sexual incidents between masters and slaves. Carrie Mason, who spent her childhood as a slave in Baldwin County, remembered that one master told his sons "ter go down ter dem nigger quarters an' git me mo' slaves." Rebecca Latimer Felton, who clearly held racist views, nonetheless recognized the plight of any women, regardless of color, who were subjected to unbridled male lust. The callousness of white masters who had sexual encounters with their slaves and subsequently ignored their mulatto offspring, appalled her. She also reported that for black women held in bondage "child bearing sometimes began at 12 years and frequent births made a heavy percent of 'profit.'"[44]

Whether or not any one sexual encounter between a master and a slave should be considered rape is almost historically irrelevant. Even the clearest cases of sexual violence would never appear in court because no legal grounds existed for such charges even if the social climate had allowed such action. The law did not acknowledge the rape of a black woman by a white man as a crime under any circumstances. White men regularly forced themselves on black women because they considered it their inviolable privilege, and no moral or legal authority restrained them. Their "absolute power" corrupted many slave masters absolutely. Lust and disdain spurred them on, and white society rarely expressed its disapproval.

Many women of color went to great lengths to avoid their masters' sexual advances. One local slave swore that she could deter her owner's attacks only when she "locked the door [and] nailed up the windows of her house." Instances of vigorous resistance were frequent and are well documented, but generally, counter-violence would have been both dangerous to the woman herself and ineffective. In a few cases, extended, intimate, and even genuinely reciprocal relationships developed between white men and women of color, but those were clearly exceptions. Acquiescence on the part of black women, even on a continuing basis, did not necessarily imply complicity. Another woman reportedly had sexual relations with her white master over an extended period of time and bore his "white child," but she was a "slave then, and had to obey his call."[45] The vastly divergent social and legal positions of black women and white men in the antebellum South is central to understanding these encounters. That enormous disparity ensured that almost any such sexual relationship would be exploitative because it pitted a white man, whose privilege and authority knew virtually no limitations, against a woman of color who would have been almost powerless to resist him. In most cases, force was redundant in a situation so inherently unequal. Physical coercion might have been involved or not, but only rarely would the woman have had any real choice in the matter.

Regardless of any possible individual extenuating circumstances, Nathan Sayre and the women of color in his life were part of that inherently coercive environment. There is no reason to believe that he needed to resort to physical violence to force his slave women to have sexual relations with him, and it seems unlikely that financial gain motivated him since he never sold his slaves and had no plantation requiring a large coterie of field hands. Nonetheless, Nathan C. Sayre probably fathered at least two children with two different slave women during his young manhood. Other than those surviving children who were born before 1828, no other mulatto slave child born after that date appeared in his household. This sort of pattern was not unusual when a master married a woman of his own race and class after years of indulging himself with sexual liaisons in the slave quarters. But officially, Nathan Sayre remained a bachelor throughout his life.

A major occurrence that significantly altered his habits seems to have changed the course of Sayre's life during the final years of the 1820s. Unlikely as it seems given the social environment and prevalent mores of plantation-belt Georgia, Sayre encountered Susan Hunt, a free mulatto–Cherokee Indian woman who probably worked as a servant for the neighboring James Hunt family at Mount Zion. He probably terminated the sexual alliances with his slaves, but instead of marrying a white woman, apparently established a permanent monogamous relationship with Susan Hunt—a relationship like those designated as "faithful concubinage" in the British West Indies. During the 1830s Susan bore three of Nathan Sayre's children. She moved from the Hunt's frontier farm near Mount Zion into the town of Sparta, where she lived for at least two decades in an impressive mansion which seems to have been planned, designed, and constructed at least in part to meet the unique needs of Nathan Sayre's free family of color.[46]

Sometime after 1830, he built that new home, called Pomegranate Hall, in the southeast quadrant of the town of Sparta. Sayre or a coachman could drive a handsome buggy drawn by his favorite team of horses through a welcoming avenue of elms, and around the circular carriageway, which culminated by the foot of an elevated verandah. Even from a distance, arriving visitors could glimpse the pitched roof, tall chimneys, and the two-storey porch with its four tall white columns. The gardeners planted much of the extensive acreage around the house in "wine grapes . . . [and] foreign experts were imported to tend the vineyards." Sayre was one of several Hancock County residents who attempted viniculture in that period. Around the house, some of the pomegranates, signifying fertility, for which the mansion was named, survive and flourish even today. Towering pines, poplars and lush magnolias, heavy with giant, waxy blossoms, now provide deep shade, and in years past, "the immediate grounds were adorned with flowers and shrubs." Smaller outbuildings including slave quarters, a stable, coach house, poultry coop, tool shed, and possibly a secondary yard kitchen, once surrounded the mansion.[47]

Unlike most other Greek Revival style houses, Pomegranate Hall's front entrance sits to the far left rather than in the middle. During this era similar residences known as "half houses" were built elsewhere around the country. Some were so designed because the owner intended to add a balancing wing at a later date and eventually locate the entrance in the center. Nathan Sayre may have had this in mind at one time, but no supplemental rooms were ever added, and the mansion's asymmetry detracts in no way from its overall style and elegance.[48]

The house is more than forty feet wide, nearly sixty feet deep, and most of it is three stories high. Ten steps led to a railed front verandah, or piazza, that stretched across its full width. Sayre had the mansion painted "monastic brown." White trim accented the door and window frames, and forest green louvered shutters and "venetian blinds" covered the rippled glass windows. The foundation is local granite and the walls throughout are two feet thick. Two smaller Doric columns to either side of the main entrance echo the massive ones on the front of the piazza. The mahogany door, eight feet high and adorned with a silver bell, is flanked by tall, narrow side windows and topped with a fanlight.

Residents and guests could enter the brick-floored ground level from another exterior door tucked beneath the verandah. Servants and tradesmen would have used the rear entrance into the kitchen—only semi-enclosed to welcome cool breezes—which featured an enormous walk-in cooking hearth. The ground floor included not only that kitchen, but also a dining room furnished with a round pine table big enough to accommodate a number of guests or a large family on twelve rush-bottomed chairs. The dining room was "finished, as is the whole house, in the finest kind of plastering." According to Sayre's cousin Mary Moragne, who visited him in the late 1830s, the ground level also included "store rooms, pantries, & every convenience of that kind which none but a Yankee could have suggested," as well as a wine cellar fully equipped with a press for making wine.

The main floor—the second level—included a grand entrance hall on the left and a parlor to the right. Nathan Sayre located his library, with its writing desks, chairs, lamps, and walls of built-in bookshelves, at the back of the house. He was an avid reader and bibliophile, and his law library was known as one of the finest in Georgia. General reading material included books on United States, international and ancient history, world travel, agriculture, the natural sciences and art, plus volumes on horse breeding and equine blood lines. The master of Pomegranate Hall enjoyed the writings of Washington, Jefferson, and Madison, as well as Shakespeare, Milton,

Homer, De Tocqueville, Adam Smith, Plutarch's *Lives,* and Lord Byron's *Journal.* Encyclopedias, Bibles, dictionaries, and atlases also lined his bookshelves.

Considering the unusual familial arrangement that Sayre established, two especially interesting books in his library were *Reveries of a Bachelor* and *Walker on Intermarriage.* In the latter, author Alexander Walker argued that his book provided "for the first time, a precise rule for the guidance of intermarriage." Walker challenged both the commonly held assumption of Anglo-Saxon racial superiority and the corollary belief that the mulatto offspring resulting from "racial amalgamation" would, like some hybrids, prove infertile. He addressed "intermarriage," finding that "the intermixture of races seems to improve the intellectual powers as much as it does the bodily proportions." He further stated that "mulattoes, unfortunately and ungenerously held in degradation, are not naturally inferior, I believe, to their fathers, either in moral or physical powers." Walker, an Englishman, attributed much of what he considered the "progress of the American republic" to the influx of many different nationalities and "bloodlines," which "offered to the world a splendid example of justice and national freedom." In many respects Sayre assimilated the traditional plantation lifestyle of Middle Georgia, but he also may have taken to heart the evidence offered in Walker's rare treatise on "intermarriage."[49]

Each of the two large rooms on the main floor are about twenty-five feet square, and Sayre covered his random-width pine floors with "Brussels carpets" and swathed the tall windows with heavy silk draperies. Couches and tables, arm chairs, a mantel clock, and gilt mirrors furnished his parlor and hall. Throughout the house framed engravings of prize-winning horses and of President Zachary Taylor and sketches of the nearby towns of Madison and Augusta covered the walls. The principal rooms on both the main and the top floors featured elegant fireplaces faced in variously colored marble. Handsome woodwork framed the windows as well as the mahogany interior doors. An "intricately carved arch" divided the main hallway, which extended the full length of the house on the main level. Beyond that divider, the massive central staircase led to a landing, angled right, then continued up to the top floor.

Only three bedrooms whose windows "attracted all the breezes & commanded views of the whole town and surrounding country," occupied that top floor. Nathan Sayre's own large chamber contained his bed—made up with linen sheets and covered with a "Marseille" counterpane—a bureau, wardrobe, rocking chair, and a stand where he may have laid his gold watch and ring before retiring. For his personal grooming and hygiene, he kept a wash stand, towel rack, soap dish, toilet glass, bowl and pitcher, looking glass, and a LeCoultre razor.

Except for its unusual asymmetry, Nathan Sayre would seem to have built an elegant, well-furnished, but otherwise undistinguished Southern antebellum mansion. That, however, is an incorrect conclusion, because Pomegranate Hall was unique in one remarkable respect. The original design, a local woman noted, included "more doors, intricate passageways & cul de sacs . . . [than] the Castle of Otranto," or, as Sayre's cousin Mary Moragne said, "many winding stairs and private passages." Those observers accurately described, but declined to admit the personal and social significance of Pomegranate Hall's architectural complexities.

The house included a hidden suite of rooms which comprised its entire right rear corner:

> From the back room on the third floor, a short stair leads down into a split-level room. This is small and its ceiling much lower than that of the principal apartments. There are three of these small rooms — one under the other and [they] had no connection with the outside world except by way of that third floor room . . . They are said to have been built that way "so that an eye could be kept on the children." The passage leading to the stairway to the roof also opens into this room which . . . must have been that of the "Master."[50]

When he designed and built his elegant home, Sparta's eligible "bachelor," Nathan Sayre, ingeniously adapted its classical architecture to facilitate this private apartment.

Above the ground floor level, the major body of Pomegranate Hall had two storeys. Each of those floors had rooms with fifteen-foot ceilings, which when combined created an elevation of about thirty feet. The private suite, on the other hand, included three rooms, one above the other, connected by narrow halls and sharply angled staircases. Each of those three rooms had a ceiling of about ten feet, which also created a total height of thirty feet. The three lower-ceilinged rooms fit neatly into exactly the same elevation occupied by the two higher-ceilinged floors in the main part of the house.

The rooms in the private apartment were twelve feet square, snug, and cozy. Each had one shuttered window on the side and another looking out onto the garden behind the house. They included just space enough for a bed or two, bureau, chair, and possibly a wash-stand. The hidden suite's bottommost chamber (most likely the children's nursery,) opened on a passageway leading to a small door outside Nathan Sayre's library. The room just above, apparently Susan Hunt's bedchamber, had two doors. One opened onto a private rear porch and the other to the master bedroom. A small landing just beyond Susan's interior door was only three steps down from Nathan Sayre's room. The door in Nathan's chamber that led to her room was both lower and narrower, but featured the same carved woodwork as the other interior doors of the house. The rear chimney serving the unadorned fireplaces in the private apartment, led down to the semi-enclosed kitchen on the ground floor level. The uppermost room included ladder-like steps leading to a trap door in the roof which could be opened for ventilation. As needed, that top floor room may have been another child's bedchamber, or Susan Hunt's own maid may have slept there. The evidence provided by the architecture at Pomegranate Hall is abundantly clear. The private suite could not have been added as an afterthought. It was an integral part of the mansion's original design. It may have been the ultimate manifestation of the ingenuity that, his cousin said, "none but a Yankee could have suggested." The only reasonable explanation for its existence is that Nathan Sayre, a leading citizen, elected official of Hancock County, and a lifelong "bachelor," built that apartment and organized much of his personal life around his free family of color: Susan Hunt and their children. They were not accorded the honored treatment given a white family, with legal sanctions, full visibility, and unquestioned social acceptance, but neither were they ignored or relegated to inferior or external quarters. Influenced by his lasting relationship with Susan Hunt, Nathan Sayre planned, wanted, and needed to "keep an eye on the children." His own children. Pomegranate Hall was Nathan Sayre's mansion—the imposing residence of one of Sparta's leading citizens—but within its walls Susan Hunt and their children occupied an intimate, privileged, and protected place.

Susan and Nathan's oldest daughter, also named Susan, was born in 1830. Three years later Great Britain ended slavery in the West Indies, and in November of 1833 people throughout the South watched the dazzling Leonid meteor shower when the "stars fell" over Georgia. "Judgment day is here!" one witness cried. Another marvelled that "worlds upon worlds from the infinity of space were rushing like a whirlwind to our globe. . . and the stars descended like a snow fall to the earth." "Saint or sinner . . . master or slave," everyone agreed that "the memory of that awe-inspiring spectacle, the grandest and most sublime perhaps ever staged in the high heavens endured with him as long as he lived." Harriet Powers, a slave born in Middle Georgia, heard the story repeated often and stitched brilliant replicas of shooting stars, astonished observers, and the little "varmints [who] rushed out of their beds," into her quilts. Susan Hunt and Nathan Sayre's second daughter, Mariah Lilly, was born at Pomegranate Hall that year of the falling stars. Their son, James Herbert, arrived several years later. All three children bore the Hunt, not the Sayre, name. Susan may have relied on traditional Native American pharmacology to space her pregnancies, but she would not have had her own mother or grandmother to administer the old herbal remedies or attend her deliveries in keeping with Cherokee tradition. More likely, Nathan Sayre's family physician, E. M. Pendleton, one of Hancock County's most respected practitioners—also a poet of some local repute who advocated the emigration of free people of color to Liberia—probably assisted her labor.[51]

Nathan Sayre lived for over twenty years at Pomegranate Hall with his family of color, but only a few stories elucidate his life prior to that time, one of which appeared only after his death in the Milledgeville *Southern Recorder*. As a boy in New Jersey he had boarded with a woman who remembered him as "a most excellent youth and a general favorite in the school and town." She also believed, however, that he had never paid the final installment on his bill for room and board, in the amount of thirty-eight dollars. Nathan thought that all of his debts had been paid by "a guardian, who had means in his hands for defraying all my expenses." Years later when he finally learned of the woman's claim, he sent her a check by return mail, not only for the balance due, but also "with interest to date."[52]

The Sayres' cousin by marriage, Mary Moragne, also reported that Aaron Burr once visited the attorney with whom young Nathan and Robert Sayre were reading law and advised the novices that "you have commenced the study of law, young gentlemen, and if you ever expect to gain distinction in it you must have a flower garden no bigger than a horse blanket." Burr's graphic illustration of the law as a jealous mistress became family legend. Nonetheless, Nathan built Pomegranate Hall with its landscaped grounds, and soon thereafter Robert Sayre finished his even more elaborate mansion, noted for its formal gardens, on the other side of Sparta. Neither heeded Burr's advice, neither married, and both became attorneys—extensive gardens notwithstanding.[53]

Mary Moragne called Nathan Sayre her "worthy cousin" and described him as "excellence itself, united with Yankee wisdom."[54] He was a lawyer by training and a politician and businessman by choice. Real estate investments constituted much of his wealth. In addition to the family's first home at Mount Zion and the extensive acreage in Sparta where he built Pomegranate Hall, Sayre "held property all the way down to Linton" in the southernmost reaches of the county. His will mentions "the lot of land owned by me in Milledgeville," as well as "a small parcel near this village [Warrenton] on the Augusta Road," and at the time of his death his holdings included nine other undeveloped lots, plus six others, presumably commercial property "with offices." Sayre first purchased land in Hancock County in 1822, continued to accumulate property through the 1830s and 1840s, and was party to at least twenty-nine land sales during the final decade of his life. In addition, he functioned as a private banker and money lender. After his death about twenty people including members of his own family, proprietors of a large cotton mill in Sparta, and a woman of color called "free Elizabeth"—probably a local laundress named Elizabeth Garnes—all paid off notes with interest to his estate. He also promoted railway development in Middle Georgia and owned a number of shares of Georgia Rail Road stock that issued regular dividends.[55]

In 1826 Gov. George Troup appointed Nathan Sayre solicitor general for the northern district of Georgia. Hancock County voters first elected Sayre their state senator in 1829 and returned him to that office in 1830. He was initially affiliated with the States Rights Party, and along with many other prosperous Georgians he later became a Whig.[56] Over the next few years he served in an unspecified role on the personal staff of Gov. George Gilmer, went to Georgia's house of representatives in 1833 and then back to the senate in 1838, 1842, and 1843. From 1845 through 1849, he was elected superior court judge for the state's northern judicial circuit. Because these positions were part-time or seasonal in nature, Sayre continued to practice law and pursue his other financially successful interests in Sparta during his more than twenty years of intermittent public service. "After taking the opinion of several gentlemen of the profession," stated Garnett Andrews, Sayre's associate on the superior court, "I have no doubt that more lawyers in Georgia make under than over one thousand dollars per annum." He added that "it is very unusual for a Georgia lawyer . . . to die worth one hundred thousand dollars, or even half of it." Sayre, however, was a successful exception to Andrews's generalization.[57]

As a legislator, Sayre was reliable, cautious, and generally undistinguished. His actions and his votes indicate that he served his constituents' interests well. He was a member of the judiciary and education committees and sponsored bills of incorporation for Sparta's Presbyterian church and for the town of Mount Zion. He worked to improve the condition of Hancock County's roads and to clarify its boundaries. Few private bills requesting the emancipation of individual slaves came before the state legislature during his years in office; when they did he sometimes voted for manumission and sometimes against, but almost always stayed with the majority. In 1830 he opposed the pending proposal to manumit the wife and child of Solomon Humphries, but later in that session he favored granting freedom to "Joy, Rose, June and John, formerly slaves of Raymond Danere." He said "yea" to the manumission of Peninah, a slave in Butts County, in 1838, but voted against the emancipation of "Nancy and John, property of Peter Ray."[58]

In 1843 he supported, and in his capacity as a member of the judiciary committee perhaps even initiated, an atypical bill to "exonerate and discharge certain free persons of color from all pains, penalties and forfeitures." That legislation forgave such people as his consort Susan Hunt who had failed to register in the county courthouses, though it did require future compliance. It also protected children such as his own from any possible punishment for continued infractions.[59]

The state representatives who boarded in Milledgeville—described by one visitor as a "mere village"—during legislative sessions enjoyed dubious personal reputations. One woman, "a neatly dressed coloured maid," apologized to some incoming guests for the appearance of a hotel bedchamber, reporting that everything was in disarray because the previous occupants, four members of the legislature, "turned the room into a hogpen, by smoking and spilling their brandy and wine about the floor."[60]

During Sayre's tenure on the Georgia superior court his associate Garnett Andrews remembered that the judges first traveled on "horseback, then sulkies became general, and then buggies . . . succeeded them." Innkeepers welcomed them hospitably, and "spirits were always placed in our rooms, as well as in the bars of the hotels at which we stopped." Living conditions on the judicial circuit, however, were less than ideal. The hotels provided "clean tablecloths once a week . . . clean [towels] every Sunday morning; sheets changed when very much soiled and without reference to the previous number of occupants."[61]

Like a number of other prominent citizens of Sparta, Nathan Sayre joined the Hancock County Planters' Club, which became a significant regional institution. Unrelieved cotton cultivation during the early decades of the nineteenth century had seriously depleted the soil by the 1830s. Formerly fertile lands had become unproductive and valuable topsoils had washed away, leaving much of the Middle Georgia landscape ravaged and scarred with deep gullies. Land and homes frequently sold for a pittance or were even abandoned. One local planter stated in 1843 that "at every point the eye meets the evacuated and dilapidated mansion, . . . fields that once teemed with luxuriant crops are disfigured with gaping hillsides, [and] chequered with gullies . . . the sure indices of barrenness and exhaustion."[62]

Those factors, combined with alarm over fluctuating cotton prices, were the conditions that the Hancock County Planters' Club sought to ameliorate. Hancock County farmers, encouraged and supported by the club, became widely known and respected for the agricultural reforms they championed, their progressiveness, and their optimism and enthusiasm for Southern agrarian life. Over a period of twenty years the Planters' Club attracted a considerable measure of public acclaim for its role in stimulating the region's economic turnaround.[63]

Reforms that the club promoted included heavy fertilization, deep seeding, hillside ditching, contour plowing, crop rotation, labor management, use of improved strains, and more efficient machinery. Hancock County reportedly employed more and better labor-saving devices than any other county in the South. The club also sponsored an annual fair highlighted by a parade led by a local band and club members who marched from the grounds of the Sparta Female Model School to the town hall square. In a few short years, the fair became a well-known regional event that attracted large, enthusiastic crowds.[64]

When the Planters' Club was founded in 1837, membership was restricted to affluent members of the community and was an indicator of lofty social status and respectability. By 1841, however, its officers stated that "any person may become a member by subscribing [to] the Constitution and paying the sum of one dollar on or before the 1st Monday in December." Nonetheless, it never would have welcomed such hard-working farmers and landholders as Valentine Bellamy and John Ross, who were free men of color. Robert Sayre was a charter member of the club and a signatory of the original constitution. His brothers Nathan and William joined a few years later, as did four brothers in the Hunt family. The club also bestowed honorary membership—the status granted to a very few "deserving" women—on William Hunt's wife Martha Ann, who managed a large plantation called Oakland that she had inherited and managed following the death of her first husband. Nathan Sayre became the club's corresponding secretary and exchanged letters with reform-minded community leaders and agriculturists throughout the South. He had little interest in crops, but served enthusiastically on its "equine committee" and cared a great deal about horses—their breeding and bloodlines—judging from his numerous books and pictures at Pomegranate Hall.[65]

Membership in the Planters' Club was not the sole manifestation of Nathan Sayre's involvement in local endeavors. His older brother Robert stimulated the establishment of the Sparta Female Model School when he purchased just under four acres of prime town land in 1833. That land became the site of the new school's three white-columned classroom and dormitory buildings plus its elegantly turreted chapel, all of which faced a street "called Maiden Lane because young ladies from the female seminary used to walk there beneath the trees." Teachers as well as students from outside Hancock County boarded nearby. Neat fences surrounded the grounds on all sides, and the bells that chimed in the chapel's clock tower could be heard throughout the town. Robert and Nathan Sayre, plus three other men, formed the academy's original board of trustees, which soon expanded to eleven, including their brother William. The academy they supported "was quoted as being amongst the top in the nation." Nearly one hundred girls from all over Georgia, the neighboring states of Tennessee and Florida, and as far away as New York attended the school in 1838.[66]

Under the direction of headmaster Sereno Taylor, a minister and former functionary of the American Colonization Society, the school grounded its curriculum on "Seven Disciplines": language, mathematics, "cosmics," history, "geotics," government, and philosophy. The academic program was unusual for its time in that "the students are taught not merely by hearing lectures and seeing experiments, but they lecture and experiment themselves." Adiel Sherwood, who wrote about education in Georgia, reported that "the most distinctive feature . . . consists of making every branch practical and causing the pupil to take the place of the teacher in all exercises." Music comprised an important part of a Southern "lady's" training, and the academy's "music department had in its heyday sixteen pianos . . . [and] the young ladies were taught many fazes of the arts, music and of course dancing." Katherine DuBose, the wife of Nathan Sayre's close friend, taught piano and harp. The academy's brochure noted proudly that "Madame E. Salmon Hantute, of Paris, has been engaged as Teacher of the French Language, Piano Forte and Singing." Tuition for the academic year 1838–39 ranged from $35 for students in the "Primary Department" to $125 for the "Collegiate Department" and included instruction in both harp and organ.[67]

Robert, Nathan, and William Sayre were well-educated, public-minded citizens who devoted themselves to increasing educational opportunities for girls and young women in their adopted town. The birth of his own daughters may have further stimulated William Sayre's interest, but Mary Moragne's visit in 1839 as her cousin's guest at Pomegranate Hall suggests another reason for Nathan's support of the academy.

By that time, Nathan Sayre and Susan Hunt had two daughters of their own: young Susan, who was nine, and Mariah, about six. His two older children by his former slave mistresses may have lived at Pomegranate Hall as well. Moragne's sensibilities as a close relative and an elite white Southern woman would have made it impossible for her to openly acknowledge the presence of those "illegitimate" mulatto children who would have been her own cousins, but she cryptically acknowledged the presence of "the boarders, some young ladies" and several "neatly dressed young gentlemen workmen," expressing surprise at their impeccable demeanor and manners. Pomegranate Hall had only three bedrooms in the main part of the house—Nathan occupied the master bedroom, his brother a second room, and the visiting Mary the third—making it unlikely that the "boarders" could have been anyone but Nathan's consort, Susan, their children—the younger Susan, Mariah, and the baby James Herbert—and possibly their older half-brother and sister. On her last day in Sparta, Moragne came home and "found the girls on top of the house." The roof was accessible only by climbing the steps that led up from within Susan Hunt's private family suite. Although she found the view from the top of Pomegranate Hall "imposing and beautiful," Mary Moragne suffered from vertigo and became decidedly queasy. "I can not bear to stand on such high places," she complained. She admired the striking vista from a safe distance away from the edge, but then turned "with a sickening feeling of horror to see . . . the girls approach the parapet & actually climb up on it."[68]

During her visit, Mary's entertainment as the honored guest of her cousin, academy trustee Nathan Sayre, included a concert at the Sparta Female Model School. She, her host, and others in their party went by carriage across town to the school where they were graciously escorted to, and seated in, a salon furnished with twelve pianos. "As if by magic spell," she said, "twelve young ladies seated themselves, & went in concert through evolutions from the first book to the fourth or fifth." But the amateurish performance disappointed Moragne. She "imagined" herself in "Bedlam," and privately complained that "nothing less than the novelty of the scene could have induced us to tolerate for a moment such a discordant concatenation of sound."[69]

Following that introductory musical disaster, however, the situation improved. Headmaster Sereno Taylor's daughter discreetly ushered in to the the room a young music student "with large dark eyes, soft and beautiful as the Turkish dream of a Houri . . . accompanied by a little dark complectioned girl apparently of eight or ten years." Moragne was pleased to "see this strikingly contrasted couple sit down & play in concert the most beautiful & difficult airs and overtures." Following the piano recital, the visitors "were next taken into a room filled with Organs, & this interesting couple again played together." When they concluded, the presumably unknown and "dark complectioned" children described as "prodigies" were surreptitiously whisked away, and the concert abruptly ended. The visitors then expressed their "thanks to Mr. Taylor for his trouble, [and] the amiable teacher assured us in a melancholy voice that it was not often . . . that they were honored with such visits."[70]

Mary Moragne would hardly have described any elite Southern Anglo-American girls—who religiously shaded their skin with hats and parasols to retain its milky whiteness—as "dark complectioned" or "the Turkish dream of a Houri." As one Georgia woman observed, "a pretty white complexion was the call of that period . . . the young women were emphatic on that line." Similarly, it would have been thoroughly uncharacteristic for a devout Christian such as Moragne to refer to two proper Anglo-American girls as "houris"—nymphs of the Mohammedan paradise—with the associated pagan implications of that word. Propriety and antebellum Southern social mores would have prohibited her from openly acknowledging what she undoubtedly considered the embarrassing relationship between her cousin Nathan Sayre and the children whom she described as his boarders, yet the young musicians who performed at the Female Model School and the bold, agile children who scrambled across the "parapets" of Pomegranate Hall, surely were the same little girls. Almost certainly they were Nathan Sayre and Susan Hunt's daughters. Traditions in the white community would not have allowed Sayre to officially enroll his daughters as regular students at the Sparta Female Model School, and indeed the younger Susan and Mariah were only minimally literate. The compromise arrangement was decidedly unconventional, but it seems likely that Nathan's political prominence, his position as an academy trustee, plus the promise of a generous bequest in his will, yielded him the opportunity to have his girls study music at the school with some kind of unique and privileged status. As a former Northerner who had been involved with the work of the American Colonization Society, headmaster Sereno Taylor and music teacher Katherine DuBose, a trusted friend, may have been conspirators in his subterfuge. The girls apparently were gifted musicians, and several generations of women in the Hunt family have displayed similar talents.[71]

Sayre's attempts to have his daughters acquire some of the "graces" expected of Southern ladies were unusual but not unparalleled. Another Southern judge also reportedly had a longtime mistress, a woman of color who lived in a cabin on his own property near his home. The woman and the judge had three daughters, whom he cherished. He sent two of them to a music conservatory and the other to a Northern woman's school.[72]

Susan Hunt and her family enjoyed the patronage of a powerful white man in the person of Nathan Sayre. His presence as master at Pomegranate Hall accorded the Hunt children unusual privileges and protections in their home town, where he was a prominent citizen. Alethea Taylor, another mulatto woman from Sparta, lived with her children in a house of her own in nearby Augusta. She supposedly had been manumitted according to law and had an officially designated guardian in the person of her consort, but, unlike Susan Hunt, her "husband" did not live with her. Because of strict legal prohibitions against teaching any persons of color to read and write, she, who previously had been educated covertly alongside her white mistress, had to teach her own children secretly in the basement of her house. David Dickson, Hancock County's wealthy "prince of planters," defied the law and handled the problem of education for his family of color by bringing in a private tutor and building a schoolhouse on his plantation for his daughter and then his grandsons. County authorities apparently did not elect to challenge Dickson on his own property.[73]

Nathan C. Sayre was honest, diligent, well-educated, well-dressed, erudite, and also hospitable and sociable. He was a professionally, economically, and politically successful man and a pragmatic, civic-minded citizen who worked to better his community. He also cared for and about his and Susan Hunt's children and provided them with at least some of the privileges accorded young people in upper-class white families.

Sayre also remained close to his white family, as evidenced by the brothers' common efforts in the Planters' Club and on behalf of the Female Model School. His cousin Mary Moragne's visit demonstrates that the Sayres' extended family maintained its strong ties. During her sojourn at Pomegranate Hall, Moragne spent time with Nathan's brothers and sister-in-law, his sister Delia Sayre Watkins, her husband, and other cousins as well. Nathan was also a better businessman than his older brothers, whom he helped, even as they fell into his debt. His will bequeathed slaves, individual stipends, and the body of his substantial estate to those brothers and to his nieces and nephews.[74]

Adella Hunt Logan, 1900.
Speaker at the 1897 Atlanta
University Conference on
Negro City Life.
From D. W. Culp's Twentieth
Century Negro Literature.

W. E. B. Du Bois, author,
sociologist, coordinator of
Atlanta University
Conferences on Negro Life,
and friend of the Hunt family.
From Du Bois's The Souls of
Black Folk.

Cherokee woman,
nineteenth century.
The Hunt family shared this
Native American heritage.
*Courtesy of
the Smithsonian Institution.*

Judge Nathan C. Sayre, 1795–1853.
An affluent lawyer and public offi-
cial, Sayre lived in Sparta, Georgia,
for many years with his free family
of color.
From Caroline Bond Day's A Study of
Some Negro-White Families in the
United States.

Mariah Hunt, "Cherokee Mariah
Lilly," 1833–95. Daughter of Susan
Hunt and Nathan C. Sayre. Born at
Pomegranate Hall, she later lived
on Hunt's Hill in Sparta.
From Caroline Bond Day's A Study of
Some Negro-White Families in the
United States.

POMEGRANATE HALL

Pomegranate Hall, Sparta, started in 1830. Home of Judge Nathan C. Sayre, Susan Hunt, and their three children.
From John Linley's The Architecture of Middle Georgia.

Exterior, showing smaller windows in the family apartment.
Photo by
Virginia Kent Anderson Leslie.

Right rear corner of
the mansion, showing back
windows and chimney of
the family apartment.
*Photo by
Virginia Kent Anderson Leslie.*

Looking from Nathan Sayre's
bedchamber at the door and
steps leading down to Susan's
room, as well as stairway to
upper level room.
*Photo by
Virginia Kent Anderson Leslie.*

Sparta Female Model School, ca. 1840. Nathan C. Sayre was a trustee and financial supporter, and his nonwhite daughters apparently studied music here.
Courtesy of the Hargrett Rare Book and Manuscript Library, University of Virginia.

Liberty Hall, Crawfordville, Georgia, home of Alexander H. Stephens, vice president of the Confederacy. Stephens allowed several of his "servants" to live as free people of color.
From Stephens's Constitutional View of the War between the States.

Rev. Wilkes Flagg, 1805–77.
*Courtesy of the Georgia Department
of Archives and History.*

Lavinia Robinson Flagg, b.1812.
*Courtesy of Lois W. Lane, Flagg's
Chapel, Milledgeville, Ga.*

Former slaves, the Flaggs purchased their own freedom. Wilkes worked as a
blacksmith in Milledgeville prior to the Civil War. They both went to trial
when they defied laws pertaining to people of color. During Reconstruction
they established an agricultural enclave for freedpeople, and Wilkes was a
Baptist clergyman.

Elmcroft, Jones County, Georgia. Members of the Hunt family built this typical Middle Georgia plantation house around 1820.
Courtesy of the Georgia Department of Archives and History.

Daughter of a Hunt family slave working in the cotton fields at Elmcroft planatation, ca. 1900.
Courtesy of the Georgia Department of Archives and History.

Amanda America Dickson, 1849–93, daughter of Hancock County planter David Dickson and his slave, Julia Lewis. Amanda attended Atlanta University and inherited most of her father's vast wealth. *Courtesy of Virginia Kent Anderson Leslie.*

Lula Hunt McLendon, b. 1860, married, raised her children, and remained on Hunt's Hill in Sparta. *From Caroline Bond Day's* A Study of Some Negro-White Families in the United States.

Adella Hunt Logan, 1863–1915, educator and suffragist. Her life at Tuskegee Institute ended tragically. *From Caroline Bond Day's* A Study of Some Negro-White Families in the United States.

The two older daughters of Mariah and Henry A. Hunt.

List of free people of color who lived and registered in Washington County, Georgia, from the Sandersville *Central Georgian,* August 8, 1860.

Turnwold plantation, Putnam County, Georgia. Childhood home of Joel Chandler Harris, 1848–1908. Chandler's popular writings about people of color reflected the biases of the local planter class.
Courtesy of the Uncle Remus Museum, Eatonton.

Henry A. Hunt, Jr., 1866–1938, educator and member of Franklin Delano Roosevelt's "black cabinet."
Courtesy of Archives/Special Collections, Atlanta University Center, Woodruff Library.

Sarah Hunt Rogers, b. 1869, became an educator. In her middle years she married her widowed cousin, Felix Rogers.
From Caroline Bond Day's A Study of Some Negro-White Families in the United States.

Ella Hunt Payne, b. 1872.
A divorced woman, she lived and worked in Savannah and then New York City.
Photo by C. M. Battey.

Tom Hunt, 1879–1942, became a professor at the University of California, Berkeley. He concealed his racial heritage in order to "pass" as a white man.
From Caroline Bond Day's A Study of Some Negro-White Families in the United States.

The four younger children of Mariah and Henry A. Hunt.

Louisa, a property owner on Hunt's Hill, was the mother of Felix Rogers.
Courtesy of Arthur Silvers.

William reportedly fought with the Union army during the Civil War.
From Caroline Bond Day's A Study of Some Negro-White Families in the United States.

Louisa Horton, b. 1830, and William Handy Horton, b. 1833, thought to be the children of Nathan Sayre's brother Robert and an unidentified slave.

Susie Hunt Rogers, b. 1864,
a daughter of the younger Susan
Hunt. She became her cousin Felix
Rogers's first wife.
Courtesy of Arthur Silvers.

Felix Rogers, b. 1862. Son of
Louisa Horton and Hunt overseer
Jim Rogers. Felix first married
Susie Hunt, then later wed their
mutual cousin, Sarah Hunt.
Courtesy of Arthur Silvers.

Susie Hunt Rogers and Felix
Rogers with two of their
daughters.
Courtesy of Arthur Silvers.

Edmund Asa Ware, Freedman's Bureau superintendent
of education, State of Georgia, and founder and first
president of Atlanta University, 1867–85.
*Courtesy of Archives/Special Collections, Atlanta University
Center, Woodruff Library.*

Atlanta University, 1880.
Courtesy of Archives/Special Collections, Atlanta University Center, Woodruff Library.

Samuel Wynn.
From Caroline Bond Day's A Study of
Some Negro-White Families in the
United States.

Louise Wynn, b. 1831.
From Caroline Bond Day's A Study of
Some Negro-White Families in the
United States.

Jennie Wynn, b. 1858.
*Courtesy of Archives/Special Collections,
Atlanta University Center, Woodruff
Library.*

Louise and Samuel Wynn lived as wife and husband in Augusta before the
Civil War. Other white men from the extended Wynn family served as
guardians for free people of color in Middle Georgia. Jennie Wynn, Louisa
and Samuel's daughter, graduated from Atlanta University and taught in
Milledgeville.

Hancock County courthouse, Sparta, Georgia, completed 1882. Site of first Dickson trial and proceedings concerning the will of J. M. Hunt.
Photo by Fred Zimmerman. Courtesy of Virginia Kent Anderson Leslie.

Received of C. W. DuBose Ex⁓
J. M. Hunt de⁰ʳ Two hundred and
thirty six 50/100 dollars dividend 86 shares
Geo R R⁰ Stock due July 15th 1889
Rec⁰ also Two hundred & thirty six
50/100 dollars from C. W. DuBose Ex⁓
of James M. Hunt de⁰ʳ dividend
due Oct 15th 1889
This 23ᵈ October 1889
In presence of

R. A. Graves

Susan X Hunt
her
mark

Susan Hunt's acknowledgment that she received stock dividends from the
Georgia Rail Road. Hancock County Courthouse, Sparta, Ga.

Much about Nathan's role as a father and consort to his free family of color is based on informed speculation and family tradition. One of Susan and Nathan's great-granddaughters always heard that he was "a sensitive white judge . . . who had only one family and this was his Negro family." "Opponents would try to use this fact against him, but he was a devoted father," she continued, who "would proudly parade his family before his constituents, and despite the opposition tactics he managed to be re-elected time and again." Another family member stated that "any white man in that day and time in the state of Georgia, who defied tradition and lived openly with the Negro woman of his choice, deserves the fullest respect of manhood."[75]

Susan Hunt's free family of color never appeared in the census until after the Civil War, but their tenuous legal status and the nature of their personal lives provide reasonable explanations for that absence. During this period, one respected citizen from each county in the country attested to the validity of the United States census for that county. In 1840 Nathan Sayre was that person in Hancock County, and he certified and signed the local enumerators' results. If for any reason he did not want his own "wife" and children to appear, he would have had enough influence to see that they did not, and no one would have challenged that decision. The Hunt elders also recall that the family's white patriarchs always advised their non-white kin "that when the census taker came around, we weren't supposed to be there." Until the end of the Civil War any person of color in Georgia was unquestionably presumed to be a slave unless he or she could definitively prove otherwise. Susan Hunt and her children had always been free, resulting from the status of her Cherokee mother, but they may not have had the requisite documentation needed to establish that freedom beyond a reasonable doubt. Susan had a mentor, but never an officially designated legal guardian, nor did her children, and none of them ever registered as free people of color in the county courthouse. That failure placed them in technical violation of the law. Their legal as well as their personal and social status was both ambiguous and tenuous. Discretion was apparently the preferred course. Better, perhaps, that they remain "invisible" and absent from all official documentation.[76]

Manumission was a risky business in Georgia as Nathan C. Sayre knew all too well from his years of governmental and legal experience.

Technically, it was possible only by a rare private act of the legislature, or through carefully structured wills. Manumission through a will required the slave in question to leave the state prior to being granted freedom. Sayre had built a remarkable mansion in Sparta with his family's needs in mind, and he cherished them and wanted to keep them near. A relationship such as his that may have originally been stimulated by sexual attraction could blossom over time into strong, genuine affection. Although rare, an enduring association between a white man and his mistress, a woman of color, might signify lasting devotion by both parties. Such men as Sayre could easily become enmeshed by sincere love for their children. He had a successful professional and political life in Hancock County. As a pragmatic man he would not have wanted to disrupt his comfortable arrangement by attempting to make any drastic changes in the life of his family. He could not under law legitimize either his relationship with Susan or the birth of his children in the state of Georgia. Officially petitioning for their manumission might easily fail, but in any case it meant that the law would require them to leave the state. They could be subject to arrest, confinement, and fines if they remained illegally. Sending them away might have been Sayre's most altruistic option. If Susan Hunt and the children had gone to a distant free state where their background remained undisclosed, they might have passed for white, benefitted from his secure financial standing, and even taken his name. But Nathan did not want to leave Georgia himself, and his paternalistic possessiveness ruled out the option of having Susan and their children leave without him. She too may not have wanted to leave the only home she had ever known for a distant and amorphous promise of greater freedom.

Susan Hunt's private relationship with Nathan Sayre can only be imagined, but her personal appeal and attributes must have been impressive. She influenced a noteworthy and, by all speculation, conservative man of substance to defy tradition on her account. Their alliance was not a fling or passing fancy. It endured for a full quarter century. It may have been a misshapen marriage, but if it began as the result of erotic attraction, it certainly endured based on much more. Sayre risked his political career, his economic security, and his social status. Because he never married a white woman, he denied himself the male badge of honor of leaving his name to legal descendents, and he probably could not have taken Susan Hunt and their children into the parlors of Sparta's elite white families.[77]

One Warren County scribe argued at the time that the wife of a "man of sense" should have the following attributes: "it is a companion whom he wants . . . who can reason and reflect, and feel and judge, and discourse and discriminate, one who can assist him in his affairs, lighten his sorrows, purify his joy, strengthen his principles . . . such is the woman who is fit for a mother and the mistress of a family." Susan may have provided all that for Nathan, though he could not have included her in his political life and many social diversions. This may not have been important, however, because the same local writer further asserted that "a woman of the former description may occasionally figure in the drawing room . . . but nothing more."[78]

Although she probably did not participate fully in Nathan's social life, Susan Hunt presided over a substantial domestic establishment. She was the mother of three active children. Her spouse would have been absent frequently while he traveled, served in the legislature, and rode the judicial circuit. Susan would have worn the mansion's keys clipped to her belt and managed the household in his absence. Unlike a number of female slaves who lived on plantations and had to succumb to the sexual demands of married masters, Susan never served under the direction of a white mistress. The presence of a white wife created almost insurmountable problems for the woman of color who was her master's sexual companion. A wife would be infuriated by her presence, and not only would she view that woman of color as a rival for her husband's affections, but any children that he had by her would visibly document his infidelity and might also compete for a share in his estate. The white wife had the power of law and tradition on her side, but the slave woman had no support. No white woman ever became the mistress of Pomegranate Hall, and Susan Hunt supervised a staff of servants that may have included two of her consort's former mistresses and his slave children, who were just a few years older than, and the half-brother and -sister of, her own two daughters and son.[79]

The "Southern lady" or "plantation mistress" has always been presumed to be white, but Susan Hunt's experiences certainly paralleled at least some elements of those women's lives. She would have needed to oversee the full panoply of domestic functions at Pomegranate Hall. That would have included everything from providing food and clothing for the entire household to caring for both the physical and spiritual well-being of her own family as well as that of Nathan's slaves. Supervising the work of the domestic servants—household maintenance, cooking, cleaning, and laundering at the least—was always the mistress's responsibility in a large household. Susan routinely would have negotiated with tradespeople, gardened, smoked meat, preserved fresh fruits and vegetables, nursed the sick, mended, and made candles, soap, and household linens. Successfully coordinating and carrying out those responsibilities challenged privileged white women and would have been even more demanding for an illiterate woman of color who probably had less external support and routinely faced open hostility from the white community.[80]

Pomegranate Hall's immediate neighborhood, however, included several other free people of color who may have been supportive friends to Susan and her children. In 1840 free people of color lived in four nearby households. They included three young men, one young woman, and two older women more than fifty-five years of age. By 1850 the people of color who had resided with three of those white families ten years earlier had left the town of Sparta. A young black man named David Coleman lived nearby with the town postmaster, and Mary Scott, a mulatto woman, and her little girl still resided within walking distance of Pomegranate Hall with their guardian Benjamin Pritchett.[81]

Susan's three children at Pomegranate Hall—the younger Susan, Mariah, and James Herbert—were bold, adventurous, and agile enough to clamber across the roof. In addition, the girls were accomplished musicians. Nathan Sayre provided them with velvet ribbons, fancy bonnets, silk gloves, scarves, and crepe shawls, and he bought silk, velvet, cambric, calico, and fine muslin for Susan to make their dresses.[82] They matured into unusually handsome women. Both were dark-eyed and dark-haired and resembled their Cherokee ancestors. They looked much like each other, except that long curls framed Susan's face, and Mariah pulled her straight hair into a severe bun at the back of her head.[83] They had no regular schoolmates, and their friends are not known. The relationships with their half-sister and -brother who lived nearby if not in the same house and remained the slaves of their mutual father can only be imagined.

No one knows where or how Susan and Nathan's children played or the chores they performed. When she was about ten, their daughter, known as "Cherokee Mariah Lilly," was baptized in the Presbyterian church to which both the white Hunts and the Sayres belonged, but her older sister and younger brother apparently did not join. Mariah later became a member of the Colored Methodist Episcopal church, where her gravestone declares that "hers was a life of trust in God." In addition to sponsoring them in his church, a man of Nathan Sayre's achievements might have educated his children, and some of his books such as *Arithmetic, Schoolcraft, Godman's Natural History*, and *The Bridget Bubble Family* clearly focused on a growing family's needs and interests. He must have believed in educating young women, judging by his interest in and financial support of the Female Model School. Nonetheless, the girls' academic attainments were minimal, though they were accomplished musicians and musical evenings were regular events at Pomegranate Hall.[84]

What would the white women of Sparta have thought and done about Susan and Nathan's unusual living arrangement? One of Middle Georgia's most eligible "bachelors," a professional, sociable, educated man of taste, moderate habits, ample wealth, and reasonable looks, was ensconced in an elegant mansion that he had built for and lived in with a free woman of color and their family. If those women had no husbands themselves, could they observe that situation dispassionately? "Spinsterhood" was generally a despised status in the Victorian South, one that often undermined a woman's sense of personal worth and self respect. Even Mary Moragne spoke shrewishly of one "ugly and rather *blueish* . . . 'old maid'" who lived in Sparta. If that kind of self-loathing was as endemic as observers believe, could an unmarried woman accept the apparent indissolubility of Susan and Nathan's union as she would with a white couple, or would she have been consumed with jealousy? Did people in Sparta gossip about Nathan and Susan, attempt to undermine the relationship, look upon them with contempt, or simply ignore the situation as best they could? Their responses can only be speculated about, and Mary Moragne's elliptical observations during her visit carefully avoided these questions.[85]

Since they lived among white people who almost certainly disapproved of their domestic arrangement and may have acted with open hostility, it seems likely that Susan and her children turned to the Sayre and the Hunt families for support. These were complex and tangled clans. By 1850 Nathan Sayre's white kin in Middle Georgia included two brothers, a sister-in-law, two nieces, and two nephews not far removed in age from Nathan and Susan's children. His brother Robert, a bachelor, completed a home only a short distance away, and local and family accounts argue that Robert also had two or more children with a slave woman who lived in a cabin on his property.[86] Their sister Delia Watkins and her husband Joseph both died in the late 1830s, and Nathan Sayre was Delia's executor, empowered to distribute her property, including slaves, "amongst her heirs."[87] Nathan's mulatto slave children, two former mistresses, several of their relatives and other slaves who were not kin resided within his household or nearby. The white Hunts with whom Susan had formerly lived included five brothers, three of whom were married with children. In addition, at least one of those white men had also fathered a child by a slave woman. The Sayres had been the Hunts' neighbors at Mount Zion, Susan Hunt probably first met Nathan while she lived there, and the two families maintained their associations through common membership in the Presbyterian church and the Planters' Club and probably had other social and business contacts as well. This was the extended, interracial family with which Susan Hunt was linked between 1830 and the early 1850s.

With little question Susan led a complicated life, but unlike slave women she was not regularly and uncompromisingly exposed to racial and sexual abuse. On the other hand, she never enjoyed the security of a white woman who might have been married to a man of Sayre's wealth and status. In some ways her life resembled the lives of slave women, yet other aspects were far more like those of white plantation mistresses.

Susan Hunt resided in a fine house where she enjoyed the physical accoutrements of wealth, yet she could not share Nathan Sayre's social life or even be enumerated as an official resident of that mansion. Her little girls studied music as "special students" at the Sparta Female Model School, but they had no access to the quality education it offered to whites. They received personal gifts and financial support, but probably could not inherit directly from Sayre or enjoy any financial advantages except those which he chose to give them. Susan lived, probably with considerable shared affection, with her consort, but she could not have that relationship sanctified by marriage, she did not carry his name, and she could not provide her children with the obvious advantages of legitimacy.

Unlike slave women, Susan Hunt was not an easy target for sexual exploitation because she maintained her relationship with a white man who provided her with moral and physical protection. But like slave women, that "marriage" was neither legally recognized nor protected. Many slave marriages defied all countervailing obstacles and showed extraordinary durability in the face of adversity. Nonetheless, in the slave quarters marriage was insecure at best, and family life was inherently tenuous and always subject to unforeseen and unpreventable disruption and separation.[88]

Susan and her children were not chattel, but they had no solidly grounded legal or economic status. Also unlike women of color who labored in the cotton fields of Middle Georgia and gave birth to children who in turn supplemented their masters' net worth, Susan was not a financial asset. In fact, she and her children required support and were therefore financial liabilities. Female slaves were considered valuable capital investments. They were "property" who worked, bore children, and also could be sold. Where Susan lived in physical comfort, most slave women endured meager surroundings at best. Few other women of color like Susan Hunt played such complex dual roles. On one hand, she was a "wife" who lacked any confirmation of her status under the law, and on the other, she was a mistress or concubine whose life included none of the romance those words usually connote. Susan's life combined and integrated elements from both slave women and from affluent white women in antebellum Middle Georgia. She and her family precariously negotiated a tightrope between the worlds of black and white, slave and free. Regardless of the difficulties they encountered, any undifferentiated and oversimplified depiction of the unrelieved, degraded, and marginal status of free people of color misrepresents their lives at Pomegranate Hall.[89]

Sometime during the early 1850s, Nathan and Susan's younger daughter, Mariah, followed in her mother's footsteps to establish a permanent relationship with a white man, Henry Alexander Hunt, youngest of the five sons of the Hunts at Mount Zion. Whether this relationship was arranged by either or both of the families can only be guessed. Family tradition argues that Henry and Mariah legally married each other under some circumstance or another. One of their sons stated with no hesitation that his mother's name was "Mariah (Hunt) Hunt," but Georgia law and custom erected almost insurmountable barriers to any such interracial marriage.[90] Although

Mariah showed "no negroid features so far as can be judged from a photograph," she may have been somewhat darker skinned than the average Anglo-American. But far more relevant than any slight gradation in skin color was the fact that her racial heritage never could have been concealed in their own home town, where both the Hunts and the Sayres were well known. She was acknowledged as a mulatto, and no justice of the peace or minister of the gospel could have legally married her to a white man. Interracial marriage was not recognized, the ceremony itself was illegal, and performing it would even jeopardize the presiding justice or clergyman in the eyes of the law. Of course, Henry and Mariah could have married elsewhere, even as close as a neighboring county where her parentage was unknown and she could pass for white. Or their descendents may be mistaken in their belief that the couple actually married according to law.[91]

Although white Southerners winked at masters' forays into the slave quarters, publicly they almost unanimously condemned intimate interracial relationships. Some people of color concurred. Sparta's Lucius Holsey, a mulatto himself who later became Mariah Hunt's pastor, said that "the way amalgamation has been brought about in these Southern States is enough to make the bushmen in the wild jungles blush with shame." For the most part, however, people of color did not condemn miscegenation as such, but they deplored the resulting degradation that their women usually endured, and they knew that most white men bore no guilt and took no responsibility for their actions. Women of African descent almost always suffered the consequences and bore the burden of "illegal and damnable miscegenation."[92]

If Mariah and Henry did actually marry, one possibility seems likely, although no proof or documentation survives. As a judge, Nathan Sayre should have had the legal authority to perform the ceremony, and he could have married the couple at Pomegranate Hall. Solemnizing his daughter's marriage would have demonstrated his familial devotion. Both Mariah and Henry were churchgoing Christians who would have wanted to legitimitize their union, and Susan would have been pleased to know that her daughter's relationship had been granted the official imprimatur that her own always lacked.

State laws erected sturdy legal walls barring marriage for people of color. Some slaveholders agreed to non-binding ceremonies between their slaves, but marriage was a contract, and at best people of color were treated like perpetual minors under the law. Statute demanded that a white guardian must represent a free person of color who wanted to enter into any legal contract. Judging from the examples of Mary Ross and Wilkes Flagg and Lavinia Robinson, practically speaking, free people of color could not even marry each other, and miscegenation in any form was a crime in Georgia. In 1852 the state stiffened and clarified the penal code by stating that a white man and a "woman of color, of any shade or complexion whatever, free or slave," who lived together "in a state of adultery or fornication" could be fined and imprisoned for three months.[93] Any extramarital sex also constituted illicit and punishable behavior. Paradoxically, Mariah and Henry would have violated the law if they did not marry or if they did.

Nonetheless, the setting at Pomegranate Hall, with its elegant verandah, parlor, and formal gardens, provided an ideal environment for a wedding, and Nathan Sayre's authority and influence may have outweighed the legal technicalities. The young couple and their families would have been happy had they somehow convinced themselves that Judge Sayre, a retired member of Georgia's Superior Court, had performed a legitimate ceremony, and they had married both under the law and in the eyes of God.

In the South parents on both sides helped provide newlyweds with the household furnishings they needed, but this usually became the special responsibility of the bride's family. Bestowing the dowry was an almost obligatory ritual among well-to-do whites, but the inventory of Nathan Sayre's possessions and one piece of material evidence argues that this ritual of transition could well have been extended to Mariah Hunt, a young woman of color. After Nathan's death, his executors inventoried his belongings with meticulous detail, down to curtain rings, penknives, razors, and washbasins. Yet those lists included not one piece of silver, china, or crystal. This could not have been an oversight. In addition, the furniture shown in the inventory was inadequate to furnish a house the size of Pomegranate Hall. Only one bed was mentioned, and candlesticks, trays, teapots, bric-a-brac, pots, pans, and other kitchen equipment were notable by their absence. Neither piano, harp, nor organ appeared. One or more of those instruments surely would have been essential accoutrements in a well-furnished home where music played an important part in the family's life. Some of those missing household belongings would have provided handsome dowries for both Mariah and her sister Susan, and others could have been considered the older Susan's personal property.[94]

A single coin silver teaspoon from an original set of eight or twelve, crafted by Otis Childs, a silversmith in neighboring Baldwin County, has been handed down in the family of Mariah Hunt. Although fire temporarily destroyed his place of business in November of 1853, Childs plied his trade in Middle Georgia with little interruption from 1837 up to the Civil War. In 1844 he advertised "tea, mustard and salt spoons, soup ladles, sugar tongs and butter knives" for sale. The Hunt family's spoon bearing his hallmark, plus the unexplained absence of other silver from the Sayre inventory, suggests that Nathan Sayre carried a bag of coins over to Otis Childs in Milledgeville and had him create a set of table silver for his daughter's dowry.[95]

Nathan Sayre may or may not have ordered handcrafted silver and officiated at his daughter's wedding during the final months of his life, but nonetheless, Susan Hunt and the children would have been jolted by his sudden death on Saturday, February 3, 1853. An obituary in the Milledgeville *Southern Recorder* stated that he died "while yet in the prime of life and usefulness" at his home in Sparta, "from a disease, it is supposed, of the heart." The *Central Georgian* attributed his death to "bilious colic" and praised him as "an amiable gentleman, an able lawyer, and an upright judge." Understandably, neither obituary mentioned his unconventional family. Rev. Carlisle Beman performed the funeral services at the local Presbyterian church. Sayre was interred in Sparta's town cemetery beneath a tall granite obelisk engraved:

> In Memory of Nathan C. Sayre
> Born in Newark, N.J. July 22, 1795
> Died in Sparta, Geo. Feb. 3, 1853
> An Honest Man

His will left the body of his estate to his white family, particularly his brother William's children, a generous endowment for Sparta's Female Model School, and personal bequests to a few selected friends. The most unexpected provisions, however, were contained in the carefully worded paragraphs that provided for the emancipation of six slaves.[96]

Between 1830 and the mid-1850s only a very few similar wills from Middle Georgia attempted to manumit slaves. George Murray from Baldwin County left three of his young "negroes" in the care of his executors when he died in 1839, and directed "that they may be protected from slavery . . . and that when they shall severally arrive to the age of 21 years or sooner, they may . . . elect a free state to live in." Murray also instructed that they should be given one thousand dollars and "any and all instruments of writing as may be necessary to insure their freedom." He did not want to free any other slaves. Since Murray had no white wife or children, it can reasonably be assumed that the three young people he wanted to manumit were his own sons and daughter. No further trace of them appears in Middle Georgia. With the assistance of Murray's executors, they may have been able to move North to freedom.[97]

Putnam County's Robert Bledsoe declared in his 1846 will that he wanted his executors to purchase "good, arable land" in Indiana and Illinois and directed that his slaves should be sent there and given "farming utensils, including the wagons and teams used in their removal," plus enough provisions for one year's "subsistence after their removal." Before the will could be executed, however, those states both passed laws that "have forbidden the introduction of negroes into their prospective limits." Since Bledsoe did not specify that the people could be freed elsewhere, Georgia's Supreme Court invalidated those provisions of his will in 1855. One justice, clearly doubting the wisdom of any form of manumission, even queried:

> what friend of the African or of humanity, would desire to see these children of the sun, who luxuriate in a tropical climate and perish with cold in higher latitudes, brought into close contact and competition with the hardy and industrious populations which teem in the . . . northwest . . . and who loathe negroes as they would so many lepers?[98]

In 1853 Thomas E. Beall directed that his slaves should "be sent to Liberia, California, or any free State or Territory . . . as they choose to elect." He carefully added, however, that "the hand of the Executor is upon these slaves as the hand of the master until they leave Georgia." And Thomas McCoy's 1854 will ordered his executor to convey his slaves "to some one of the free or non-slave-holding States and there left." These are among the few known instances in Middle Georgia during the middle decades of the nineteenth century when masters attempted to manumit slaves through their wills.[99]

In electing to free some of his slaves, therefore, Nathan Sayre placed himself among a very small group of white Georgians. He divided the six slaves to whom he wished to offer freedom into two groups—each a separate family. The first consisted of Nelly, Augustus, and Mary Louise Watkins. Sayre bequeathed them "to my friend John DeWitt." The second group included the older woman named Susannah Watts, her daughter Chloe, and Chloe's son Marcellus. Sayre directed that those three should go "to my friend Seaton G. Day." In both cases Sayre crafted the explanatory passages with a wily lawyer's cautious attention to the letter, intent, and application of Georgia law. Those provisions read: "If [Nelly, Chloe, etc.] should desire to remove to another Country, I require my friend to allow [Nelly, Chloe, etc.] to go." Furthermore, Sayre added, the slaves named were "not to be emancipated in this State, but are slaves while here." If the wording in any will carelessly indicated the testator's intent that a slave was first to be freed within the state of Georgia and then transported elsewhere, those provisions could be challenged and invalidated, and had been in other instances. Nathan Sayre had encountered similar cases when he served as a legislator and judge. He knew and fully understood the vagaries, complexities, and subtleties of the law.[100]

If Sayre provided for the manumission of six slaves, does that prove that they were his kin? Other explanations seem implausible. If he held strong moral convictions that slavery was evil and wanted to clear his conscience as an owner of human property, he would have emancipated of all of his slaves, but he did not. If he thought that his heirs would be irresponsible or cruel masters, he would not have willed them other slaves, but he did. If the slaves were old or non-productive and could prove a burden on his heirs, that too would have been understandable, but most of those named in his will were not. Their total appraised value was well over two thousand dollars. Their individual value varied from nothing in the case of Susannah, who was almost eighty, to one thousand dollars for Marcellus, for whom Nathan Sayre had incurred substantial medical expenses, as he had for Mary Louise as well. A thousand-dollar slave was clearly an asset, not a liability. None of the slaves was singled out as having performed special meritorious service, as was occasionally indicated in cases of individual manumission. Coupled with their ages and the knowledge that they were mulattoes, the most reasonable supposition is that the paternalistic Nathan Sayre wanted to keep his former mistresses, his children, and their close relatives near him during his lifetime, and offered them freedom after his death.[101]

The question is whether and how Nelly, Mary Louise, and Augustus Watkins and Susannah, Chloe, and Marcellus Watts chose freedom, if indeed they did. For them to "remove to another Country" might have disrupted their lives. In a case occurring several years later, another testator offered to free his slaves under similar circumstances, but found that "he could not manumit [them] in Georgia, and the negroes did not want to go off." Would Nathan's slaves have wanted to leave Middle Georgia to create new lives for themselves far away? Susannah was very old, nearly eighty in 1853. Even Chloe, her daughter, was fifty-five. Augustus, almost sixty, was listed as worth only seventy-five dollars. He too was probably unwell or disabled, though he worked as a tanner in Macon. But the others, who were appraised much higher, would have been healthy and able.[102] Emigration lists from the ships that transported free people of color to Liberia in that period show no passengers who could possibly have been these people. Sayre's slaves may have considered moving to the North or to Canada in order to take advantage of his offer, but apparently at least some of them preferred to stay near their kin and the only homes they had ever known.[103] Considering the options of departure for distant places or continued slavery, the solutions they fashioned were not surprising.

Nelly Watkins, one of Sayre's former mistresses, remained in Sparta, where, although she technically violated state law by doing so, she lived as a free woman of color with her brother Augustus, his wife Nancy—also a free mulatto—and their son. Nelly and Nathan's daughter, Mary Louise Watkins, disappeared from the region shortly after her father's death. She may have gone North or perhaps just left the county and passed for white some place where she was not known. Augustus probably died in the 1850s, and by 1860 the Watkins household, presided over by Nelly and Nancy, two free women of color, also included two slaves in residence. Some of the mahogany tables, looking glasses, vases, and other elegant accoutrements that furnished their house may also have come from Pomegranate Hall.

Susannah Watts may have died soon after Nathan Sayre; she never again appeared in any local records. Even before that time, however, Susannah's daughter, known as Chloe Watts (also a former mistress), though technically a slave, had already established herself as a free woman of color. She had moved to neighboring Baldwin County, where she lived on "the lot of land owned by [Nathan Sayre] in Milledgeville." Like Mariah Hunt, Mary Louise Watkins and Chloe Watts had also "proclaimed the faith" in the same Presbyterian church the Sayres attended. Chloe and Nathan's son Marcellus Watts had worked as a free man of color in nearby Wilkes County for some years, but nothing is known about his life following his father's death.[104]

The other puzzle surrounding Nathan Sayre's will is the omission of any recognition of Susan Hunt and their free family of color. Most likely Sayre, a cautious and pragmatic lawyer, understood the difficulties that they would have had collecting from his estate. Real property could not easily be willed to free people of color. Without papers to confirm their free status, without official white guardians, and because—either ignoring or defying state law—they never registered in the county courthouse as all free people of color were required to do, they lacked any definitive status or legal standing. Their attempts to make claims under the provisions of Nathan Sayre's will could have been challenged in court and might have subjected them to exposure or even enslavement.[105] The voids in Sayre's inventory indicate that a substantial portion of his personal household effects probably went directly to his companion Susan and their children by unwritten agreement. By the time of his death, Nathan and Susan's younger daughter Mariah was securely "married" to Henry Alexander Hunt, a farmer and tanner. At sixteen, their only son, James Herbert, would have been fast approaching independent manhood. Their older daughter, the second Susan, had settled into an independent life by 1853. Her first child, Alexander, given the middle name of her sister's new husband, was born a year later.

The older Susan however presented a different problem. She was in her forties, and because of her age and her precarious legal status probably would not have been considered "marriageable." She had no obvious means of support, and most likely could not have been a direct beneficiary of Nathan Sayre's will. Throughout her adult life she had been the mistress of Pomegranate Hall, but she had no marketable trade. She had never farmed as most people of color did in Middle Georgia, nor had she served as anyone's employee for several decades. She had no legal guardian, and initiating any such dependent arrangement would have been demeaning and difficult for her to contend with. But the presence of one of her own "kin" in Hancock County offered a viable solution. James M. Hunt—called J. M. by the family to distinguish him from the other Jameses—a widower and farmer in his forties with no children, had known Susan all of his life.[106] She had lived with the Hunts during her youth, her daughter Mariah had recently established a home with J. M.'s youngest brother Henry, and the two brothers had even lived together. J. M. Hunt had had a passing brush with the law in 1848 when he was accused of creating a public disturbance, and the grand jury asserted that he "did act unlawfully and fight to the terror of the citizenry of said town of Sparta." The minor charges were apparently dismissed, however, and within a year he was himself serving on local juries as an eminently respectable citizen.[107]

The inventory of Nathan Sayre's holdings showed that he, who had long promoted the development of rail transportation in the region, owned a substantial amount of Georgia Rail Road Company stock, which paid substantial quarterly dividends. Shortly before he died in 1853, Sayre and J. M. Hunt apparently entered into a "gentleman's agreement," confirming that those shares would be transferred to ensure Susan's future security. She, in turn, left Pomegranate Hall and returned to the Hunt farm at Mount Zion following Sayre's death. More than a quarter of a century later, when J. M. Hunt died, he left the body of his estate—largely consisting of that railroad stock—to this same woman whom he and others in Hancock County called "Susan Hunt, a free woman of color."[108]

DESCENDANTS OF MARTHA AND JUDKINS HUNT:
FROM THE GEORGIA FRONTIER THROUGH THE CIVIL WAR

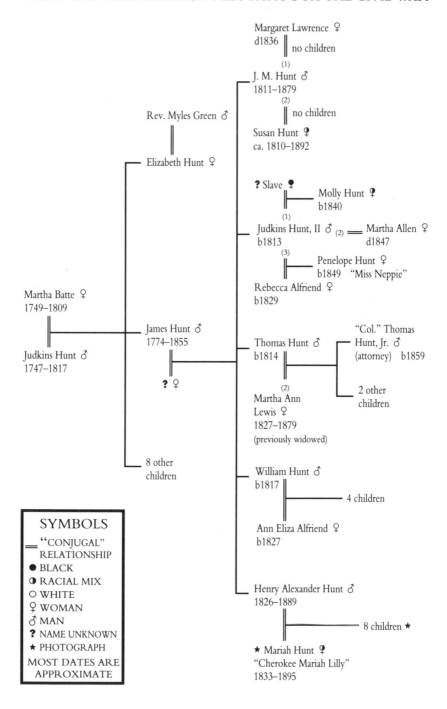

Margaret Lawrence ♀
d1836 ‖ no children
(1)

J. M. Hunt ♂
1811–1879
(2)
‖ no children

Susan Hunt ♀
ca. 1810–1892

Rev. Myles Green ♂

Elizabeth Hunt ♀

? Slave ♀ — Molly Hunt ♀
b1840
(1)

Judkins Hunt, II ♂ (2) ══ Martha Allen ♀
b1813 d1847
(3)
Penelope Hunt ♀
b1849 "Miss Neppie"

Rebecca Alfriend ♀
b1829

Martha Batte ♀
1749–1809

Judkins Hunt ♂
1747–1817

James Hunt ♂
1774–1855

? ♀

Thomas Hunt ♂
b1814

"Col." Thomas
Hunt, Jr. ♂
(attorney) b1859

2 other
children

(2)
Martha Ann
Lewis ♀
1827–1879
(previously widowed)

8 other
children

William Hunt ♂
b1817

4 children

Ann Eliza Alfriend ♀
b1827

SYMBOLS
── "CONJUGAL"
RELATIONSHIP
● BLACK
◑ RACIAL MIX
○ WHITE
♀ WOMAN
♂ MAN
? NAME UNKNOWN
★ PHOTOGRAPH
MOST DATES ARE
APPROXIMATE

Henry Alexander Hunt ♂
1826–1889

8 children ★

★ Mariah Hunt ♀
"Cherokee Mariah Lilly"
1833–1895

CENTRAL HANCOCK COUNTY, GEORGIA

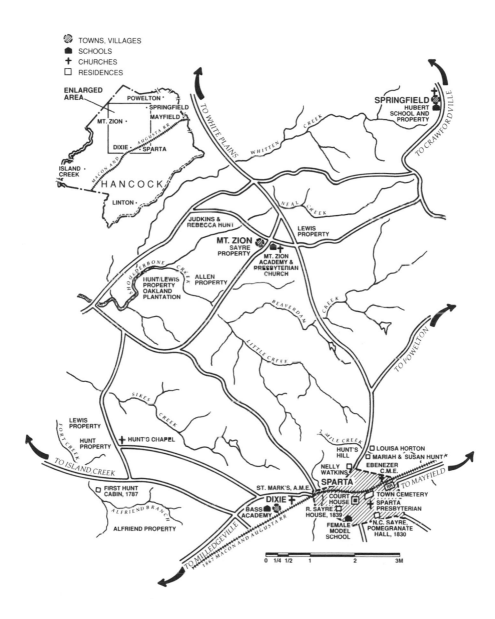

TOWNS, VILLAGES
SCHOOLS
CHURCHES
RESIDENCES

ENLARGED AREA

POWELTON •
• SPRINGFIELD
MAYFIELD
MT. ZION •
DIXIE •
• SPARTA
ISLAND CREEK •
HANCOCK
LINTON •

TO WHITE PLAINS

WHITTEN CREEK

SPRINGFIELD
HUBERT SCHOOL AND PROPERTY

TO CRAWFORDVILLE

NEAL CREEK

JUDKINS & REBECCA HUNT

LEWIS PROPERTY

MT. ZION
SAYRE PROPERTY

MT. ZION ACADEMY & PRESBYTERIAN CHURCH

SHOULDERBONE CREEK

HUNT/LEWIS PROPERTY OAKLAND PLANTATION

ALLEN PROPERTY

BEAVERDAN CREEK

LITTLE CREEK

TO POWELTON

SIKES CREEK

LEWIS PROPERTY

FORT CREEK

HUNT PROPERTY

HUNT'S CHAPEL

2 MILE CREEK

LOUISA HORTON

HUNT'S HILL

MARIAH & SUSAN HUNT

EBENEZER C.M.E.

NELLY WATKINS

SPARTA

TO MAYFIELD

TO ISLAND CREEK

FIRST HUNT CABIN, 1787

ST. MARK'S, A.M.E.

COURT HOUSE

TOWN CEMETERY

SPARTA PRESBYTERIAN

DIXIE

BASS ACADEMY

R. SAYRE HOUSE, 1839

FEMALE MODEL SCHOOL

N.C. SAYRE, POMEGRANATE HALL, 1830

ALFRIEND BRANCH

ALFRIEND PROPERTY

TO MILLEDGEVILLE

1867 MACON AND AUGUSTA RR

0   1/4 1/2   1   2   3M

III

Plantation Life
through the Civil War

---

*All dem Mount Zion member, dey have many ups
and downs;
But cross come or no come, for to hold out to the end.
Hold out to the end,
Hold out to the end.
It is my 'termination for to hold out to the end.*

Middle Georgia plantation song
Slave Songs of the United States, *1867*

After Nathan Sayre's death in early 1853, Susan Hunt left Pomegranate Hall and returned to the Mount Zion farm with the widowed and childless James M. Hunt. Both Susan and J. M. were in their early forties at the time. J. M.'s youngest brother Henry, a leather tanner who lived nearby, had recently married Susan's daughter Mariah.[1]

In that same period, the whole country became embroiled in bitter debate over a book: Harriet Beecher Stowe's *Uncle Tom's Cabin,* which sold a staggering three hundred thousand copies in the first years following its publication. Jovial Uncle Tom, the spirited Topsy, evil Simon Legree, and the tragic Eliza became instantly recognizable folk characters. The book moved readers to tears, rallied reformers to abolitionism, stimulated retaliatory writings by Southerners who lauded the patriarchal virtues of slavery, and Harriet Beecher Stowe's very name became anathema in the South.[2] Meanwhile, Congress passed the controversial Kansas-Nebraska Act, and bloody border incidents erupted between antislavery Kansans and proslavery Missourians. Also in Missouri, the Dred Scott case began its arduous journey through the state courts and up to the United States Supreme Court, which ruled in 1857 that no American of African descent, slave or free, could claim the rights of citizenship. These events swept Northerners, Southerners, and Westerners alike into the maelstrom of debate over the status of African-Americans.

In 1852, the general assembly of the state of Georgia, seeking to further control the lives of the small number of free people of color in the state, decreed that laws restricting land transactions made on behalf of minors by their legal guardians would also apply to free men and women of color. It also passed a new requirement making both slaves and free persons of color "liable to perform road duty" in the town of Sparta—a local bill no doubt reflecting the demands of Hancock County's legislators. That same year the legislature further attempted to discourage miscegenation by subjecting a white man and any woman of color to fines and imprisonment if they committed adultery. A few years later, aggressive local law enforcement officials in Glascock County charged a married white man and a free woman of color under the provisions of the antimiscegenation law. Separate juries acquitted the white man, but found the woman of color guilty as charged and presumably imprisoned her. The legislature, however, temporarily retained a small loophole in the manumission law when it affirmed the validity of such testamentary documents as Nathan Sayre's will, which allowed the emancipation of slaves who were first transmitted to free states before being granted their freedom.[3]

In 1854 the legislature reinforced laws that required free people of color to register annually, insisted for the first time that they must have written certification and approval to travel to another county, and again charged that any of their children who were "not being raised in a becoming or proper manner" could be involuntarily bound out for service to others until they reached adulthood. In 1857 and 1859 the legislature further tightened the screws on this group when it reinstated the requirement that they must live with their guardians and subjected those guardians to stiff fines for any violations. In Warrenton and Crawfordville, free people of color could no longer operate "eating houses" or "traffic in chickens, butter, eggs, ducks, turkeys, etc." because, presumably, these activities would "induce blacks to steal." Milledgeville taxed white men $1.50, free women of color $7.50, and free men of color $15, "for the benefit of the city." Those who failed to pay that head tax could be hired out as "temporary slaves." Furthermore, any free man or woman of color found "wandering or strolling about, or leading an idle, immoral or profligate course of life . . . [could] be sold into slavery" by local sheriffs for two years following a first conviction, and for life pursuant to a second. This slavery, the legislature emphasized, would be "absolute and not nominal bondage." Any free person of color from another state who ventured into Georgia was subject to immediate arrest and also could be sold into slavery, and by the end of the decade revised legislation barred all testamentary manumissions of slaves whatsoever.[4]

The state supreme court also decided several important cases concerning free people of color. In 1856 it affirmed that "one-eighth African blood" determined a person's status as a Negro, and as such she or he had no "civil, social, or political rights or capacity whatsoever, except such as are bestowed . . . by statute." This decision reinforced the inability of free men and women of color to legally function as adults. Another case concerned Baldwin County's Wilkes and Lavinia Flagg, who reportedly violated the law by reentering the state once having left. They also had "lived at large"—apart from an owner or legal guardian—and had not registered in the courthouse. The Flaggs already had been tried and acquitted locally, and in this uncharacteristic instance the state supreme court affirmed that protections against double jeopardy did indeed still apply to people of color.[5]

State legislation and supreme court decisions concerning free people of color affected only a few more than 400 persons in Middle Georgia in 1850, and that number decreased to only 365 in the eight-county region a decade later. In fact, this "troublesome" intermediary caste still comprised only about 0.5 percent of the total population of Middle Georgia. Nonetheless, this small substratum of antebellum society continued to aggravate white Georgians. It attracted inordinate attention from the legislature and the courts because its very existence challenged the precise dichotomy between the dominant free white and the enslaved black population. The presence of free people of color—particularly those who led successful independent lives—undermined the rationale for maintaining the institution of slavery based on an assumption of the inherent racial inferiority of all people of African descent.[6]

Most Hancock County residents in the early 1850s probably knew little about the few free people of color who lived among them. White people in the region would have been surprised to learn that two free women of color—Betsy Foard, a thirty-four-year-old seamstress, and her daughter, Virginia Bugg, a spinner and weaver from Milledgeville—boarded the steamer *Adeline* in June 1853 and sailed from Savannah under the auspices of the American Colonization Society, seeking a new life in Liberia. In 1855, however, the Georgia Supreme Court discouraged such emigration when it cited technicalities invalidating the will of a Putnam County man who had hoped to emancipate all of his slaves. By doing so, the court thwarted the appeal of the American Colonization Society, which planned to transport those blacks to Africa. Nonetheless, in spite of laws and court decisions that might have stopped them, the departure of Foard and Bugg presaged the 1860 emigration of thirty-seven additional women who were among seventy-four slaves emancipated by Eatonton's John Cuthbert, a member of the American Colonization Society.[7] These incidents would have been unfamiliar to most local whites, who were far more cognizant of reforms stimulated by the Hancock County Planters' Club that had brought about improvements in the county's agricultural and financial well-being.

That same spring, when the Foard women left Middle Georgia, a notice in the Milledgeville *Southern Recorder* announced the upcoming auction of "the entire Library, Law, Literature & Miscellaneous, of the late Hon. Nathan C. Sayre, being one of the most extensive & best selected private libraries in the State." The sale would be "conducted after candlelight from night to night during the . . . approaching April Term of Hancock, Superior Court." Among the more than fifty area residents who acquired books from Sayre's estate were his brothers, his physician, author Richard Malcolm Johnston, Georgia supreme court justice Linton Stephens, and John DeWitt, whom Sayre had charged with caring for one of the children he had fathered by his slave mistresses. William Hunt bought several books about horses, and Sayre's son-in-law Henry Hunt purchased a dozen miscellaneous volumes.[8]

William and Henry were but two of the five Hunt brothers who lived with their families in Hancock County during the decade prior to the Civil War. The eldest, J. M., was born in 1811. He had married in 1832, but his wife died soon thereafter without bearing children. He never remarried, although following Nathan C. Sayre's death in 1853, Susan Hunt lived with him for many years. As the family's oldest son, J. M. Hunt would have inherited the original late eighteenth-century log cabin built by his grandparents, Judkins and Martha, and much of the surrounding lands. By 1850 the livestock on his nine-hundred-acre plantation included horses, mules, cattle, cows and oxen, swine, and sheep. J. M. and his slaves sheared sheep and sold the wool, kept bees and made honey. They also raised cotton, oats, barley, and a variety of vegetables. J. M. owned thirty-nine slaves in 1850, but ten years later that number had decreased to thirty-two.[9]

The second Hunt brother, Judkins, named after his grandfather, was born in 1813. In 1846 he first wed Martha Allen, who died a year later, but then married Rebecca Alfriend. Thomas Hunt, the third son, was born about 1814, and in 1848 he married an affluent widow, Martha Ann Lewis, an honorary member of the Planters' Club who managed Oakland, her own nearby plantation. Thomas's one-thousand-acre estate placed him among the elite group of the county's largest landholders. Except that he raised wheat instead of barley, his plantation's output closely paralleled that of his brother J. M.[10]

William, the fourth son, was born in 1817. In 1848, in keeping with the common Southern practice of family consolidation that encouraged an advantageous merger of assets, he married Ann Eliza Alfriend, the sister of his older brother's wife. William and his family were the only Hunts who left Mount Zion in this period, and they moved only a few miles south to a plantation near the village of Linton. William's one thousand acres placed him too among the county's largest landowners. His agricultural production resembled that of the other men in the family except that he kept a large herd of dairy cows and produced more than six hundred pounds of butter a year. In 1850 thirty-seven slaves lived and worked on William's plantation, but in ten years that number had almost doubled to seventy-one people who lived in twelve cabins. Only thirty planters in Hancock County owned more than fifty slaves. Most of William's were black, but seven were young mulattoes, raising the possibility that William may have fathered several children born to some of the slave women on his plantation.[11]

Henry Alexander Hunt, the family's youngest brother by almost a decade, was born in 1826. During most of his young adult years he lived on or near the plantation of his oldest brother, J. M. For the first time, Henry appeared as a tanner and a slaveholder in his own right in the census of 1860, which listed him as the owner of five men, three women, and five children, all black. Henry took care of most commercial transactions for J. M.'s plantation as well as for his own business. He bought his saddle girths and blankets, kitchen equipment, "negro shoes," camphor, toothbrushes, and fishing line in Sparta's general stores, where he also purchased leather processing materials. Plug tobacco, cigars, and whiskey attested to the brothers' personal habits. Henry worked in his tannery, but often dressed—wearing cravats, three-piece linen suits, silk and velvet vests—as a successful businessman. In addition to making substantial sales of grain, Henry Hunt brought different grades of leather—raw hides, calf skin, and leather for soles—into town for sale. Henry would have brought his new wife, Mariah Hunt, a free woman of color who looked almost as white as he did and with whom he lived in violation of Georgia's antimiscegenation and fornication laws to his home and tannery near Mount Zion. Henry and Mariah had eight surviving children born between 1854 and 1879.[12]

The old log cabin built by the first Judkins and Martha Batte Hunt before 1800 survived at least through the Civil War, but the Hunt brothers of the third generation in Hancock County developed four more homesteads in the county on their extensive acreage. Except for Henry, the youngest, they married and constructed those new homes between 1840 and 1850.[13]

It is impossible to map out the exact landholdings of early Hancock County residents, but the area between Sparta and Mount Zion clearly became home for the interlocking—and interracial—families that included Hunts, Sayres, Allens, Alfriends, and Lewises, who were tied together by bonds of blood and marriage. Geographical proximity reinforced those relationships and their common affiliation with the Presbyterian church linked the families as well.

Much like the patterns established by white Middle Georgians, and in spite of their small numbers, free families of color in Hancock and the contiguous counties also bonded together to form both neighborhood clusters and extended interlocking families during the 1850s. Nine residential clusters of free people of color emerged in the eight Middle Georgia counties. Each cluster included twenty or more free men and women of color who had at least two different surnames, and lived in three or more separate residences in close proximity with one another. The clusters can be further divided into town groups and rural groups. Households in the town groups were small, averaging only about three persons each, whereas the rural clusters had almost six persons per household. The people in these household clusters in the towns of Middle Georgia worked as housekeepers, laundresses, spinners and weavers, smiths, shoemakers, carpenters, and the like, while most of those in rural areas followed agricultural pursuits, either as hired laborers or on their own farms.[14]

Further demonstrating the extent of this neighborhood clustering, although free men and women of color comprised only about one percent of the total population of Warren County, within the town of Warrenton itself almost twenty percent of the households included one or more free people of color.[15] When they lived close to one another, these people could work, cook, quilt, worship, and socialize together and create their own small but viable communities. These communities in turn became nuclei for the rest of the region's free nonwhite population.

Free people of color also established strong area-wide networks through family affiliations. These linkages are probably even more extensive than can be definitively documented, but at least five extended families can be clearly identified within the eight-county region. The most remarkable network tied together families with eleven different surnames living in five separate counties. Branches of the large Ruff family alone lived in Glascock, Greene, Hancock, Taliaferro, and Warren counties, and members of the Jones and Moss families turned up in three of these counties. Intricate consanguinal, conjugal or affinal, and co-residential relationships characterized this extended family linking them roughly as follows:

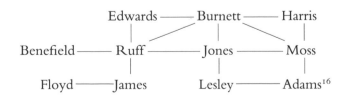

These families of free people of color spread even beyond the eight-county region. People named Benefield, Burnett, and Ruff lived in Augusta. Four families of Hunts turned up in Athens, north of Greene County, and surnames of several free people of color in Macon, to the southwest, duplicate those found in Milledgeville. Because their overall numbers were so few in the plantation belt, it seems unlikely that these people were unrelated to those in the eight core counties.[17]

Family ties also linked some free people of color with the slave community. A number of free women and their children—all described as "black"—lived without an adult male in residence in family units near large plantations. The women's status established their children's freedom regardless of the fathers' condition. The fathers and husbands in those families probably were slaves living nearby. Conversely, such men as Baldwin County's Henry Foard had wives and children who remained slaves. Others—the roughly one quarter of the group who were acknowledged as mulattoes such as the Hunts—had consanguinal or affinal relationships with white families as well. They, too, often had no adult man in residence. Certainly not every free person of color lived in a residential cluster, nor were they all related to other families within their subgroup. A few had no identifiable family ties at all, and some lived in isolated cabins scattered around the countryside among the farms and plantations belonging to whites and worked by slaves. Nonetheless, their small numbers notwithstanding, most free men and women of color in Middle Georgia managed to establish small but coherent communities characterized by clustered residential living and family networks.

Susan and Mariah Hunt and Mariah's children did not live within a residential cluster prior to the war, but they were among the free people of color enmeshed in an interconnected family network. The older Susan had a son and another daughter who had several children of her own before the end of the Civil War. Nelly Watkins had been Nathan Sayre's mistress and had borne their child Mary Louise. Mary Louise apparently left Middle Georgia, but Nelly remained in Sparta with her brother's widow Nancy—also a free mulatto woman—and Nancy's son John, who worked as a porter in a Warrenton hotel. Nancy had a personal estate valued at $2,000, and, most surprisingly, she owned two slaves who lived in their house. These slaves, a young woman and a baby, were John's wife Caroline and their son, named

Sayre Watkins. Caroline once may have been a slave in the Sayre household, but almost certainly Nancy Watkins established her "ownership" of these two in order to keep her family intact. After Nathan's death, she and Nelly astutely maintained an ongoing relationship with his brothers, who were local lawyers, and with other white friends.[18]

Chloe Watts was also a former mistress of Nathan Sayre whom he had made provisions to free in his will. Even before Sayre's death, however, Chloe Watts had already established herself as a free woman in nearby Milledgeville. On the eve of the Civil War, she lived alone, worked as a seamstress, owned real estate valued at $450 in the form of a lot previously held by Nathan, and had personal property in the amount of $500. Nathan Sayre had probably acquired Nelly Watkins and Chloe Watts from his sister Delia and her husband Joseph Watkins, both of whom died in the late 1830s. These women took their surnames from the white Watkins family, with Watts probably evolving as a distortion of Watkins. According to Georgia law, and specified and reinforced by Sayre's carefully structured will, they could be legally emancipated only pursuant to their departure from the state of Georgia. The promise of freedom elsewhere might have tempted them, but they clearly did not choose to leave their homes, friends, and relatives.[19]

The older Susan Hunt, young Susan, Mariah Hunt, Nelly and Nancy Watkins, and Chloe Watts lived within several miles of one another. Unlike Susan Hunt and her family, Chloe Watts and Nancy Watkins did appear in the census, clearly listed as free women of color, yet none of these women had legal guardians, nor did any of them ever register in the Hancock and Baldwin county courthouses. They used their advantageous affiliations with leading white families and combined those connections with determination and independent willfulness. They thereby managed to live in relative comfort as free, propertied women of color, countervailing legal strictures, prejudices, and practices notwithstanding. Although smaller by far than the eleven-family network centered around the Burnetts, Joneses, and Ruffs, this extended family in antebellum Hancock and Baldwin counties included at least the Watkinses, Watts, and Hunts.

Susan lived with J. M. Hunt, and her daughter Mariah lived with his youngest brother Henry from the 1850s through the Civil War, which makes their households especially intriguing. Nonetheless, two other Hunt residences in Middle Georgia are interesting as well and illuminate various aspects of Middle Georgia plantation life, especially as they pertain to this one extended family. The first belonged to some cousins of the Hancock County Hunts who had moved a few miles west to Jones County, where they built a home called Elmcroft.[20] Even as seen in 1900, Elmcroft was little changed from its original 1820 design. The main house, a simple but spacious two-story farm residence, was located some distance from any neighbors, surrounded by broad lawns and shaded by tall overhanging trees. The white wooden house with its dark shutters had an ample front porch and vine-covered arbor. Three brick chimneys denote the fireplaces within, which were topped and faced with heavy oak mantels. One oversized fireplace and hearth provided cooking facilities in the attached shed kitchen. Blacks working at the Elmcroft plantation at the turn of the century still drove mule-drawn wagons, churned butter, cured meat in open smoke sheds, and cultivated cotton much as they had in the mid-1800s. These men and women were the children of slaves. They packed the cotton they had picked into large baskets made from white oak splints, smoothed with glass, which they wove as their ancestors had for generations. The Hunt's Jones County plantation was the typical home of a family of successful, white Middle Georgia farmers, much like their cousins in Hancock.[21]

In Hancock County itself, ex-slave Henry Rogers knew the Hunt family well because he lived seven miles from Sparta on one of the Hunts' Mount Zion plantations. Rogers was born near the start of the Civil War, but retained vivid memories about the old homestead because he remained there and on the neighboring farm belonging to the Hunts' in-laws, the Alfriends, until 1895, and stories from friends and relatives reinforced his own recollections.[22]

Henry Rogers was a slave of "Jenkins" (Judkins) Hunt and his wife "Miss Rebecca." Molly Navery Hunt, the plantation's housekeeper and seamstress, was Henry's mother. Molly also may have been a daughter of Judkins himself, conceived during his bachelor days. Henry said that his father was Jim Rogers, the overseer, and in 1860 "J. Rogers" was the only white man on that plantation, excluding members of the Hunt family. Jim Rogers was probably related by marriage to the Sayres as well, and in roughly the same period he fathered a son by yet another woman of color. Henry Rogers remembered the plantation as "a big place [with] fifteen or twenty slaves" who lived in "comfortable log cabins . . . in the Quarters over a high hill 'cross the springbranch from the white peoples' house." He actually underestimated the number of slaves. Just before the Civil War thirty-one slaves—twelve females and nineteen males whose ages ranged from three months to fifty years—lived in six separate cabins on Judkins Hunt's plantation.[23] The workday began when "Ole Uncle Alex Hunt . . . ev'ry mornin' at 4:00 o'clock blowed the bugle fer us ter get up."

Judkins and Rebecca had one daughter of their own plus several children from Rebecca's earlier marriage living with them. They owned a sizable spread of almost one thousand acres and kept a variety of livestock including horses, mules, dairy cows and cattle (Henry Rogers's first chore was "'tendin' the calves"), and forty-five pigs. They raised and baled substantial amounts of cotton and other crops including corn, peas, beans, white and sweet potatoes, wheat, and hay. Local accounts report that Judkins "was the creator of Hunt's Meadow . . . the biggest hay meadow ever cleaned up on the bank of Fort Creek."[24]

"Aunt Winnie" cooked for everyone on the plantation, and Henry Rogers remembered that her "kitchen wuz a big old one out in the yard an' had a fireplace that would 'commodate a whole fence rail it wuz so big, an' had pot hooks, pots, big old iron ones, an' everything er round to cook on . . . [and] in one corner of the kitchen set a loom my mother use to weave on." Food was plentiful, but communal meals disregarded even rudimentary hygienic standards. All of the slave children dipped their spoons into a food trough and ate together out of one "big wooden tray." Before puberty, young slaves and the masters' children often played freely together, and on the Hunt plantation the black and white children enjoyed marbles and mumblety peg and, when necessary, received their punishment together as well from "Ole Miss" Rebecca. As for clothing, Henry wore only a loose shirt in warm weather when he was a youngster, but had "plenty of good heavy warm clothes" for the cold months. His mother wove the cloth, and his "Mistess" made his "'nits an' lice' pants and hickory stripe waists."

Henry Rogers also remembered such community work projects as "log rollings, corn shuckings, house coverings and quilting parties." Everyone from miles around pitched in "when a neighbor cleared a new ground and needed help." The host family summoned both blacks and whites from surrounding plantations and later fixed supper and provided a fiddler—perhaps even Judkins Hunt himself—for dancing after the work had been completed.[25] Excitement abounded when the Hunts and Alfriends held joint festivities celebrating the Fourth of July:

> On the evenin' of the third of July all plows, gear, hoes an' all sich farm tools wuz bro't in frum the fields an' put in the big grove in front o' the house where a long table had been built. On the Fo'th a barbeque wuz cooked, when dinner wuz ready all the han's got they plows an' tools, the mules wuz bro't up an' gear put on them, an den ole Uncle Aaron started up a song 'bout the crops wuz laid by an' res' time had come, an' everybody grabbed a hoe er sumpin', put it on they shoulder an' jined the march 'round an' 'round the table behind Uncle Aaron singin' an' marchin' . . . It wuz a sight to see all the han's an' mules er goin' 'round the table like that. Den when ev'ry body wuz might nigh 'zausted, they stopped an' et a big barbeque dinner. Us use ter work hard to git laid by by de Fo'th so's we could celebrate. It sho' wuz a happy time on our plantation an' the white peoples enjoyed it as much as us niggers did.[26]

Henry Rogers testified that he "allus been to Church," and religious training played an important part in his upbringing. Before every meal he recited the prayer that his "white peoples" had taught him: "We humbly thank Thee, our Heavenly Father, for what we have before us." The Hunts allowed their slaves both Christmas and Easter as holidays—a well-established compromise intended to quell incipient slave insurrection—and at Easter a picnic followed the "big church service." But other Sundays as well, the slaves went to "the white peoples' Church" where "the white folks had services in Mt. Zion in the mornings an' the niggers in the evenin's," and the congregation sang such hymns as "Go Tell Marse Jesus I Done All I Kin Do." Some other local slaves "went to de white folkses' churches and set in de gallery," and still others worshipped in brush arbors "constructed of a brush roof supported by posts and crude joints" where they sat on stumps and listened to their slave preachers.[27] When someone in Judkins and Rebecca's slave quarters died, the blacks on the plantation "sat up with the dead and had prayers for the living." "Mr. Beman," Mount Zion's minister, built "home-made coffins," and "on the Hunt place old Uncle Aaron Hunt helped him."

The white Hunts maintained strong ties with the Presbyterian church. Henry Hunt had been baptized at Mount Zion Presbyterian, and Judkins and his first wife had married in the same church. Although a justice of the peace officiated at Judkins's second marriage to "Miss Rebecca," Rebecca Alfriend Hunt already had abandoned the Methodists for the Presbyterians by 1841, when her mother purchased and donated land for the Sparta Presbyterian Church.[28]

The free people of color in the Hunt family may have attended church with the whites, or they may have gone "with the niggers in the evenin's," but whatever the time of day might have been, Reverend Beman definitely baptized Susan Hunt and Nathan Sayre's daughter, known as "Cherokee Mariah Lilly," in 1843 at the Presbyterian church.[29] Although Mariah Lilly Hunt joined the Ebenezer Colored Methodist Episcopal Church during Reconstruc-tion, the influence of the Presbyterians, widely viewed by African-Americans as a somber and undemonstrative group, remained with her children. Years later a student of Mariah's son who knew about his Presbyterian upbringing commented, "Pshaw! Mr. Hunt don't mind us getting happy. I saw him patting his foot. Soon he will be as good a Baptist or Methodist as any of us!" Few nonwhite Southerners became Presbyterians, and those who did seemed so dour that one old adage asserted that "dem Presbiteriums is de wuss uv all, case who ever hyar uv a Presbiterium nigger? Taint none. . . . nobody ain't never hyar de true blue Presbiterium laugh."[30]

The planters' church introduced many of the slaves at Mount Zion to Christianity, but their own African traditions, practices, and beliefs, metamorphosed in the New World, also strongly influenced their lives. Henry Rogers thought that a sudden wave of heat was "a sho sign hants is somewheres 'round," birds nesting near the house promised good luck, a red bird forecast bad weather, and a crowing rooster signaled either a stranger's approach or death, depending on the direction it faced. He remembered how the slaves mixed "devil's snuff and cotton roots chipped up together and put into a little bag . . . hidden under the front steps . . . [to] make all who came up the steps friendly and peacable." He prescribed "life everlasting tea" to cure a cold and "soft rosin, fat meat and a little soot mixed up and bound to the wound" for other aches and pains.

Henry Rogers also remembered that many of the local white men, and his owner in particular, enjoyed cockfighting and horse racing. One Mount Zion plantation even featured a private race course. Hunt family members confirm that Judkins Hunt relished cockfights and gambling and also had a well-deserved reputation as a philanderer. A young mulatto woman named Molly lived on Judkins Hunt's plantation, and she may have been Molly Navery Hunt, Henry Rogers's mother. As an older woman, Molly Navery Hunt (Harper) complained bitterly that her younger white half-sister Penelope (called "Miss Neppie"), Judkins and Rebecca's daughter, was "mean to all the colored children." Family stories portray Judkins as a profligate rascal who enjoyed a good time, good sherry wine, and good food and "ate up all his money and gave it away to people who needed it more than he did." Several loans made to Judkins at exorbitant interest rates corroborate the tales of his financial woes. The white members of the Hunt family all suffered financial setbacks following the Civil War, but personal excesses exacerbated Judkins's misfortunes. An apocryphal story persists that he was impoverished when he died and the family could not afford a funeral, so they just wrapped his body in a sheet and tossed it into an open grave. Some Hunt descendants still brand any family member who displays irresponsible or hedonistic behavior "a Judkins."[31]

In addition to Henry Rogers, six other men and fourteen women who had been slaves in Hancock and the surrounding counties during the late antebellum years have provided accounts of their early years. Their stories illuminate many aspects of plantation life including family and friends, the home, work, diet, and health.[32] Henry Rogers spoke with some fondness about the "comfortable log cabin" where he lived on the Hunt plantation, but his life may have been at least minimally privileged as the master's probable grandson and the overseer's son. Female former slaves recalled more meager surroundings. Rachel Adams lived near Eatonton in a "mud-daubed" cabin with its "stack chimblies made out of sticks and mud." In Greene County, Minnie Davis remembered that three slave families often shared one cramped cabin, while Dosia Harris said that most children had to sleep on their parents' rough wheat straw mattresses or on the floor.[33]

Women performed specific jobs designated for them, such as quilting, spinning, weaving, and cooking, but they also did the more physically demanding farm labor. At harvest time, masters promised liquor to men and women alike as a reward for the satisfactory completion of their work, and Dosia Harris remembered how her grandmother labored in the fields alongside the men until she was quite elderly, when she was relegated to slopping the hogs.[34]

Although they performed arduous labor, slaves in the Georgia plantation belt may have been somewhat better nourished than generally has been thought. Most of the former slaves ate a variety of vegetables and fruits when they were young and had milk, plus chicken, turkey, beef, kid, wild game, and fish to supplement the fatty "hog meat." Such women as Della Briscoe from Putnam County, however, remembered little fresh meat or chicken, and on the Baldwin County plantation where Snovey Jackson grew up slaves tended gardens but could not keep poultry. Not one of the women from Hancock and the surrounding counties reported that she ever went hungry during her childhood. Slaveholders did not provide a costly diet, but they wanted to maintain the efficiency of their work force, and slaves ate what was locally produced, cheap, and readily available.[35]

Although black plantation women in Georgia may have eaten somewhat better than might be expected, poor hygiene generated serious health problems. Other sources confirm Henry Rogers's descriptions of communal wooden eating troughs, and those troughs would have been only one factor contributing to the contagious diseases that devastated some Middle Georgia plantations. Dosia Harris's mother died during an epidemic that killed twenty-five people on their plantation. Polluted water was commonplace. Middle Georgians often were ignorant of and inattentive to cleanliness and disregarded such preventive methods as inoculation. Malaria, dysentery, cholera, smallpox, and deadly respiratory diseases regularly swept through the region.[36]

On many plantations, childbearing stimulated cooperative efforts between plantation mistresses and slave women. In Baldwin County, Carrie Mason recalled that "didn't hardly nobody have a doctor in dem days. De white folks used yarbs an ole 'omans to he'p em at dat time." Some plantations did contract with physicians, however, and E. M. Pendleton, the Sayre family's physician in Sparta, was surprised to find that his own empirical evidence disproved the common belief that slaves gave birth with unusual ease. "One would suppose," Pendleton wrote in 1856, "that a delicate white female would have had a much oftener demand for the physician than the coarse muscular negress. But such is not the case." Low birth rates among slave women disturbed Pendleton, and he suspected several causes. He found that they frequently suffered from uterine infections and endured harsh physical conditions such as overexposure and overexertion during their pregnancies, and he also suspected that they knew "secret[s] by which they destroy the foetus at an early stage of gestation." African-American women, of course, may have had good reasons to choose to limit their childbearing.[37]

Although even a mild physical reprimand could be insulting and demeaning, most masters and overseers in Middle Georgia seem to have whipped black women only occasionally and moderately. The former slaves nonetheless recalled memorable exceptions to that overall restraint. Ferebe Rogers of Baldwin County remembered the time when her "aunt was beat cruel . . . When dey got ready to beat yo' dey'd strip yo' stark mother naked . . . den dey'd lay de rawhide on yo' and cut yo' buttocks open." "Sometimes," she continued, "dey'd rub turpentine an salt in de raw places, and beat yo' some mo'." Similarly, Snovey Jackson stated that "I seen 'im cut womens on dey shoulders wid a long whip 'till it looked like he wuz gonna cut de skin offen 'em." Such incidents as these suggest a perversion of sexual attraction into sadistic cruelty.[38]

Family life in the slave quarters was characterized by mutual, and often intergenerational, support and concern. Slaves established and maintained enduring two-parent families as best they could, but masters often showed little respect for kinship ties in the black community. When their mother was sent off to work as a housemaid in the town of Eatonton, Della Briscoe and her siblings remained on the farm in the countryside where their grandmother raised them. Slaves almost always knew the parentage of the mulatto children in the quarters but understood that a white father did not guarantee special treatment or privileges. Rachel Adams's white father sold her when she was just a baby, and Minnie Davis confirmed that a "lot of the girls was sold by their masters who was their father." As for her own brother, she confided, "I know who his father was," but then added, "of course you won't ask me that."[39]

The few free women of color in Middle Georgia lived somewhat differently from slave women in the late antebellum years. Lucretia Ruff, a black woman known as "Free Creecy," was the proprietor of a substantial farm near Mayfield where she lived with her twelve children. Apparently the children's father was a slave. Families with eight, ten, and even fourteen children were not unknown among the farm-dwelling free people of color. Lucretia raised cotton, wheat, oats, and a variety of vegetables. She owned a horse, several mules, some milk cows, and twenty-five pigs. Her brother Jim resided and worked on a neighboring farm, and other members of their family lived in two additional residences nearby. Like successful white farmers in the region, Free Creecy considered and described herself as a "planter." She owned land plus a personal estate valued at a total of two thousand dollars. All told, just before the Civil War, over fifty members of the Ruff family lived in the extended strip of land that curved around the county lines on the north and east of Hancock, abutted by Greene, Taliaferro, Warren, and Glascock counties. Similarly, four branches of the Ross-Bellamy family, each with moderate holdings in land and personal property, left Hancock and moved a few miles west where they flourished in Baldwin County.[40]

Not far from the Ross-Bellamys, more than a dozen free women of color lived near one another in the Georgia capital of Milledgeville. A number had been born in Virginia or North Carolina, and they worked as spinners, nurses, washerwomen, cooks, and seamstresses. Like Chloe Watts, most owned small amounts of personal or real property valued from $25 to $950. Some of the women were single, others lived in permanent conjugal relationships with men who shared their free status. Some were described as "black," as were their children. The spouses of these particular women who had no adult male in residence would have been slaves from nearby plantations. Other such women had mulatto children, leading to the inevitable conclusion that local white men had fathered them. In 1853 Wiley Tompkins—a white man—bequeathed one single dollar in his will to his sister and brother and left the rest of his estate to Mary Moss and her five children, "free persons of coller." Tompkins almost certainly was the father of those mulatto children. He had no wife, and Mary Moss officially had no man at all living with her.[41]

In contrast to the slaves, most free women of color seem to have lived in moderately comfortable circumstances, whether they stayed with white guardians or in independent households. Some of them accumulated a little money or property, and they apparently resided in adequate quarters and often had large families. However, unlike white women, most of them worked regularly in addition to taking care of household and family responsibilities. Susan, her daughter Mariah, and Mariah's children—the free Hunt women of color in

Hancock County—clearly lived in physical comfort. Those children knew their white fathers and saw them regularly. At different times, both Nathan Sayre and the Hunt men supported them, lived with them, and acknowledged the mulatto Hunt women as their kin.

The Hunt women never served white mistresses, but many other free women of color worked as cooks, maids, and housekeepers, and as such, certain aspects of their lives may have closely paralleled those of some domestic slaves in the region, many of whom were also mulattoes. A household servant from the Macon area described how she would "come in an dress my Young Missus in de mawnin', wash her face an' hans an go 'long by her when she take her mawnin' walk. Wait on her when she's eatin', an fan her when she take her nap." Late in the day, she would "undress her, bathe her feet in warm water, put on her night gown an' rub de aches erway what she got endurin' de day." While visiting Middle Georgia, one Englishman observed that "domestic slaves about the houses of respectable families . . . are as well fed and as well clad as the free domestic servants of many countries of Europe." But he added that "even these are wholly uneducated, and entirely without the hope of benefitting their condition by any exertions of industry or economy to the practice of which they have no inducement whatsoever." Special privileges that house servants may have enjoyed, or the relative physical comfort in which they sometimes lived never altered the constant reality of their perpetual bondage. In addition, what these women gained in trivial creature comforts and relief from gruelling field work, may have been more than offset by the lack of privacy and the round-the-clock demands of a white family. Free women of color who worked in the houses of affluent white Georgians experienced similar working conditions, they too had little opportunity to acquire an education, and they may have been disparaged because of their race. But they always knew that they were not slaves, and they could and did try to "benefit their condition" by their own "exertions of industry or economy."[42]

In Hancock and the surrounding counties during the 1850s, most free women of color worked because of economic necessity and because state law and county regulations demanded that free women as well as men must have regular employment. Nevertheless, a few women of this free caste told authorities that they had "no occupation" or described themselves as housekeepers much like white women of substance. Whether or not his presence in the household was openly acknowledged, some man—often white—would have taken primary financial responsibility for those women and their children. A propertied woman such as Lucretia Ruff, who considered herself a "planter," would have had a good deal of independence on her own land, but many others who lived out in the countryside worked for whites as farm laborers. Free women of color, however, did not have the options available to their hardworking fathers, spouses, and sons to become artisans or establish their own businesses as blacksmiths, tinners, carriage makers, wheelwrights, stonemasons, carpenters, shoemakers, barbers, or hatters, nor did they work on the railroads, another common occupation for the men. Georgia law severely limited the economic opportunities and the fields of commercial endeavor that free people of color could pursue; nonetheless, they generally functioned effectively in the areas that remained open to them.[43]

In their work and in many other aspects of their lives, free people of color faced daily anxieties, and they constantly had to negotiate their anomalous roles in a society strictly divided along the lines of black and white, slave and free. State laws restricted their movement, denied them an education, compromised their freedom, limited their economic opportunities, and insulted their dignity. Nonetheless, although law and society demeaned them because of their race, they could find satisfactions in life that slaves could not. They could work, enjoy the fruits of their labor to a limited extent, and in most cases, as evidenced by the large intact households that survived over many decades, they had a good deal of control over their own families. Slaves certainly tried to do the same, and paternalistic impulses on the part of some masters may have helped to keep some slave families together, but the planters' economic interests always came first. A notorious slave market flourished less than a day's journey southwest of Hancock. "Macon, you must know," reported a visitor in 1858, "is one of the principal marts for slaves in the South." On a smaller scale, slave auctions occurred regularly, even in the Hunts' home community and in others like it throughout the region.[44] But for the most part, planters neither sold many slaves away from their families nor physically punished them to the point of permanent injury. That would have been economically counterproductive, and some owners also had moral and religious compunctions about abusing their "people." Nonetheless, rigid laws and a master's virtually unlimited power over his own slaves narrowly circumscribed most aspects of those black people's lives and routinely reinforced their degradation. They could not acquire an education, own property, enter into contracts, control their own labor, enjoy legally sanctioned marriage, or do very much at all to protect their children. Patrols and pass laws strictly enforced the conditions of bondage, and severe punishment awaited recaptured runaways. Realistic fears of reprisal notwithstanding, the yearning to escape, resist, and rebel always ran deep in the slave community.

Slave resistance took on many subtle guises: an order misinterpreted, dinner burned, ironing scorched, a task uncompleted, tools misplaced or broken. One Greene County slave ran away in the 1850s and successfully hid out in nearby swamps and woods for years. The Milledgeville *Southern Recorder* reported numerous escapes from plantations in the surrounding counties, and those notices represented only a small percentage of the total number of similar incidents. That same newspaper advertised the services of a runaway-slave bounty hunter in Hancock County—no doubt a lucrative profession.[45]

Rebellion among African-Americans occasionally assumed more violent forms. In the early years of the nineteenth century, Hancock County's first legal hanging took place in the backyard of a farmhouse. The condemned and executed slave was a woman who had poisoned five white people. In 1841 the *Southern Recorder* reported that a black man in the same county murdered an overseer, and in 1865 another white man was killed, "presumably by former slaves." These killings and others could be provoked by personal animosity, vengeance, or frustrated retaliation against the degrading nature of slavery itself.[46]

Slaves in Middle Georgia unquestionably resented and resisted their condition, but for African-Americans freedom remained almost impossible to come by and difficult to sustain. Slavery was deeply entrenched—an integral element of the social and economic structure of plantation life and the cotton economy. One former slave reported from Milledgeville that "the law was well settled in Georgia, that every negro was presumed to be a slave, until he proved his freedom by the clearest evidence." The law considered a dark skin "*prima facie* evidence of slavery." Nonetheless, a few free people of color managed to document and maintain their "freedom by the clearest evidence."[47]

By the years immediately preceeding the Civil War, most free people of color in Middle Georgia had been born to their condition. For decades self-purchase and almost all manumissions through wills had been outlawed. Runaways were common, but lasting escape was rare. The Fugitive Slave Act of 1850 kept an escapee in continued jeopardy any place in the United States. Slaves could be manumitted only through private act of the state legislature, but that rarely happened, and that body freed its last slave in 1856.[48] Most free people of color had been born to African-American women who themselves were already free. A few others were the children of Creek, Cherokee, and in some cases even white women. Taliaferro County's Jane Lesley, a white woman, continued to go to the county courthouse every year to reconfirm the free birth of her son. The Anglo-American family of Permelia Hutchinson, a free mulatto woman, recorded her birth in their Bible, and she lived for many years with her white grandmother.[49] By 1860 it was difficult to trace the routes by which most of these people in Middle Georgia had initially gained their freedom. It was apparently just as difficult to accurately establish their numbers as to document the ways by which they had achieved their free status. Nonetheless, the census that year reported these numbers in the counties of Middle Georgia:

Baldwin:	92
Glascock:	24
Greene:	25
Hancock:	36
Putnam:	31
Taliaferro:	42
Warren:	92
Washington:	23

That total—365 in 1860—dropped from just over 400 ten years earlier. The count may be accurate and reflect the departure by some members of the group for larger towns in the South or even for less repressive but distant venues in the North. On the other hand, it may indicate that a number went underground and made themselves unavailable when the census takers—representing an inquisitive and repressive governmental authority—came around.

In spite of persistent legislative efforts designed to keep close track of these people, the difference between census records and county registers shows their understandable reluctance to have their lives controlled by stifling official regulations. The 1860 census for Hancock County enumerated thirty-six free people of color who bore the names Clark, Ridley, Ruff, Sharp, and Watkins, but the official register maintained by the county between 1859 through 1861 included the variously spelled surnames Bellamy (Bellerma), Coleman, Found, Garnes (Goins), Ruff, Shopp (Sharp), and Woodley.[50] Thirty-five persons registered at that county courthouse in 1859, twenty-one in 1860, and seventeen in 1861. The Bustles, who had lived in Washington County in 1820 and then moved to Hancock, disappeared completely by the late antebellum years, and the Shopp family alone remained from the 1834 list of free persons of color in the Milledgeville *Southern Recorder*. In 1860 only the Shopps and Ruffs appeared both in the census and on the county's free register. Similarly, in Glascock the census included twenty-four people, yet the county register listed but thirteen; in Warren the census included ninety-two people, and the register listed fifty-seven; in Washington, the census had twenty-one, but courthouse officials registered thirty-six; in Baldwin, the census showed ninety-two, and the register listed only fifty-eight.[51]

The disparities between these records surely had several causes. Spelling variations indicate low literacy on the part of white officials as well as the free men and women of color. The fluctuation in both numbers and names shows that those officials often maintained their records erratically. It further suggests that some members of the free caste did not want to be pinned down and vigorously resisted complying with laws that they disliked and cooperating with authorities whom they mistrusted.

In an 1857 incident that is an example of the petty harassment free people of color faced, a white man in Taliaferro County brought charges against Allen James, William Lesley, and Wilson and James Lloyd and accused them of not registering in the county courthouse. The four men were arrested and taken to court and then had to secure the services of an attorney. The court heard the complaints but, evidently judging them nuisance charges made by a vindictive crank, dismissed them and assessed costs to the accuser.[52]

At other times free people of color were sold into slavery either temporarily or permanently for some minor infraction of law, and as a result, disappeared from the records. A few may have led itinerant lives. However, since the majority were described as "black," most of these officially documented people of color in both the federal census and county records could not have been the "privileged" mulatto children of white planters.

This raises the question of how many free persons of color may have been excluded from both the federal census and county registers. For many reasons, a number of people of color living outside of the bonds of slavery no doubt wanted to avoid any form of registration or any official acknowledgment whatsoever of their ambiguous status. Some of the mulattoes may have tried to pass for white, others could have been involved in legally questionable endeavors. A number may not have been able to pay the required head taxes, and for still others proof of their freedom might have been very tenuous. Both the census and county registries may have substantially underestimated the numbers of free men and women of color living in Middle Georgia and throughout the South.[53] Hunt family members, all of whom are certain that their family was free in antebellum years, state firmly, more than a century later, that their antecedents in Hancock County avoided the census enumerators, and, in fact, they never appeared in those records until 1870. In neighboring Baldwin County, a man named July De Saussure, "a farmer, . . . minister of the gospel," judged to be "much above the average in intelligence" was a neighbor of the large Ross family with whom he engaged in livestock transactions before the war. To have traded in cattle as he did, he would seem to have been at least nominally free, though his name appears neither in Baldwin's county registry nor census records prior to the Civil War.[54] Solid evidence illuminates details of their lives, but they never appeared in official listings. Information concerning the Hunts and July De Saussure hardly indicates that thousands of others like them also led undocumented lives, but surely they were not alone.

The Hunt's case argues that a sub-caste of free people of color—perhaps more often than not men and women with mixed racial parentage—sometimes may have been protected as "family" by white men who enjoyed considerable community status and who would not be casually challenged by local authorities. Susan Hunt originally acquired her free status from a Cherokee mother, but she then spent her early years with the Hunts. Following that period, she lived for over two decades at Pomegranate Hall. If Judge Nathan Sayre thought that his free family of color should not be enumerated in the census, a lowly census marshal would hardly argue with a man of his authority.[55] After Sayre's death, Susan returned to J. M. Hunt's plantation. Her daughter Mariah and her grandchildren lived nearby with Henry Hunt. The Hunt brothers were respected citizens as well, and they were among the county's largest landowners and slaveholders. On their own plantations, they too would have wielded enough influence to decide whether members of their family would or would not be included in the census and listed in the county registry as officially required by law.

Living as an undocumented family of color may have involved risk, but, considering the alternatives, that risk might have been acceptable. If Susan and, in turn, her daughter Mariah, and Mariah and Henry's children lived with and were treated as kin by the white Hunts, who loved and protected them, the idea of labelling them slaves would have been distasteful, even for traditional plantation masters who held other men and women in bondage. Free people of color, on the other hand, needed definitive documentation validating their manumission or free birth, and the burden of proof lay entirely on them to affirm that status beyond any possible doubt. State laws demanded that they have legal guardians to serve as surrogate masters and guarantee their "responsible" behavior. Susan and her family presumably had no such irrefutable proof of freedom. They held themselves above those humiliating requirements of law and neither registered nor acquired legal guardians at any time. Lacking the requisite documentation, and not being in compliance with the law, they could not act to untangle or clarify their status because any attempts to confront the situation could have embroiled them all in extended legal wrangling and might have resulted in unhappy and unforeseen personal consequences. Everyone concerned may have wisely decided not to stir up those already muddied waters.

Particularly in New Orleans, but elsewhere in the slaveholding South as well, wealthy white men sometimes coerced attractive quadroon and octoroon women into concubinage. A contractual system known as *plaçage* sometimes circumvented the prohibition of marriage between the races and helped to protect the women and their children. However, many men who entered into these relationships never guaranteed the financial security of their mistresses and children in any way, and ultimately their unprotected "wives" and daughters sometimes found it necessary to support themselves through prostitution. Slave markets throughout the South advertised "fancy girls for fancy purchasers."[56] Light-skinned women who resembled the Hunts could have fallen into that sort of life had they not retained the protection of their white families.

Mariah and her children could have passed for white had they been willing to leave home, deny their heritage, and abandon family and friends. But people in the county knew their parentage, so they could never have carried off a successful masquerade in Sparta, even if they had wanted to do so. After 1840 the status of anyone suspected of trying to pass for white could be challenged in court, and the Georgia code defined "all persons having one-eighth or more, of African or negro blood in their veins" as Negroes. In the early 1860s a quadroon who had lived as a white woman for many years was "promptly hurled from her position of social equality" when her parentage became known. Considering the circumstances and the other unpalatable options open to them, it is easy to understand the discreet invisibility that the Hunts and others like them seem to have chosen.[57]

In the late antebellum years most white Southerners continued to view free people of color as problems and unfortunate misfits. Joel Chandler Harris, who grew up at Turnwold, a large Putnam County plantation, recorded black folk tales with some degree of paternalistic affection but clearly wrote from the perspective of a white man who identified with the interests of the planter class. He created a character called Free Joe, described as a "black atom, drifting hither and thither without an owner, blown about by all the winds of circumstance." According to Harris, Free Joe believed that "though he was free, he was more helpless than any slave [and] having no owner, every man was his master." As for the slaves, if they "secretly envied him his freedom (which is to be doubted considering his miserable condition), they openly despised him, and lost no opportunity to treat him with contumely." Harris projected the prevalent bias concerning free people of color when he created the rootless Joe, because no free black man in Putnam County conformed with his description. All of the free men of color in that county lived with their own families or with white people, and all of them, even the elderly, worked. Not one could be accurately described as Harris depicted Joe. Nonetheless, a few free people of color did feel disoriented and insecure in a hostile environment that called them free even as it discouraged and disparaged them at every turn. In 1861 Elmira Mathews from Greene County requested and received legislative permission to "sell herself into perpetual slavery" to John Doherty, a tailor, for whom she had previously worked as a housekeeper. Several other frustrated and apprehensive free women of color in Georgia followed the same course.[58]

Many whites harbored hostile feelings towards free Negroes. One white man who spent extended periods of time in Middle Georgia vowed that he loved "the simple and unadulterated slave" but viewed free people of color as a "nuisance" and singled them out for his "especial abomination." He accused them of "leading careless, lazy, and impudent lives, [and] treating white freemen with superciliousness if they happen to be poor." Their "dandified" manners, "illimitable jewelry," and style of dress particularly infuriated him.[59]

Although blatant racism colored that Southerner's observations, he recognized that grooming, fashion, dress, and personal possessions helped to define free status and also reinforced the limited privileges of a racially mixed heritage. Hair, shoes, diamonds, and gold all became indicators of the relationship between interracial ancestry and freedom.

Many stories survive about the Hunt women and their hair. Mariah and Henry Hunt's daughters all grew theirs to an extraordinary length. Adella bound hers up in a chignon, and her younger sister Sarah's hair reached her knees. Years later, Sarah's students watched with rapt attention as she ritualistically brushed, parted, twisted, and then pinned it on top of her head. Ella, Mariah's youngest daughter, had thick braids long enough to sit on. An elderly storyteller from Sparta recalled that when one of the Hunt women returned home to care for an aging relative, townspeople marvelled over the visitor's hair, which reportedly extended down to her ankles. That account sounded unbelievable, and one local girl decided to creep into the woman's bedroom at the crack of dawn and see for herself. At that early hour the visitor still wore a night dress and, as reported, her unbound hair reached all the way "down to the hem" of her gown. Caring for such a weighty mane required great time and effort, but for the Hunts, the hair epitomized their desirability.[60]

The Hunts thought that the long hair set them apart from the slave women, who usually wore their short curls covered by bandannas or tied up with twine or rags. One of Joel Chandler Harris's characters observed that a "nigger 'oman kep' 'er h'ar wrop up wid a string night en day," and at least one Georgia mistress refused to allow the women on her plantation to take off those bandannas because she complained that "their black woolly heads did look too ugly without their usual covering." At the same time, white women always yearned for curls and ringlets and obsessively crimped and twisted their own hair to acquire them. The Hunt's African-American ancestry provided that much-desired wave with no artifice. Their Cherokee forebears bequeathed them hair that was longer, thicker, and glossier than white women's, which they considered unattractively thin and limp. Hair has always been viewed as a measure of female desirability, and the Hunts cherished the strategic advantage that they believed they had over both black and white women, grounded in the substantively insignificant ability to grow an abundance of pretty hair.[61]

If long hair was their proud badge of beauty and femininity, shoes seem to have symbolized their unique free status. Throughout the Western hemisphere slaves often, but not necessarily by choice, went barefoot. Brazilians even called shoes "the badge of freedom." Pictures of children on plantations in the Southern United States show small white girls bedecked in frills and petticoats and wearing dainty slippers. Their young black companions wore plain shifts made from coarse material, and almost invariably appeared shoeless. Former slaves from Middle Georgia substantiated this image from personal experience. Minnie Davis, who grew up near Penfield in Greene County, said, "we went barefooted most of the time. I remember one particular time when the ground was frozen and I went about without any shoes." No illustrative material shows what the Hunt girls wore on their feet in childhood, but years later, Mariah and Henry's second daughter chided her young niece, who was cavorting about barefoot, and chased her briskly inside with an admonition that "you must never let a man see your bare feet." She later confided to a friend that her own husband had never seen her feet uncovered—so persistent was that ingrained aversion on the part of a free woman of color who considered bare feet an indicator of low and enslaved status.[62]

A story about the free *gens de couleur* in Saint Domingue further illustrates the breadth of this perception. In the 1760s, French administrators decided that the stylish free mulatto women on the island should no longer be allowed to wear shoes in the streets of town as, of course, white women did. But the outraged women of color forced the colonials to repeal the regulation when they marched in protest through the city, en masse, wearing diamonds on their feet instead of the forbidden *chaussures*.[63]

That display of diamonds by those women from the Caribbean also recalls similar cases from Middle Georgia. Hancock County's wealthiest planter, David Dickson gave his slave mistress Julia a diamond when their daughter was born. Apparently, this was not an uncommon practice because the Hunt family carefully preserved four almost identical diamonds, one of which had been bestowed on each of the four daughters of Henry and Mariah Hunt.[64] And diamonds were not the only treasures that the nonwhite children of affluent white Middle Georgia planters might acquire. David Dickson's cherished daughter Amanda, called "Miss Mandy" on her father's plantation, had her own silver engraved with the initials "A. D." At least one of Henry Hunt's children drank from a white Old Paris porcelain baby cup decorated with a gold leaf rim and laurel wreath encircling the name "Adella Hunt." Antebellum Southerners greatly admired and collected this imported china, which Henry would have had to custom order from France.[65]

In *The Autobiography of an Ex-Colored Man,* a fictionalized account of a life similar to his own, James Weldon Johnson wrote that his light-skinned protagonist was "born in a little town in Georgia." Johnson described the boy's relationship with a "tall man with a small, dark moustache" modeled after his own white father. Johnson's young hero remembered the day he "sat upon his [father's] knee and watched him laboriously drill a hole through a ten-dollar gold piece, and then tie the coin around my neck with a string." Much as in Johnson's account, three gold coins—a French five-franc piece with a small hole drilled in it, a one-dollar piece, and a larger five-dollar coin—were given to children in the Hunt family.[66]

J. M. and Henry Hunt lived on their farms where the census acknowledged them as single men, but their reported "bachelor" status notwithstanding, local store ledgers reveal that Henry bought many yards of white silk, fine cambric, calico, and Irish linen, plus needles and thread, hooks and eyes, pearl buttons, trimming, and white kid gloves. He would hardly have purchased those supplies for himself, his brother, or his slaves. In addition, J. M. Hunt, who did little shopping on his own and reportedly could neither read nor write, bought a spelling book in 1862. A surprising purchase for an illiterate "bachelor," but not so perhaps for the doting uncle of five- and eight-year-old nephews.[67]

When Middle Georgia planters bestowed such elegant or humble gifts on their spouses and children they accomplished several purposes. They must have enjoyed the simple satisfaction of giving to people whom they cared for and the pleasure that those gifts—large or small—evoked. In addition, owning such possessions would have given their loved ones special status and set them apart from the slave community. Finally, the more valuable gifts comprised a kind of portable wealth and security. In the 1930s Europe's dispossessed Jews fled Naziism bearing small bags of diamonds. With their country in turmoil in recent years, Lebanese women often wear armfuls of gold bracelets wherever they go. When the security of banking institutions is in doubt and the legal system becomes a questionable ally, portable wealth has always provided individual and family financial security. It would have accomplished the same purpose for some free families of color in nineteenth-century Middle Georgia.

A few free persons of color managed to become registered property owners in the region, and most of them acquired that property with the assistance of white intermediary agents because the law did not allow them to enter into legal contracts on their own. This was true for members of the Ross and Bellamy families in the 1840s and early 1850s. In 1862 Nelly Watkins, who had borne Nathan Sayre's child and was sometimes even known locally as Nelly Sayre, purchased a half-acre lot and house in Sparta for $790 from the estate of a man named Richard Fears through the agency of a family friend, Eliza Terrell. Nelly's snug house included at least a parlor, bedrooms, cellar, and attic.[68] Nonetheless, it would have been difficult for undocumented women like Susan and Mariah Hunt to have held deeds to real property. With a few specific exceptions, prior to 1866 no married women of any race in Georgia could hold property in their own names. With their legally indeterminate status Susan and Mariah remained dependent on the largess of the men whom they and many others considered their "husbands." Their limited personal wealth may have been more secure when it was kept in the form of tangible possessions.

In plantation belt Middle Georgia, the few free men and women of color lived somewhat differently than they did in many other places in the slave states. By the outbreak of the Civil War, the number of free blacks in the border states, many of whom lived in rural areas, almost equalled and in some localities even surpassed the number of slaves. For both economic and political reasons, slavery was declining in those areas.[69] In the deep South, on the other hand, most free people of color congregated in the cities where some worked as skilled artisans and tradespeople, but others moved in and out of a shadowy and economically insecure world. The port cities of New Orleans and Charleston attracted relatively large numbers of these people, as well as other nonwhite foreigners with whom the local men and women of color sometimes mingled. More than half of the free blacks in Georgia resided in Savannah, with another large cluster around Augusta. In Georgia as in most of the other Southern states, fears about the disruptive example and supposedly insurrectionary proclivities of this group caused legislatures and courts to continually tighten the economic, social, and legal nooses that circumscribed their lives. They could not own property in the larger cities of the state. They could not leave Georgia and then return, and generally they retained few of the rights accorded white citizens.[70]

Free persons of color in rural Middle Georgia were few and far between, even though they probably managed to establish a real sense of community through their extended families and by congregating in residential clusters. In those rural counties they could rely on little support from the law. Nonetheless, when necessary, they did confront the power of the white establishment. In 1862, for example, Washington County's Eliza and Solomon Hagans and their family challenged the authority of their guardian who was even a county official. They accused him of "inhumane" treatment and took him to court charging that he kept them "ill clad and half fed, overwrought . . . liable to much suffering if not ultimately death."[71] But, for the most part, free people of color avoided confrontations and interaction with the legal system and depended on personal and family resources and friends within their own group and in the community of slaves. When they had white kin, they took advantage of those relationships as best they could.

During the years leading up to and continuing through the Civil War, Mariah Hunt lived near Mount Zion with her husband Henry. About 1854 she bore a first son named Will, for his uncle William Hunt. A second boy, James (called Mac), after J. M. Hunt, was born in 1857. The oldest daughter Lula (probably christened Louisa for her grandfather Nathan Sayre's sister-in-law, Louisa Rogers Sayre) was born around 1860. In February of 1863, Mariah gave birth to a fourth child, Adella, who later stated firmly that she "was not born a slave, nor in a log cabin." Although Adella may have been born in the Hunt's original "log cabin," she clearly differentiated between that old family homestead and a slave cabin.[72]

That generation of free Hunt children born prior to and during the Civil War did not grow up in an elegant mansion as their mother, Mariah, had. Rather, they lived on a relatively prosperous farm—a rural homestead most likely appointed at least in part with silver, china, crystal, and furnishings that Susan and Mariah had brought from Nathan Sayre's home. Unlike Nathan Sayre, their father, Henry Hunt, was not a cultured man of letters, but he was a successful farmer and tanner—a well-dressed, churchgoing man of substance in his community who managed a good business and fulfilled his civic responsibilities. He must have cared deeply for his free family of color, because he maintained an enduring relationship with Mariah and their children and probably sacrificed social status and respectability in the white community because of them.

Henry Hunt was unusual but not completely alone in his alliance with a woman who was not white. Louis Snopes and Olivia Jones stayed together for many years with their two mulatto children in Taliaferro County. In nearby Augusta, Samuel Wynn had no wife other than an elegantly well-groomed and beautifully dressed woman of color named Louise who lived with him for many years. Samuel and Louise Wynn also had two children born in the late 1850s. Elsewhere in the state another planter, referred to as a bachelor, "lived on the farm [where] among the negroes . . . were a family of mulattoes, to which [he] for reasons not necessary to be repeated, had a strong affection." Right in Hancock County, David Dickson frequently entertained on his huge plantation, but some members of "polite society" in the county reportedly kept their distance due to the presence of his slave mistress, Julia. Those whites disdained David Dickson not because he had fathered a mulatto child—most antebellum Georgians expected that sort of behavior—but rather because of the respect with which he treated Julia and his open affection for and acknowledgment of their daughter and her sons who lived with them. White visitors asked Dickson, "have I got to eat with them?" He replied, "By God, yes, if you eat here!" Henry Hunt too lived with Mariah for a number of years. He cared enough to present her with diamonds when their daughters were born, buy fine fabrics to clothe them all, and provide personalized porcelain cups from which those children drank their milk.[73]

For her part, Mariah was Henry's wife and the mistress of his home. She apparently retained his attention and affection for decades. Although barely literate herself, she made certain that most of her children acquired a solid education. Her girls also became proficient in the requisite social and domestic skills expected of Southern ladies. Mariah's mother Susan had cultivated Pomegranate Hall's elaborate gardens and probably shared that art with her daughters. Mariah, in turn, passed the knowledge along to her children. Mariah and her sister studied music at the Sparta Female Model School and later taught their own daughters to play the piano. The girls became accomplished seamstresses and musicians, but as a child Adella Hunt, at least, never learned to cook. Household servants may have performed those particular domestic functions for the family.[74]

Mariah must have faced constant conflicts as Henry's wife, the mother of many children, and a free woman of color who presided over a large domestic establishment that included a number of slaves. She needed to constantly negotiate her way through sometimes difficult relationships with those slaves and simultaneously had to interact with numerous white in-laws. Mariah, however, had been raised in an even more affluent home than that which she made with Henry Hunt. Her own mother had been the spouse of a wealthy and influential white man. She too had slaves in the house and white relatives just a short distance away. Managing a house full of servants would not have been unfamiliar to Mariah. In addition, her mother lived nearby, and Mariah would have had her support and guidance throughout her adult years. Nelly Watkins and her widowed sister-in-law also lived in Sparta as did a handful of other free women of color. But the extent to which these women turned for friendship and support to each other, to the female slave community, or to white women is not really known. Just who might have helped or shunned them during those late antebellum years remains open to speculation.

The Hunts apparently experienced few upheavals in their lives through most of the 1850s, but the sentiment for secession and ultimately the threat of war became paramount issues throughout the South by the end of that decade and inevitably touched the lives of everyone in the region. In October 1859 the messianic Kansas abolitionist John Brown and a handful of supporters unsuccessfully tried to raid the Federal Arsenal at Harper's Ferry, Virginia, in the belief that slaves would join their insurrection. At the same time, John Pool, a young Hancock laborer, was overheard to say that "he was going to take care of himself by joining the strong side." If war came, he planned to "black himself" and go over to the Yankees. A "vigilance committee" of local slaveholders charged him with "uttering abolitionist statements." That tribunal did not believe his protestations of innocence but, fearing that he might be perceived as a martyr, finally dismissed him with a "stern lecture." Middle Georgians vigorously debated the wisdom of secession, and the region's most renowned politician, Alexander Stephens from Taliaferro County, vehemently opposed it. Of course, secessionist opinion ultimately prevailed, such holdouts as Stephens rallied to the cause, and Stephens himself even became vice president of the Confederacy. Georgia withdrew from the Union in the winter of 1861. By that spring Abraham Lincoln had been sworn in as the new president of the United States, and, with the attack on Fort Sumter, the Civil War began.[75]

The war brought economic hardship to the entire South, but for three years the fields of battle remained geographically remote from Middle Georgia. On May 8, 1861, Katherine DuBose presented a "banner blazoned with the glorious stars of our holy Southern Confederacy" to the Sydney Brown Infantry, Hancock County's first unit to go off to war. In spite of continuing strife between wealthy planters and poor local conscripts, the Hancock Volunteers, Dawson's Artillery, and the Bullard, Pierce, and Turner Guards followed the Sydney Brown Infantry. In August 1863 the final company formed in Hancock County was Capt. Linton Stephens's militia, designated "for a term of six months . . . to serve anywhere in Georgia." Corp. Henry Alexander Hunt was one of its noncommissioned officers.[76]

Throughout the South younger men went off to war while older planters stayed at home raising cotton and food crops to help support the Confederate forces and for consumption in Middle Georgia. White women gave up many luxuries and shredded their best linens for bandages. In spite of shortages, and proclaiming their undying support for the cause, they defiantly created a new "Southern-rights" cake, rich in eggs and butter, redolent with cinnamon, allspice, and ginger, and heavily laced with brandy.[77]

A wedding between two of Hancock County's self-described "colored 'swells'" helped to alleviate the depression and monotony of the early war years. Methodist Bishop George F. Pierce believed that slaves should be married in the sight of the Lord, so he opened his home, known as "Sunshine," and officiated over one such occasion. In 1862 young Lucius Holsey married Harriet Turner, a girl of fifteen—like himself, one of Pierce's slaves. The mistress of the household surely would only have dressed a bride of her own race in pristine white, but Mrs. Pierce adorned young Harriet in "the gayest and most artistic style, with red flowers and scarlet sashes predominating in the brilliant trail." To her bridegroom, Harriet "looked like an angel in the dwarfed splendors of heaven." The Pierces provided "a splendid repast of good things to eat . . . turkey, ham, cake, and many other things." "'The house girls' and 'the house boys' and the most prominent persons of color" attended the gala event. The guests most likely included such people as the Hunts and Amanda Dickson, whose own son married Harriet and Lucius Holsey's daughter a generation later. A few years after the Civil War, Holsey himself became minister to those same "prominent persons of color" as a bishop of the Colored Methodist Episcopal Church.[78]

Events such as the Turner-Holsey wedding provided only a brief respite in an otherwise anguished period. The secessionist government ordered large plantation owners to decrease cotton production and concurrently increase the acreage devoted to food crops. Except for Mariah's husband Henry, who was thirty-seven when he joined Linton Stephens's company, the Hunt brothers fell into the category of "old experienced planters" exempted from active service. During the war years Henry and J. M. Hunt's households, presided over by two free women of color, Mariah and her mother Susan Hunt, provided blankets and rugs for the Confederate army to use as saddle blankets and bedding.[79]

The war often divided families in unexpected ways—even those living in the same locale. Nathan Sayre's two white nephews fought with the Confederate forces in Virginia and Pennsylvania, but his other nephew, William Handy Horton, believed to be the son of Nathan's "bachelor" brother, Robert Sayre, and a slave woman, ran off to join the Union forces.[80]

The Confederacy took a number of slaves out of the fields and forced them to work constructing military defenses and performing other menial jobs, and some blacks went off to war as personal attendants to their masters. At least a few young free men of color such as Levi and Henry Ross from Baldwin County were reluctantly "pressed into service as cooks for the officers." Confederate officials informed the Ross family that "they had the authority to take them." "They were forced to go, [but] did not want to go because they were for the Union," their relatives explained. In the latter days of the war, however, the young Rosses got away from Milledgeville and, like William Handy Horton, volunteered to fight with the Yankees.[81]

With the implied support of new state legislation, in July 1861 a Hancock County "vigilance committee" hanged a black man accused of arson. As the war progressed and news of widespread slave unrest and desertions spread throughout the South, local fears of upheavals in the black community increased. Further rumors of rebellion shook Middle Georgia just a few months following the issuance of Lincoln's Emancipation Proclamation. "Eighteen Negroes have been lodged in Sparta jail, Hancock County," reported the Milledgeville *Southern Recorder,* "for . . . attempting to excite an insurrection." Local officials charged the cabal with committing "many depredations—thieving, killing, and driving off cattle." Supposedly, the group planned to join up with Union forces, "after first killing off all the old white men and women and appropriating the young white women as wives." White men had relatively free access to women of color, but the specter of any possible sexual relations between black men and white women triggered resounding alarms in the minds of white Southerners. The initial panic over the incident subsided somewhat in a few weeks, and a subsequent issue of the *Southern Recorder* stated that only four of the "ringleaders" had been indicted and would be held over for trial.[82]

The accused slaves' actual testimony differed markedly from newspaper accounts. Their own statements revealed a group of somewhat rowdy young men who liked to march around in secluded fields and groves drinking, smoking, and trading tall tales. Apparently, they had a rifle that had fired accidentally. They probably did hope to escape to the Union lines—an understandable aspiration—but did not intend to murder the local people or "to fire Sparta." The fears of local whites notwithstanding, the reputedly conspiratorial men were hardly part of an insurrection plot generated by "rascals from Lincolndom." Nonetheless, their activities reflected the pervasive restlessness within the slave community and an impatient desire to do whatever they could to facilitate and accelerate their own emancipation.[83]

The trials of the four leaders of "The Emeute in Hancock"— Richard Shaw, Cornelius "Mac" Simmons, John Cain, and Spencer Beasley—took place between November 26 and December 11. The presiding judge articulated the views of the white population when he stressed the importance of enforcing laws enacted "for no other purpose, but the keeping of the slave in subordination." Four separate juries found the men guilty and sentenced them to be hanged "by the Sheriff of Hancock County or some deputy appointed by him for the occasion." Almost immediately, however, Gov. Joseph E. Brown recommended clemency for Shaw.

Soon after sentencing, two of the men escaped from the Sparta jail. William Hunt was one of three local white men who put up a two thousand–dollar reward for their "apprehension and delivery," and the fugitives were recaptured in short order. In spite of his brief flight, a petition circulated that urged commutation of Beasley's sentence to four hundred lashes. Alexander Stephens argued that reducing the punishment "would have a good effect upon the negro population," because Beasley had apparently urged the others to avoid violence.[84]

J. M. Hunt was a member of the jury that found Beasley guilty and sentenced him to death. Hunt may not have recognized the irony in the fact that he helped to convict a man for crimes attributed to blacks "who had been permitted to perambulate the country and make their own contracts contrary to law, and live separate and apart from their owners." The *Southern Recorder* editorialized that this "unlawful privilege not only breeds disaffection among other servants, but opens the door to much mischief." In other words, J. M. Hunt, who lived with one free woman of color and near her daughter and grandchildren—who were also his own nieces and nephews—had sentenced to death a black man whose criminal behavior, most white

Georgians agreed, came about largely because he lived as if he were free.[85]

The judge, prosecutor, and the four juries all wanted to make an unequivocal statement about the potential dangers of laxity concerning the behavior of black people. With increasingly bad news about Confederate losses in the war, these white men desperately hoped to tighten the grip of authority and enforce strict discipline over the restless black community, and they sought to teach all African-Americans a lesson by this example. Slaves elsewhere might be running free—"let other communities take warning," cautioned one Atlanta newspaper—but white men still remained in control in Middle Georgia.[86]

That abortive rebellion rocked Hancock County in 1863, but the frenzy of battle remained distant until the fall of 1864 when Gen. William Tecumseh Sherman and his troops captured and burned Atlanta and started to march toward the sea at Savannah. Their routes took them directly through Middle Georgia. The Northern forces moved east and south through Putnam and Baldwin, down the roads, by river banks and railroad beds, along the southern borders of Hancock and Glascock, and on through Washington County. Foraging bands of soldiers even engaged in skirmishes as far afield as the northernmost reaches of Greene County near Scull Shoals. Throughout that fertile region, one Union soldier commented, the "sweet potatoes and negroes seemed to grow spontaneously."[87]

Women of color seem to have been a novelty for many of the soldiers, though they had sometimes been fighting in the South for several years. One Yankee observed that some of the women "had the octoroon lightness of color and clearness of feature, others approached the brown olive of the Indian, while others displayed the thick lips, woolly heads, and dusky skins of the pure Ethiopian." He added that "such a medley would send your miscegenation disciples into ecstasies, but it would take a whole herald college to trace their relationships to one another." The soldiers also came across a few "negro wenches, particularly good looking ones, decked in satins and silks," and slatternly, ragged backwoods white women who boldly accosted the troops and offered to trade personal favors in exchange for chewing tobacco.[88]

One soldier watched awestruck as hundreds of African-Americans streamed out "from abandoned plantations or miserable hiding places, to join in the march with the Yankees." Throughout Middle Georgia black people wanted to follow along with the liberating armies, one Milledgeville woman vowing that "I walks till I drop in my tracks." The soldiers tried to turn them away, but the blacks formed wretched refugee caravans that trailed in the wake of the Union troops. Scrawny mules pulled wagons filled with meager belongings, and women trudged alongside leaning heavily on sturdy walking staffs, with large bundles of clothing balanced on their heads and small children clinging to their legs. Other more exuberant blacks "waved to the regiments as they marched by and called them 'de Lawd's deliverin' army.'" A group of youngsters in Baldwin County piled into a "big wagon" on their plantation and went down to see the Yankees marching by. "We did see 'bout 5,000 soldiers," one remembered from when she was only a girl of eight, "dey was tryin' to git back home . . . I had alluz been skeered o' soldiers, but after I seen dem I warn't skeered no mo'." Another local woman embraced one Yankee officer and greeted his men crying, "Bress de Lord! Tanks be to Almighty God, the Yanks is come! de day ob jubilee has arribed!"[89]

White Southern women also encountered the Yankee soldiers. Near Sandersville, one young "belle" searched in vain for a Union officer crying piteously, "we've been robbed of our jewels. My sister's diamonds were rudely snatched from her . . . Surely your officers will not permit such an outrage." Miraculously, the misappropriated diamonds were returned to their owner. Marion Alexander Boggs, a white woman, wrote from Eatonton that Yankee troops marching through Putnam County had deeply offended Southern women of her race. They "found out the names of the young ladies, and called them all by their first names," she complained, "and wherever there was a piano, they forced them to play and they would all sing their national songs." However Boggs disparaged reports of more savage outrages. "They say in Milledgeville they violated several respectable females," she continued, "but I don't know how true that is and I am inclined to doubt it." Boggs also recognized that Union soldiers sometimes treated blacks more brutally than they did whites. "Two negro women were confined at their camp on that Sunday," she said, "and after they left, and our own men went out there, both these women and their infants were dead."[90]

Rebecca Green, a white girl, lived by Buffalo Creek in Hancock County. When her family heard that the Yankees were coming imminently they buried trunks filled with fine clothing and other treasures. Most planters' families in Hancock County took the same precautions, and on the Dickson plantation, Julia, David Dickson's slave mistress, and their daughter Amanda, buried the family silver "under a locust tree" just as many white people did. Union troops destroyed much of the Dickson plantation. The white Fort family abandoned Milledgeville for safer surroundings, and their former slave, Wilkes Flagg, "was intrusted . . . with all the silverware and jewelry." Flagg "buried it on his own lot, in the floor of an old stable, then burnt the stable so as to conceal the evidence of the burial of the valuables." Near Sparta, after days of fearful anticipation, Rebecca Green "saw a column of smoke, flames bursting out in every direction." The family's losses were all-inclusive. "In less than an hour the ginhouse, the whole crop of cotton, seed of last year's crop, carriage house, wagon shelters, packing screw, my good carriage and harness, two fine buggies, a six horse farm wagon [and] a new iron-axle oxcart," went up in smoke, Green said. The Yankees even destroyed "every utensil used on the plantation."[91]

Union soldiers also appropriated property belonging to free people of color. "Thousands of soldiers" stopped for a week close to the farms belonging to the Ross and Bellamy families near Milledgeville. For several years young Mary Ross Bellamy had efficiently farmed twenty-five acres that her uncle had allotted her, and she proudly declared her pro-Union sentiments. She vigorously opposed the Confederacy because "free persons of color had no rights, had to have passes and guardians and could not go anywhere." On the other hand, if the "Old Government succeeded," Mary reasoned, "we would be free and have some chance." Her cousin, another free woman of color, echoed those sentiments. "We had no rights as we were then situated," she said, "and what we had we could not enjoy."[92]

When Sherman's troops came by and camped only four hundred yards from her home, Mary Ross Bellamy "rejoiced with the balance of us . . . I never saw such rejoicing as we had among the colored people at Milledgeville when the Union army came." Mary gladly "fed them, cooked for them, washed for them and treated them with kindness." In exchange for her generosity—explaining with some embarrassment that they were cut off from their supply lines— "officers ordered the soldiers to take the property . . . [because] they were obliged to . . . feed the men and stock." Mary complained bitterly, but to no avail. The soldiers emptied her corn from the cribs and hauled it away in wagons, dug up sweet potatoes from the fields, carried off white peas in gunny sacks, took white and red wheat, fodder, almost two hundred pounds of bacon, and gallons of syrup as well, loading the supplies onto their mules and wagons. They took the mare that Mary Ross Bellamy had raised from a colt—the family saw a Union soldier riding her a few days later—a yearling, "four fat hogs . . . around 200 pounds apiece," many young shoats, and some cattle. The Yankees camped so close by that Mary could hear the men talking, laughing, and singing and see them cooking and then eating her pigs around their campfires.

Unseasonably cold winds whipped across Middle Georgia making it feel like midwinter, and soldiers appropriated Mary Ross Bellamy's coverlets, blankets, quilts, coffee pot, pans, and skillets as well. Her uncle John and aunt Martha lost even more than she did from their two hundred–acre farm, and her cousin Currell was furious because one soldier incomprehensibly rode off wearing his "Sunday hat." Abraham Lincoln, newly elected to a second term, had just officially declared the fourth Thursday in November as a national holiday of Thanksgiving. Plundering Union troops gleefully shot and carried off fifteen of the Rosses' geese, twenty ducks, thirty chickens, and twenty guinea hens to roast and devour along with yams for their Thanksgiving dinners. Just down the road in Milledgeville, the "Federal army . . . robbed Wilkes [Flagg] of a handsome gold watch and chain, stripped his house of everything they wished [and] tied him up by the thumbs."[93]

Only a few miles away, Judkins Hunt's Mount Zion plantation became an assembly point for local Confederate loyalists when the Union troops "was goin' past Town Creek on de way to Sparta." On Friday, November 25, one of Judkins's neighbors wrote to a friend urging him to join a group that included William Hunt and a brother-in-law, at "J. Hunt's." The neighbor reported that one thousand Yankee cavalrymen had just burned the state capital, and a black woman confirmed that "Milledgeville was jes' tore up; twon't nuttin' mo'n a cow pasture when de Yankees got th'ough wid it." The soldiers then crossed over the plank bridge spanning the Oconee River and entered Hancock County. They moved quickly through Washington and Glascock, encountering little resistance, and continued their route eastward.[94]

By November of 1864, when Sherman and his army marched through Middle Georgia and on to the sea, the devastating and divisive war was all but over, and the final surrender at the Appomattox courthouse the following spring made it official. Henry Rogers remembered the end of the war on the Hunts' plantation. "When it wuz over with an' our white mens come home," he recalled, "all de neighbors . . . livin' on plantations 'round us had a big dinner over at my white peoples' the Hunts, an' it sho wuz a big affair." Henry Hunt would have been one of their "white mens" who returned. Both Susans, as well as Henry's own wife Mariah and all of their children should have attended that "big affair" which, Rogers said, included "ev'rybody from them families." "Ev'rybody" may have come to celebrate the peace at Judkins and Rebecca's plantation, but the place that the people of color in the family would have had at that sort of gathering is a question which can never be adequately answered.[95]

Even following the Confederate surrender the irrepressible Judkins Hunt, a diehard believer, remained in the thick of the action. Judkins harbored the Confederate Secretary of War, Gen. John C. Breckinridge, at his Mount Zion plantation as Breckinridge fled across Georgia in a futile attempt to escape by way of Savannah and the sea.[96]

The War between the States was over, and the South had lost. White Georgians struggled to deal with the fact that slavery was no more. "No more old mammies and daddies, no more old uncles and aunties," one local girl complained.[97] Many Southerners who had invested so much of their wealth in human property were humbled, angered, and reduced to modest economic circumstances at best. Plantation masters and slave owners such as the Hunts lost much of their capital. Union troops had burned houses, barns, cotton gins, and bridges in their path. They had torn up railroad tracks, twisted them into "Sherman's neckties," confiscated horses and mules, stolen chickens, pigs, and other livestock, and plundered personal and household possessions belonging to whites and even free people of color sympathetic to the Union.

The former slaves acquired a proud new status as freedpeople, and the free men and women of color, who had occupied a distinct role as a separate class between the white citizenry and the black slaves, lost their singular standing. They retained their familial connections, a bit of their very modest personal property, and, in a few cases, the advantage of a little education. But nonetheless, when slavery was abolished, everyone who was not white was black. New laws recognized no distinctions between the former free people of color and the former slaves.

More than a decade earlier Susan and Mariah Hunt had left Nathan Sayre's Pomegranate Hall and moved to Mount Zion with Henry and J. M. Hunt. They resided there and supervised the domestic life of those establishments through the war. The older Susan was J. M. Hunt's housekeeper, "nurse," and companion. Mariah lived as Henry Hunt's wife and she had given birth to four of his children. A rigidly patriarchal antebellum society may have tried to ignore them but somehow managed to tolerate their unconventional familial arrangement. The enormous upheavals resulting from the termination of slavery, however, did not bypass this family or others like it. The new era that both the former slaves and their former masters encountered inevitably and irrevocably also changed the lives of that small intermediary caste—the free people of color.

The war ended, and the president who led the nation through that most devastating war had not survived the peace. White Southern women mourned their men and boys who had died for the Confederacy trying to ensure states' rights and preserve the repressive slave regime and the way of life they had always known. Women of color in Middle Georgia knew as well as whites that the war had touched their lives. They did not doubt that their world had changed for the better and that black people had played a crucial role in bringing about that change. Sarah Shuften, a young woman of African ancestry—perhaps free herself—who had defiantly learned to write during Georgia's repressive slave era, spoke for many of her race in a passionate, optimistic poem memorializing the contribution of the black men who fought and died to restore the Union and end slavery. "Ethiopia's Dead" appeared in the Augusta *Colored American* just months after the end of the war:

> Their bones bleach on the South'rn hill,
>   And on the Southern plain,
> By brook and river, lake and rill,
>   And by the roaring main.

Oh! few and weak their numbers were,
    A handful of brave men,
But up to God they sent their prayer,
    And rushed to battle, then
The God of battle heard their cry
    And crowned their deeds with victory.

Fair Afric's *free* and valiant sons,
    Shall join with Europe's band,
To celebrate in varied tongues,
    Our *free* and happy land.[98]

THE HUNT FAMILY:
PEOPLE OF COLOR BORN THROUGH RECONSTRUCTION

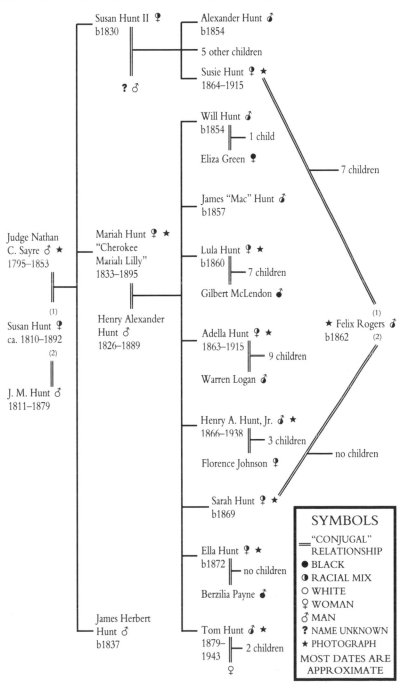

Susan Hunt II ♀
b1830

? ♂

Alexander Hunt ♂
b1854

5 other children

Susie Hunt ♀ ★
1864–1915

7 children

Will Hunt ♂
b1854

1 child

Eliza Green ♀

James "Mac" Hunt ♂
b1857

Lula Hunt ♀ ★
b1860

7 children

Gilbert McLendon ♂

Judge Nathan
C. Sayre ♂ ★
1795–1853

Mariah Hunt ♀ ★
"Cherokee
Mariah Lilly"
1833–1895

Henry Alexander
Hunt ♂
1826–1889

(1)

Susan Hunt ♀
ca. 1810–1892

(2)

J. M. Hunt ♂
1811–1879

Adella Hunt ♀ ★
1863–1915

9 children

Warren Logan ♂

(1)

★ Felix Rogers ♂
b1862

(2)

Henry A. Hunt, Jr. ♂ ★
1866–1938

3 children

Florence Johnson ♀

no children

Sarah Hunt ♀ ★
b1869

Ella Hunt ♀ ★
b1872

no children

Berzilia Payne ♂

James Herbert
Hunt ♂
b1837

Tom Hunt ♂ ★
1879–
1943

2 children

♀

SYMBOLS

═ "CONJUGAL"
RELATIONSHIP
● BLACK
◑ RACIAL MIX
○ WHITE
♀ WOMAN
♂ MAN
? NAME UNKNOWN
★ PHOTOGRAPH
MOST DATES ARE
APPROXIMATE

IV

On Hunt's Hill

There was joy in the South. It rose like perfume—
like a prayer. Men stood quivering. Slim dark
girls, wild and beautiful with wrinkled hair, wept
silently; young women, black, tawny, white and
golden, lifted shivering hands, and old and broken
mothers, black and gray, raised great voices and
shouted to God across the fields, and up to the
rocks and the mountains.

W. E. B. Du Bois
Black Reconstruction in America, 1935

"'Cordin' to my way of thinkin'," Rachel Adams explained, "Abraham Lincoln done a good thing when he sot us free . . . [and] we wuz free as jack-rabbits." At the same time, her old master in Putnam County warned his former slaves "dat from den on niggers would have to git deir own sumpin' to eat."[1] Freedpeople throughout Middle Georgia celebrated their emancipation and the end of the devastating war, but they also faced new challenges that they were sometimes ill-prepared to handle. "Dey wuz sho' in er mess atter de war," Carrie Mason said about her friends and relatives in Baldwin County. "Evvythin' wuz tore up an de po' niggers didn't know whichaway to turn."[2]

In the antebellum years, slaves had not been able to acquire any formal education, political experience, tangible assets, or virtually any knowledge of finances. The freedpeople who stayed in rural Middle

Georgia after 1865 remained in the same repressive environment in which they had been enslaved, as promises of free land soon proved a chimera. They faced the scorn of former slaveholders who, in losing the bitter war, had also lost much of their wealth, honor, dignity, and cherished way of life. For many generations white Georgians had treated blacks as chattel. Following emancipation, they were unwilling to treat those same people as equals and were certainly not prepared to support them or compensate them for several hundred years of deprivation and abuse. Suffering through their own anguish and losses, white Georgians often lashed out at blacks as they celebrated their freedom. Soon after the war freedpeople in Greensboro exultantly hoisted a Union flag and sang:

> We rally around the flagpole of liberty,
> The Union forever, Hurrah! Boys, Hurrah!

But white townspeople tore down the flagpole and quickly silenced the joyous revels.[3]

Although he listened attentively to their stories, Joel Chandler Harris viewed the former slaves from the perspective of a white plantation-bred Middle Georgian. People of color near his home town of Eatonton experienced deep conflicts as they pondered leaving their homes. Harris wrote about a woman named Jemimy who tried to balance the longing to remain with family and friends against a strong desire to leave the place of her enslavement once and for all. "Dey say if we don't go 'way from whar we b'long at, we never is ter be free," she cried, but "I wuz born here, an' ef dis ain't my house, I dunner whar in de roun' worl' I got any." But others held different views. When asked by a Northern visitor why she had left her home and former "mistress," an elderly woman near Milledgeville answered, "What fur? 'Joy my freedom!" She saw "no reason to make complaint." Such freedwomen as Hancock County's Mollie Kinsey, however, had to heed family responsibilities that sometimes prevented them from leaving the villages and farms they knew best. Kinsey remained where she had always lived because she "was set free with a blind ma."[4]

Little more than a year after Sherman's destructive march from Atlanta to the sea, Eliza Frances Andrews, a white woman, looked around the Middle Georgia region she loved and commented that "the country seems to have pretty well recovered . . . so far as appearances go; the fields are tilled and crops growing." Though most plantations did not equal their prewar productivity, for the most part, cotton, sweet potatoes, and field peas came up as they always had by the spring of 1866, but changes that Andrews saw in the fabric of Southern life enraged her. She thought that both the Yankees and the freedpeople expected "to play the masters over us." The Federal Bureau of Refugees, Freedmen, and Abandoned Lands, commonly called the Freedmen's Bureau, dispatched agents throughout the South to help facilitate the transition from slavery to freedom. Andrews also hated the postwar presence of Yankee troops garrisoned near her home town, and especially resented the relationships that those soldiers established with the freedwomen. "They had two negro balls while they were here, the white men dancing with negro wenches on their arms," Andrews complained. The Yankees opened "a negro brothel, or rather a colony of them," and she and other local white people watched with disgust as the "insolent" soldiers socialized with black women, "singing and laughing at their detestable orgies."[5]

Regardless of what such white Georgians as Andrews might have thought, the former slaves understood that they must establish new lives for themselves. From Taliaferro County, politician Alexander Stephens wrote his friend, former governor Howell Cobb, near Milledgeville, grumbling that "freedom has had a decidedly injurious influence upon the moral character of the blacks . . . the whites are inspired with contempt for [them] . . . and constantly irritated and provoked by their bad conduct." A white woman in Eatonton complained that "before they were declared free," black women on her plantation "could weave six or eight yards of cloth a day, easy. Now the most they do is about one yard."[6] The freedwomen's new assertiveness appalled Frances Butler Leigh, an affluent Georgian. "Always inclined to be immoral, they have now thrown all semblance of chastity to the winds," she exclaimed from her coastal plantation. "What has become of their yearning for better things?" she asked. One newspaper concluded from these accounts that the recently emancipated women were simply "idle, lazy and crazy, delighting in new shoes and hats," while another journal wistfully editorialized that "no joyous smiles lit up their faces as in days past." "Thousands" of the freedpeople, Milledgeville's *Southern Recorder* wishfully stated, would gladly exchange liberty for the "chains of slavery."[7] Such unsubstantiated reports as these reinforced white Southerners in their beliefs that blacks were irresponsible, morally lax, in continuing need of supervision and discipline from their former masters, and generally unready and unfit for freedom. With the advent of the Reconstruction era, many freedwomen stopped working in the cotton fields and in white people's kitchens to stay home and care for their own families and household responsibilities. Black men, who wanted to "take their wives from the drudgery and exposure of plantation toil as soon as it is in their power to do so," encouraged the women in those actions that so clearly characterized their desire for independence.[8] White Southerners recognized that the black women wanted greater control over their working conditions. To counteract that determination, the whites attempted to replicate the conditions of bondage as best they could in order to preserve an accustomed way of life and maintain their power over the apparently willful freedpeople.

Whenever possible, women of color left the houses and plantations of affluent whites who had long relied on them to care for their children, clean their homes, and prepare their every meal. One Northerner visiting Middle Georgia observed that it was important, but very difficult, to "teach the [white] women of the South that labor is not degrading." He met few white Southern women whom he believed would "know and appreciate the dignity of domestic life [or the] subtile mysteries of orderly and cleanly housekeeping." In Greensboro he ran across one black woman whom he judged to be a singular exception, but from his Northern perspective, he thought that the freedpeople hardly did much better, and he seriously doubted "the capacity of a negro woman to be a good cook."[9]

Southern food, whether prepared by blacks or whites, presented Northerners with a distinctly different culinary experience, which some of them clearly could not appreciate. For generations, many whites had black servants who cooked for them, and a unique Southern cuisine had evolved that combined African with Anglo-American traditions, supplemented by Native American influences as well. To some degree, diet differed according to income, but blacks and whites, affluent and poor alike, consumed such fresh local produce as limas, field peas, snap beans, and cabbage—always flavored with salt pork or butter. Georgians fried every imaginable food. They sautéed Indian corn or combined it with butter beans for succotash. They ground it into meal that was stirred up with water, milk, or eggs to create an omnipresent variety of baked and skillet-fried breads and fritters. They also soaked and hulled it to make hominy, often consumed as grits, which were prepared in many ways, at any time of day. Peaches, pears, berries, figs, quince, and melons grew abundantly in the fields, orchards, and woods. Middle Georgians of both races ate them fresh in the summertime, preserved them for the cold months, and processed them for beverages, jams, sauces, cobblers, and pies. White people especially delighted in such rich desserts as Georgia sponge and marble cakes and a sweet "Augusta pudding" topped with custard. They also liked Brunswick stew, spit-roasted partridge, and calipash—an elegant pastry-covered terrapin pie seasoned with herbs, mace, and sherry, baked and served in the turtle's shell. Men and women of color consumed okra, plus the collard, kale, mustard, and turnip greens that their ancestors had known in their homeland. Watermelons, figs, and pomegranates were also familiar fare from West Africa. Sweet potatoes or yams were buried and baked in the ashes, moistened with butter, sweetened with molasses, made fragrant with cinnamon, clove, and nutmeg, or mashed and heaped into pie crusts. Hogs rooted in almost every yard, and, except for the few who adhered to Islamic traditions, black people ate a lot of pork. They used all parts of the pig—head, trotters, innards, and tail included—and most African-American women in rural Georgia knew how to cure ham and bacon by cooling the fresh meat, rubbing it down with saltpeter, brown sugar, salt, and cayenne, soaking it in brine, cleaning off the skipper-fly eggs, then finally covering it with hickory ashes and smoking it for several days longer. For their own families, women of color prepared such composite dishes as hoppin' John (black-eyed peas mixed with rice), spicy gumbos—the name derived from the Angolan word *ki-ngombo*—thickened with sassafras, and fish and chicken fricassees flavored with tomatoes and onions.[10]

Resentment ran high when whites were faced with the loss of servants on whom they had always depended to prepare their food and attend to their every need. Taliaferro County officials even imprisoned a cook named Sofia Chapman because she left her employer's house for one day without permission. Once she was released from jail she was summarily fired from the job.[11]

The former slaves, of course, understood that freedom under any circumstances was preferable to their previous condition, but they soon found that freedom in and of itself was no panacea. Employers established governmentally sanctioned contract systems to control most black workers—including domestics. Often they were not as free as they had hoped or expected they would be. Intimidation was also used to attempt to keep blacks where they had once legally belonged. In nearby Wilkes County one freedwoman attempted to leave her former master's plantation "to go and try the blessings of freedom." Two white men attacked her, one of whom "shot her, while the other broke her ribs and beat her on the head with a stone 'till she died." Blacks must have wondered where they could turn for support when the captain in charge of Freedmen's Bureau operations in Milledgeville ordered that "freedmen that will use any disrespectful language to their former masters will be severely punished."[12]

A few African-Americans, disillusioned by harsh conditions in the Reconstruction South, left the United States under the auspices of the American Colonization Society. E. M. Pendleton, the Sayre family's physician and one of the society's white supporters, reported in 1868 that a small group of twenty five blacks from Hancock, "little and big, made their appearance and left today in the cars for Savannah," on their way to make new lives for themselves in Africa. A couple of years later a black legislator from neighboring Baldwin County received letters with news—most of it reporting tragic deaths—from members of two local families who had emigrated to Cape Palma, Liberia.[13]

Following passage of the federal Reconstruction Acts and operating under newly imposed voting regulations, Hancock County, which had 1,578 black and 795 qualified white male voters, elected two former slaves, W. H. Harrison and Eli Barnes, to the state House of Representatives in 1868. After the war an affluent white man from Sparta had converted a piece of his own land into a residential community called Dixie for elderly freedpeople. Dixie was just west of Sparta, and one evening shortly after the election of Hancock's new black representatives, its residents rejoiced exuberantly. They paraded around the neighborhood acclaiming their political victory with cheers and reverberating drum rolls, but a rumor soon circulated that they were preparing to march down the road and take over the town of Sparta. The Ku Klux Klan sent two scouts to investigate, but they found that the happy Dixie-ites were only cooking up a celebratory barbecue. Jubilation among blacks in Hancock over their new representation was short-lived, however, when the Georgia legislature challenged the qualifications of all the black delegates. Along with the other African-American representatives, Barnes and Harrison were expelled from the legislature soon thereafter, to be briefly reseated only in 1870 by act of the United States Congress.[14]

The freedpeople in Hancock did not hesitate to remind Barnes and Harrison that they faced harsh times. After their reinstatement in 1870 the two representatives received the following letter from a constituent:

> Sparta, April 25th, 1870
> Hons. W. H. Harrison & Barnes

> To-day about 11-oclock on the Plantation of Jas. T. Gardner my Daughter—Ida was outrageiously & Brutely Beat by one John Hall imployed by—Mr Gardner as agt. I & my wife was in the field at work at the time—when I came and went to Hall and asked him why he did not come to me he sayed he consulted no Damed Negro about Beating thare Children—Ida's head was Beat into a Jelly & I fear her Skull—*fractured* also her hands & arms cut serverly in several places to the bone—I Brought my Daughter to town to give her Medical Treatment. I also have now in my persession the Sharp edge Rock that she was Beat with and the Bloody Garments that she wore—the Garrison left here this morning & I think if they had been here thare would been no troble with me & Hall—I am not acquainted with You or Mr. Barnes but I only write to let you know what is going on aready at home I will leave the Rock at your store with Mr. Wilson—I can & will make an affadavit to this Murdious affare & produce many witnesses = but I know thare will be nothing done so I will not Ishure no warrent untill I here from you.
> Write to Wilson soon

> Your Friend
> Frank Watkins[15]

Had Ida Watkins talked back to John Hall or been slow responding to an order? Her father's letter suggests no answers, and none matter. Regardless of any possible provocation, Hall violently and unconscionably assaulted a child who could not protect herself, and, with good reason, the Watkins family anticipated that the law would not help them at all.

Not infrequently, white men in Middle Georgia abused and humiliated black women. When two women named Rhodes left their place of employment in Greene County because they had not been adequately fed, the white Spinks brothers with whom they had contracted followed them all the way to Crawfordville. They chased the women, their husbands, and their children on horseback, "with their pistols drawn." When the Spinkses finally cornered the group, they forced the women to "lay down on the *ground pulling their clothes up over their heads,*" then publicly whipped and threatened to shoot them.[16] In Warrenton, another man strung up an employee, Ellen Storey, by her thumbs. The local Freedmen's Bureau agent said that he could not condemn that abuse because Ellen Storey had been "impertinent and indisposed to labor and at all times manifesting a disposition to produce dissatisfaction." Since emancipation, he added, blacks had become very "impudent."[17] John Hall and the Spinks brothers may not have been Klansmen, but they operated freely in an environment that condoned and even encouraged the brutal intimidation of blacks—often women and children.

Even if the Ku Klux Klan was not behind those specific incidents, the secret society nonetheless flourished in Middle Georgia. The Klan had first been established in Tennessee in 1866, and within a few years it spread throughout the South. In 1871 Hancock County's black representatives, Harrison and Barnes, testified in Atlanta before a United States congressional committee that had been convened to investigate "conditions of affairs in the Southern states." Both men answered questions concerning the purported voting irregularities and intimidation tactics that had led to their expulsion from the state legislature. Harrison swore under oath that he had received threatening notes illustrated with "skeletons and coffins." In neighboring Greene County, another black legislator was almost beaten to death when he refused to voluntarily relinquish his office. "There have been more cases of whipping in the same length of time among the colored people than there were in the days of slavery," Harrison attested, and further stated that the previous year two blacks in Hancock County had been killed by "bands of disguised men." A white man had been indicted for one of the killings, but Harrison doubted that he would ever be tried.[18]

The former vice president of the Confederacy, Taliaferro County's Alexander Stephens, probably spoke for most of his race when he appeared before the same committee to refute the charges of intimidation that Barnes and Harrison had previously sworn to. His half brother Linton, suspected of encouraging several Klan-backed incidents in Hancock, may have influenced his testimony. Alexander Stephens argued that disqualifying black voters was an acceptable procedure because they refused to pay the poll tax when their people were denied the educational benefits those monies were intended to support. Stephens further asserted that the two men had not been killed by the Klan; rather he implicated local blacks for the crimes, citing robbery as the motive. He did admit that one former slave named Watson had been "whipped and maltreated by disguised persons" but justified the attack on the grounds that Watson had been "living with a white woman in a state of adultery."[19] In Washington County John Turner, another black man, and his white wife Ellen, were similarly harassed. "They will do the worst they can do if they are not stopped," Ellen Turner said fearfully.[20]

In Warren County, the Klan operated openly and brutally. Starting in mid-1868, well-organized terrorists began whipping and shooting freedpeople almost nightly. African-Americans felt the brunt of the violence, but whites—particularly Republicans—who showed blacks any sympathy or support were also victimized. The Klan focused its rage on the more enterprising people of color who did not seem satisfied to "stay in their place" economically, socially, or politically. Moderately successful and strong-minded black men faced the greatest danger, but their wives and children were also at risk. One evening in November 1868 when they failed to find her husband—their intended victim who had escaped to the nearby woods—masked riders dragged a woman and her crippled son out of their log cabin near Camak and hanged her from a tree with bed cord. They shot the boy eleven times, made a pyre from the family's household belongings, threw the boy's body on top and set fire to the whole thing. Several months later four robed Warren County Klansmen gang-raped a young black girl, beat eleven other freedpeople, and shot and killed yet another, all in one bloody and frenzied Sunday night.[21]

The Klan spread its terror in Hancock and the surrounding counties but may not have had the undivided support of the white community.

In 1869 Rebecca Green wrote an ambiguous poem from her home at Mount Zion. In one stanza she condemned the terror disseminated by the "terrible" hooded raiders:

Ku Klux Klan! and a shudder ran
Through every nerve of those who serve
In field and by fireside—
And with horror they hide
From the terrible Ku Klux Klan.

Yet at the same time, Green articulated the position held by so many members of the white community. She believed that the pervasive "vice" which supposedly accompanied Reconstruction justified the Klan's convictions if not its violence. She yearned for a restoration of what she saw as the revered standards—"religion," "Truth and Justice," "Wisdom and Virtue"—of the antebellum era:

May God speed the day when religion holds sway—
When o'er these broad lands Truth and Justice
    join hands—
When Wisdom and Virtue in places of power
Banish Vice to Hell's haunts there forever
    to cower—
No need then of the Ku Klux Klan.[22]

Fear and violence plagued many African-Americans in Middle Georgia during Reconstruction. Nightriders spread terror in the darkness, and white men could murder black men, abuse and rape black women, and batter their children in broad daylight. A number of African-Americans yielded to this intimidation and fled the area and sometimes even the country. Threats of retaliation silenced many decent people, both black and white. Nonetheless, this horror and adversity did not control the lives of everyone in the nonwhite community. For one, Adella Hunt, a privileged mulatto born free during the war, had a secure home and the continuing support, protection, and guidance of not only her mother and other "colored" relatives but her white father as well. Years later, friends attributed her political acumen to the fact that she was "the daughter of a Confederate officer and her father used to talk politics to her when she was a little girl."[23]

Only a few white girls in Georgia, such as Eliza Frances Andrews and Frances Butler Leigh, engaged in political debate with their fathers. Politics was not considered something that fell within a woman's sphere of interest and understanding, and Andrews and Leigh were exceptions among Southern females—and, of course, they were white. Their privileged position in their parents' homes and their communities was open and above board. For a rural white Georgian such as Henry Hunt to "talk politics" with his nonwhite daughter would have been even more of an anomaly.

Political discourse between a white father and his mulatto child in the Hunt household, however, constituted only a small and somewhat atypical part of that family's routine in the years following the war. At best, Mariah Hunt and her husband Henry shared the same roof only intermittently. By 1870 Mariah Hunt lived in a house near Sparta with her six children, but no adult male officially resided with them. She had no employment other than mother and homemaker. At the same time Henry, her spouse and the father of her children, lived as a "bachelor" near his oldest brother J. M. at Mount Zion, possibly sharing the home as well with Mariah's mother Susan. In addition to Mariah's four older children—Will, James (often called Mac), Lula, and Adella, all born before or during the war—two younger children, Henry, Jr., and Sarah, were born in 1866 and 1869. With the exception of the last two, all of the children, even seven-year-old Adella, attended school by 1870. Two additional children, Ella and Tom, born in 1872 and 1879 respectively, eventually completed Henry and Mariah Hunt's family.[24] Although Henry did not live with Mariah and the children on a regular basis, the four boys were named for their father and three of his brothers in a strong affirmation of their identity as Hunts and their association with the white family. Lula (Louisa), Adella, and Sarah were given the names of women in their maternal grandfather Nathan Sayre's family.

Henry and Mariah maintained separate households after the war, and several complex legal and social circumstances probably contributed to their residential separation. Among its early postwar actions, the Georgia state legislature officially sanctioned "colored ordained ministers of the gospel . . . to solemnize . . . marriages between freedmen and freedwomen of African descent only." People of color swarmed to the county courthouses to legitimatize their conjugal relationships. The legislature also specifically banned marriage between whites and any person who had as much as "one-eighth negro or African blood in their veins." For the first time that same year another new law also granted all married women, regardless of race, the right to own or inherit property apart from their husbands.[25] These statutes apparently had contradictory consequences for Mariah and Henry Hunt. On one hand, the first of these newly instituted provisions might have invalidated their marriage—if in fact their interracial union ever had any legal standing—and impelled them to live apart. Social opprobrium against interracial relationships also increased during this period. At the same time, however, since many people in Hancock County had previously considered her a married woman, Mariah finally could have held title to her own home under provisions of the new married woman's property act.

In addition to changes in the law, new patterns of residential separation by both class and color began to emerge in Middle Georgia and throughout the South during this period. Most freedpeople no longer wanted to live in the old slave quarters under the surveillance of their former masters. Many moved out into tenant cabins scattered around the large plantations, and others began to reside in all-black communities such as Hancock County's Dixie. Only a small percentage of African-Americans living in Middle Georgia during Reconstruction managed to accumulate any amount of property at all, but those who did tended to cluster together, much as a number of free people of color had lived in close proximity with one another prior to the war. These small, nascent "middle class" neighborhoods included three in Baldwin County, with the largest in Milledgeville, another in Scottsboro, and one more near the little village of Pittsburgh. In Putnam County the more comfortably situated people of color congregated in Eatonton and around the Union Chapel junction, and in Taliaferro almost everyone who owned property in the black community resided in Crawfordville. One Washington County neighborhood was in Sandersville, with another to the west in Hebron. So few blacks owned any property at all in Warren and Glascock that those counties had no middle-class clusters of African-Americans, but in Hancock that class lived in small but clearly identifiable groups near Sparta, Devereux, Culverton, Springfield, and close to Island Creek, where the free Bellamy and Ross families once farmed.[26]

By 1870 several common attributes characterized property-holding families in the the African-American community. All of these families included at least one adult woman who stayed at home as a housekeeper. This contrasted with non-property-holding families where men, women, and even young children often had to work in the fields. Although some people in the propertied group labored as tenants or sharecroppers on farms that they did not own, others worked their own land.

In 1869 Lucretia Ruff, who had been Hancock County's most successful African-American planter prior to the war, sold one hundred acres of her land on Beaverdam Creek to her sons for five hundred dollars.[27] Dilsey Fraley, a mulatto woman who had lived free in Baldwin County where she worked as a seamstress prior to the war, owned about one hundred acres. Five years after the end of the Civil War, she considered housekeeping her primary vocation. She had three children but no husband living with her. She resided and farmed in an area that included other property-holding people of color. She valued her land at six hundred dollars and her personal estate at three hundred and estimated that she paid out four hundred dollars per year in wages to the men whom she hired to do her farm work. Dilsey Fraley owned one horse, a mule, two milk cows, two other cattle, and seven pigs. She raised corn, cotton, and sweet potatoes and churned and sold her own butter.[28]

July De Saussure, another man of color in Baldwin County who had been nominally free prior to the war, and John and Martha Ross and their six youngest children owned and operated farms a short distance from Dilsey Fraley. In 1868 John and Martha had to sell one hundred acres of their land just east of the Milledgeville and Eatonton Railway tracks, perhaps partially because of the serious financial losses they incurred when Sherman's troops stripped them of livestock, crops, and personal property in November 1864. Along with John Ross's brother Currell and their niece Mary, they brought claims for those losses against the federal government, which finally granted them small cash settlements, a large percentage of which went to their white lawyers. By the mid-1870s the family had moved to Atlanta, where Martha Ross became a laundress and seamstress and her husband John worked as a shoemaker. Prior to the war, Mary Ross had lived for a time with Robert Bellamy, a free farmer. Her new husband, Allen Frazier, was a carpenter, grocer, and clergyman associated with the Union Methodist church.[29]

Right after the war when the Georgia legislature first passed legislation to recognize marriages between black people, Lavinia Robinson and Wilkes Flagg immediately had their relationship officially recorded in the county courthouse. The Flaggs owned a large farm of almost a thousand acres in Baldwin County, where they resided in a sizeable "colony, principally of kins-people."[30] They valued their land at over five thousand dollars and their livestock at a thousand. The farm produced mainly cotton and corn, plus a small amount of wheat. The Flaggs paid their agricultural laborers a total of thirty-five hundred dollars per year in wages.[31] Local planter and erstwhile politician Howell Cobb disparaged Wilkes Flagg as a "miserable creature for stirring up labor unrest among freedpeople," although Flagg, already in his sixties and a free blacksmith prior to the war, was a respected, silver-haired Milledgeville clergyman and a rare black Democrat who shunned political involvement. During Reconstruction he became increasingly conservative. At his church, Flagg's Chapel, he was known for his "piety and fanaticism." Before the church acquired its baptismal pool, in the wintertime Flagg immersed hardy candidates in a local pond even when he first had to chop through the ice. He sternly reprimanded parishioners from the pulpit and temporarily expelled them for such minor infractions as foot-tapping, whispering, lateness, or "shouting." He also told white friends "he was satisfied that the hand of the Lord was in it when the white people went over to Africa to bring them into slavery . . . this being the only way under Heaven by which they could be taught Christianity and civilization; [and] that they had progressed more in slavery than they would have done under any other circumstances."[32]

In the towns of Middle Georgia men of color who had accumulated a bit of money or property worked as carpenters, painters, shoemakers, brick masons, blacksmiths, harness makers, barbers, railroad workers, and porters. Their number also included one butcher, one dry goods merchant, one teacher, one state legislator, several clergymen like Flagg, and a couple of municipal employees. In Hancock, property holder Liburn Hunt worked at the fire station. Wilburn Scott served as an attendant at the state mental asylum in Milledgeville, and that same town had an entire "colored fire company" that included a fife and drum corps and operated "under the command of efficient white officers."[33] The few townswomen in this somewhat more comfortably situated group who did not consider "keeping house" their primary occupation, were domestic servants, cooks, laundresses, and seamstresses, and one taught school. Except that far more of the women worked only in their own homes, much as married white women did, these occupational patterns closely paralleled those of free people of color prior to the war. In addition, the children in a considerable number of these families attended school, especially in the larger towns.[34]

People of color who had been free prior to the war comprised a remarkably high percentage of these propertied Middle Georgia families in 1870. The residents in about twenty-five percent of the nonwhite households where at least two hundred dollars in property had been accumulated by 1870 seem to have had familial ties to former free people of color. Just ten years earlier, free African-Americans comprised less than one percent of the nonwhite population in the eight-county region of Middle Georgia.

Mariah Hunt and her family belonged to this small propertied minority. They lived in a house located in the northeast quadrant of Sparta by Two Mile Creek on a gentle slope appropriately called Hunt's Hill. The neighborhood got its name, one former Hancock County resident explained logically, "because of the many Hunt families that lived there." The hill was "nothing spectacular, just an unpaved road of red clay, slightly inclined." Some people in Sparta think that Martha Ann Hunt gave her "colored family" the land that became known as Hunt's Hill, but no record substantiates that understanding.[35]

Several transactions in Hancock County, however, do document the acquisition and ownership of land in that neighborhood by the Hunts and their kin during Reconstruction. In June 1866 Nelly Watkins, one of Nathan Sayre's mistresses, bought a piece of property known as "the Haynes lot" from James Thomas for $530. Interestingly, Thomas had acquired the same lot from Sayre's estate in 1860.[36] When Nelly Watkins died in 1874, she willed her home and property on Hunt's Hill to her nephew John Watkins and his wife Caroline, and she provided that her sister-in-law, Nancy, should have a "comfortable log house" built there for a sum not to exceed one hundred dollars.[37]

Another woman of color on Hunt's Hill was Louisa Horton. She apparently was the daughter of Nathan Sayre's bachelor brother Robert. Louisa Horton's son claimed that she was one quarter

Cherokee, and, like Susan Hunt, she may have been at least nominally free prior to the war, although she never appeared either in the census or the county's free register. Louisa Horton dressed with severe elegance in dark silks, veils, and gloves and wore steel-rimmed glasses perched down on her nose. She had at least a passing relationship with Judkins Hunt's former overseer, Jim Rogers, who was probably related to the Sayres by marriage. Louisa and Jim had a son named Felix Rogers, born during the early war years, who lived with his mother on Hunt's Hill. Louisa Horton validated the transaction with her "X" when she sold a one-acre tract that was part of the property she owned on Hunt's Hill to her cousin Mariah Hunt for thirty-five dollars in 1873. Although the census indicated that Mariah could neither read nor write, she affixed her signature to that bill of sale.[38]

On December 25, 1878, J. M. Hunt deeded a lot in the same area to Susan Hunt "for and in consideration of the services rendered to him as a nurse during his protracted affliction." A welcome Christmas present, perhaps. That property, near the railroad depot, "adjoining the lands of Lou Horton on the North," had 105 feet of road frontage and ran back approximately 400 feet.[39]

Mariah Hunt may have resided in a house on the property she acquired from Louisa Horton in 1873 or on land given to her mother by J. M. Hunt several years later. Her eight sons and daughters, as well as her sister, the younger Susan, with her children, lived in the same immediate neighborhood. A cousin, Molly Hunt Harper, the natural child of Judkins Hunt, plus Louisa Horton and her son, lived nearby. In addition, Nelly Watkins, Nathan Sayre's first mistress, resided a few houses away with her sister-in-law, her nephew, his wife, and their children. The women of the Watkins family were seamstresses and ran a laundering business out of their comfortably furnished home. Nelly Watkins, who had surely learned from Sayre about the importance of legal documentation, formally willed her house and modest estate to her family when she died in 1874.[40]

Sparta's townspeople described the residents of Hunt's Hill as light-skinned, comfortably situated, educated, and "well-connected" through their associations with the influential white Hunt and Sayre families. One woman reported that they "were not what you'd call wealthy," but they enjoyed "good lives." In addition to the Hunts, the extended family living on the hill included Hortons, Harpers,

Rogerses, and Watkinses, with whom they shared many social, economic, and physical characteristics.[41]

In the 1870s Mariah Hunt was a well-dressed, handsome though somewhat ascetic looking middle-aged matron. Her pale skin, angular features, dark eyes, and straight, swept-back black hair revealed only her white and Cherokee heritage. One of Mariah and Henry Hunt's granddaughters, who grew up on Hunt's Hill, knew that although her white grandfather lived elsewhere, everyone understood that "he was her [Mariah's] known support. He took care of her." The families on Hunt's Hill enjoyed a few privileges denied to most African-Americans, but they reportedly treated the people who worked in their houses and gardens, as well as other less affluent blacks, with great courtesy and never "set themselves above" anyone else.[42]

Mariah Hunt's children sometimes perceived, or at least described, their home life on Hunt's Hill in different ways. Writings about Henry Hunt, Jr., who became a noted educator, assert that he grew up in a "weather-stained cabin on a red hillside" where he "spent the early years of his life chopping cotton, hoeing potatoes, dropping corn and shelling peanuts for planting." The Hunt boys apparently did some gardening at home and helped out a bit around the family farm, but they did not engage in backbreaking field labor. Other family members state categorically that the white Hunts absolutely forbade them to pick cotton because it was not considered an appropriate activity for anyone of their kin. Whites, however, often preferred to think that people of color should be poor and humble. As an African-American educator who had to go out, hat in hand, seeking the assistance of white philanthropists in the early twentieth century, Henry Hunt, Jr., may have needed to distort the reality of his comfortable childhood in order to present a more modest picture of his background and upbringing.[43]

The women in the family had no comparable need to skew the true picture. They were free to admit, for example, that the family hired part-time household help. Though "the girls," Mariah's daughter Lula explained, "did not work outside the family . . . they were diligently trained in household duties and responsibilities." Lula Hunt was taught to do fine needlework, enjoyed music, and "prized old and beautiful things." She loved flowers and gardening but never chopped or picked cotton. As a girl she learned how to drive a horse and buggy but not how to steer a plow. A family friend recalled that for many years the Hunts "lived in town in a large old-fashioned frame house with a big center hall . . . [and] a good deal of land around," where Mariah, "looking like a little old white lady," often stood out on her wide front porch.[44]

In addition to the family and their close-knit community of neighbors and kin, the churches with which they became affiliated also influenced these people of color. During Reconstruction the white Hunts gave their former slaves several acres in the area near Mount Zion where they could build a church of their own. That church, situated about five miles north and west of Sparta and known as Hunt's Chapel, remains in use today, and its graveyard contains headstones for almost a dozen persons named Hunt dating back into the latter years of the nineteenth century. One stone marks the grave of Rev. Henry D. Hunt, born in 1837. He was the first pastor of Hunt's Chapel and was related by blood to both the white Hunts and the people of color on Hunt's Hill. The families from Hunt's Hill often drove their buggies out there for Sunday picnics "in the country," where they also may have watched or joined in a "match game of base ball" with the new "sable-hued" Mount Zion Dots team.[45]

Mariah, her children, and other family members and friends from Hunt's Hill, however, worshipped at the "neat frame building painted white," officially named Ebenezer Colored Methodist Episcopal Church of Sparta, but later called Holsey Memorial.[46] Black members withdrew from most white congregations during Reconstruction hoping to gain more autonomy and control over their own religious institutions, and new churches with both African-American ministers and parishioners sprang up throughout Middle Georgia. In those years, however, the Colored Methodist Episcopal (CME) church remained affiliated with the white Methodist Church, South. The CME was a minority denomination within the Southern black community, at least in part because its members sometimes identified closely with the former slave owners. The African Methodist Episcopal (AME) church, established by black Philadelphians in the early nineteenth century and associated with the Northern branch of the white Methodist church, became a preferred alternative for many former slaves, as did the AME Zion and fundamentalist Baptist churches. Their denominational name revealed that the CMEs considered themselves "colored" rather than "African," and throughout the South CME congregations were typically more affluent and more conservative than the AMEs. Wilkes Flagg's chapel and Hamp Brown's church were friendly rivals in Baldwin County. St. Mark's AME church in Dixie became a nucleus of religious and social life for Hancock County's African-American community and held enthusiastic revival meetings throughout the summer of 1879. The extended revival attracted participants who came by train from all around Middle Georgia, and the church reported almost three hundred converts.[47]

The leader of the CME church in Hancock County, Bishop Lucius Henry Holsey, was first ordained in 1868, "in the little church that stands beneath the oaks and cedars, in the village of Sparta." Hancock County's CME circuit originally included seven small congregations—including Julia and Amanda Dickson's Cherry Hill church on the Dickson plantation—under the joint leadership of Holsey and Rev. E. B. Oliver. A magnificent voice and spellbinding delivery characterized Oliver's ministry, and Holsey lauded him as "the flying angel of the everlasting gospel." Holsey, on the other hand, possessed neither Oliver's vocal resonance nor his magnetism, but, he claimed, "it was understood by the people that I was 'the deeper reasoner.'" White Methodist officials also admired Holsey, characterizing him "quick of apprehension, apt in instruction, brilliant, brainy, gifted, and endowed by nature with an intellect destined to expand and develop."[48]

This self-proclaimed "deep reasoner" often stated that he had "no complaint against American slavery." "It was," Holsey said, expressing sentiments similar to those attributed to Rev. Wilkes Flagg, "a blessing in disguise to me and to many . . . [and] it has made the negro race what it could not have been in its native land." Holsey's heart overflowed with Christian forgiveness, and he saw no reason for African-Americans to "harbor any feelings of hate and revenge." He admitted, however, that the former slave had been freed with "nothing but his religion, poverty and ignorance" to guide him.[49]

Holsey also deplored the fact that "in the Southern States the colored man is treated and regarded as an inferior," and he saw Reconstruction as the time when "negro civilization . . . yet in its infancy and crude evolutions, [should] lay the foundations upon which future generations are to build those institutions that are to make him and his progeny solid citizens and valued citizens." Thus he offered his congregation a gospel that on one hand seemed to accept inherent black inferiority as a reality but concurrently stressed pride, community building, responsible citizenship, and strength through Christian faith. In spite of his obsequious gratitude for the "blessings" of slavery, Holsey also preached the egalitarian message that "no man is born higher, purer, and better than another, so far as his real nature and the faculties of his humanity are concerned." These apparent contradictions may have been encouraged because Ebenezer had close ties with the white Methodist Church, South, and its minister's future depended on retaining the good will and financial support of the parent denomination and the local white community, as well as his own parishioners. Southern white Methodists liked to boast that "no Christian leaders among [the CME] had ever been accused of any agitation."[50]

Holsey himself was the son of his white master and a favored slave, and his congregation included a number of other mulattoes who were considered Sparta's "colored elite." Frequent debate focusses on tensions and conflicts between these lighter-skinned people of color and others with darker complexions. Some light-skinned African-Americans did harbor at least covert feelings of superiority, and their darker-skinned cousins justifiably resented those assumptions. The unremitting imposition of prejudicial attitudes relentlessly expounded by whites encouraged people of color to share those biases. When they were repeated and reinforced often enough, those views sometimes came to be assimilated, even by some members of the diverse African-American community themselves.[51] One member of the Hunt family anguished as he observed racial attitudes in the African-American community. All too often, he said, "three hundred years of degradation was indelibly stamped, and they deeply believed . . . that people with white skins [were] superior to people with black skins." Holsey preached about the "inferiority" of the "semi-civilized" African culture, and their minister's views may have influenced some of his parishioners to think that their heritage made them somehow inferior to whites.[52]

Although their alliances in the African-American community were far stronger than their ties to whites during Reconstruction, some light-skinned people of mixed Anglo-African descent did think of themselves as both "different" and in some ways superior to those with darker skins. Resulting to a certain degree from their familial ties with whites, some of these mulattoes did enjoy greater affluence, had more access to education, worked at less menial jobs, and lived in more comfortable circumstances than their darker-skinned cousins. They had their own circle of friends and sometimes attended different churches. Because of the mulattoes' characteristic creamy-beige skin color, both African-Americans and whites at times referred to them as "yellow," just as that term appeared frequently in Middle Georgia registries describing free people of color prior to emancipation.

Stories that illustrate rifts within the African-American community based on the frivolous grounds of pigmentation have been repeated in a spirit of self-mockery, laced with a discomforting undercurrent of truth. Members of the Hunt family told one such apocryphal tale about a Sunday morning long past when a heavyset, dark-skinned woman wearing a bandanna around her head, an apron, and generally shabby clothing supposedly rushed into the service at the Ebenezer church and positioned herself in a front-row pew, interrupting Bishop Holsey's sermon. Her color, her unpolished manner, and her dress immediately told the more affluent and lighter-skinned parishioners, decked out in their finest attire, that she was neither a member nor an invited guest. The woman fanned herself, gasped for breath, and tried to recover from her exertions while the minister and church members stared in stunned silence following her unexpected intrusion. Then, slowly, a solemn hymn reportedly swelled around the visitor as the congregation began to sing:

> None but the yellow,
> None but the yellow,
> None but the yellow . . . shall see God.[53]

Their attendance at Ebenezer Methodist Episcopal Church and their associations with Holsey and members of that congregation may have influenced the thinking and behavior of the Hunt family in many ways. Mariah Hunt had been baptized in the white Presbyterian church at Mount Zion, where she was known as Cherokee Mariah Lilly, but she belonged to the Colored Methodist Episcopal church for a quarter century, and when she died in late 1895 her granite headstone, the earliest found in Ebenezer's cemetery, was inscribed "Hers was a life of trust in God."[54] Mariah's oldest daughter, Lula, remained a member of the same church, and in the 1890s, when Holsey still presided there, Lula's daughter sat in the "Amen corner" every Sunday while the family attended services "all day long." Mariah's second daughter, Adella, on the other hand, was not an intensely religious woman. She joined the Congregational church during her years at Atlanta University, often attended nondenominational services, and occasionally lectured on Biblical history and philosophy. Throughout his life the favorite hymn of their younger brother Henry Hunt, Jr., remained "There is a Balm in Gilead," which he first sang at Ebenezer. He went to church regularly, and, like many other relatives, associated himself with the Presbyterian church—his white father's denomination. Adella and Henry, Jr., both considered church membership more a part of their overall civic and moral responsibilities than a way of expressing any fervent religious devotion.[55]

Although their association with the Ebenezer Methodist Episcopal Church influenced Mariah Hunt and her children in different ways and to differing degrees, during Reconstruction education became an undeviating commitment for the entire family. Mariah herself could scarcely read and write, but she consistently urged her children to study. Will, James (called Mac), and Lula, the three older children born before the Civil War, all acquired only rudimentary academic skills, but they helped their younger brothers and sisters and encouraged them to stay in school and excel.[56] The five younger children, starting with Adella, the first child born following the Emancipation Proclamation, all completed not only elementary and high school but college-level work as well.

Members of the family possessed a gritty determination to acquire an education, but they also enjoyed unusual opportunities and good fortune. The opportunities available to a small number of fortunate families like the Hunts notwithstanding, most African-Americans in Reconstruction Middle Georgia had fewer educational options than they might have hoped for. In Greene County, Dosia Harris remembered that it was a "long time 'fore schools fer niggers was sot up."[57]

During the early years of Reconstruction, the Freedmen's Bureau established schools throughout the South, but the Bureau did not act alone. Freedmen's aid societies, churches, the Peabody Fund (a private educational foundation), and the American Missionary Association all provided supplemental assistance as well. This outside help notwithstanding, black parents bore a heavy responsibility for financing their children's education. Carrie Mason's mother in Baldwin County, who had little to spare, always spent "ten cents a mont' a piece fer all us chillun."[58]

In Hancock County J. S. W. Johnson, a white man who received a salary of twenty dollars per month, taught at the the local Freedmen's Bureau school called the Sparta Institute. A series of crises plagued his endeavor during the late 1860s. His students always needed primers, the rent frequently went unpaid, and the school even closed intermittently. The freedpeople started to build a new schoolhouse but had insufficient funds to complete it, then classes had to be moved because the building lacked a chimney. Despite shaky beginnings, by November 1868 the Sparta Institute enrolled fifteen male and twenty-five female students, and by April 1870 the total had increased to forty-five. The Bureau required that its schools stay open five days per week and six hours each day, but Johnson reported that he taught eight hours a day and twenty-five days per month, including Sundays.[59]

In addition to the Sparta Institute, the Freedmen's Bureau sponsored another school in Powelton, a third in Guillville, and a fourth near Linton.[60] If those were the only schools for the freedpeople in Hancock, they could not have begun to fulfill the tremendous demand for education. Hancock County had a nonwhite population of over eight thousand at the end of the war. Assuming that one quarter of those were either school-age children or older men and women who wanted the education long denied them, the county would have needed to provide educational facilities for at least two thousand African-Americans. Little is known about the schools in Powelton, Guillville, and Linton, but Johnson's records show that he taught fewer than fifty students in Sparta. The others hardly would have accommodated any more.[61]

In the rest of the eight-county region of Middle Georgia, the Freedmen's Bureau operated schools in Sandersville and Tennille, Warrenton, Milledgeville, Eatonton, and Greensboro. Greensboro reportedly had a large number of students but a "very poor schoolhouse," and near Sandersville there was "one Sabbath school [with] one hundred and forty pupils, [and] one day school on the plantations."[62]

The few white men and women who dedicated themselves to educating the freedpeople sometimes became fretful. James R. Smith, Washington County's teacher, was associated with the Southern

Methodist Church as well as the Freedmen's Bureau. Although his schoolhouse lacked heat and his students did not have adequate clothing for the chilly winter weather, he taught more than one hundred pupils and wanted a "lady teacher" for an assistant. Smith, however, could not imagine where a white female teacher might find a place to board in town. "She will face social ostracism . . . [and] sickness," he worried, and "would find herself isolated in the midst of strangers." He first thought his daughter might fill the position, but then decided that "the fear of ridicule was too strong."[63]

Sparta's J. S. W. Johnson complained to the Freedmen's Bureau that he could no longer teach if it did not pay him better. His monthly salary, he said, did not adequately support him, his wife, and their daughter. However, before Johnson could leave voluntarily, the Bureau's superintendent of education in Georgia wrote in July 1870 to notify him that their office "ceases today, entirely, therefore no more aid will be allowed you." The Freedmen's Bureau had lost its legislative mandate, and funding was terminated for all of its activities in the state.[64]

In 1866 the Georgia legislature had assured only that "any free white inhabitant of the State aged six to twenty-one is entitled to school free of charge," but five years later it required each county to "make all necessary arrangements for the instruction of white and colored youths of said districts in separate schools." It emphasized the necessity for segregated facilities by further stating that "the children of the white and colored races shall not be taught together in any school in this State."[65]

The Northern teacher and missionary Charles Stearns, who had bought a plantation near Augusta, expressed his outrage at the injustices that local African-American children faced each day. "At the South, any more than at the North," he asked, "why should a colored child go miles from his dwelling in quest of a colored school, when a white one is to be found near at hand?" Furthermore, he argued, "multitudes of Southern children [are] so white as to pass for white children, and yet they are . . . excluded from white schools because a small amount of negro-blood courses in their veins." Stearns also denounced the irrational response of some white Southerners when they saw any evidence that blacks might gain access to an education. "Large numbers of negro-schoolhouses . . . have been burned," he exclaimed, and "teachers have been driven from their schools." Local people told him that "the sight of a negro-schoolhouse stirs up the rabid feelings of a Ku Klux gang."[66]

R. M. Gladding, a white man who had come to Middle Georgia from Newport, Rhode Island, must have feared those "rabid feelings" when he wrote to Freedmen's Bureau officials stating that he had started a school for blacks, that he needed a pistol, and that when a midnight fire had blazed out of control "right across the street from my rooms . . . [it] gave me quite a start . . . I thought at first they were trying to give me a warning." Gladding sealed his own fate when he walked down Greensboro's main street one day holding an umbrella for a woman of color. By that gracious act he flouted the town's established social mores. White-robed Klansmen threatened him and dumped him into a fish pond. One crazed white man even fired shots into the schoolhouse, and, fearing for his life, Gladding fled.[67]

Educational opportunities for people of color did not disappear in Georgia with the demise of the Freedmen's Bureau in 1870, but schooling remained difficult to come by. Small new schools were started in Mount Zion and Dixie, and in the mid-1870s the Hubert family spearheaded efforts to establish a church-associated school in Hancock County's Springfield community. While they were building, the Klan threatened the organizers, and even some local blacks who feared reprisals from whites tried to stop the project. If black people acquired an education, one freedman cautioned Zach Hubert, they would soon "be thinking they got much sense as white folks and that's dangerous." Then he asked, "Is you trying to stir up trouble?" Promoters of the Springfield school hired a teacher from North Carolina named Fess Smith. The county regularly denied the school any financial support—supposedly out of concern that the education of white children would suffer if funds were diverted to blacks—so Smith's "salary was paid through contributions of food and money from the community."[68]

In neighboring Baldwin County, the Milledgeville *Southern Recorder* reported on graduation observances at the local Eddy "colored free school," commenting that "the juveniles of the Caucasian race might learn a lesson from the young freedmen on behavior." The Eddy School, sponsored by the American Missionary Association, was a large one. In 1868 five white instructors taught almost three hundred children, and the school sent reciprocal contributions back to its parent organization whenever possible. The most deserving graduates received books as prizes, and in addition to such leaders from the black community as Wilkes Flagg, the *Southern Recorder* commented, "several of our most talented ladies of the white population, to whom the front seats were given by the freedmen" attended the ceremonies and stayed on to enjoy a barbecue lunch, eating at "a separate table prepared for the whites present." The African-American hostesses "attended to their [white guests'] appetites first, and afterwards to the wants of their own color." The newspaper reassured its readers that "no attempt at social equality was exhibited."[69]

People of color who had been free prior to the war may have participated in educational programs designated specifically for the freedpeople. Mariah Hunt's older children could have started out at J. S. W. Johnson's Sparta Institute, but they also may have studied elsewhere. At least part of Adella Hunt's early education was described as "of a private nature," and she and her siblings may have been tutored by her white aunts in their own homes.[70] Her younger brother Henry, Jr., remembered that the family sent him "and his sisters and brothers to the little, unpainted school house that was open for three months each year," where "on those crude benches, [they] caught in some miraculous way the desire for book learning and the determination to get it."[71]

Adella did not think that she encountered the enormous barriers that confronted so many people of color who sought an education during Reconstruction. She did, however, have the same "desire" and "determination" attributed to her brother. "To tell the truth," she reminisced, "I got my education by no greater hardship than hard work which I regard as exceedingly healthful." Henry Hunt, Jr., expressed similar sentiments. "Discipline, *discipline*, DISCIPLINE," he declared, "the first, second, and third requisites for all training worth having."[72]

The Hunt family's gritty determination and the former slaves' general hunger for education notwithstanding, Sparta's Treena Threatt Nelson candidly recalled the attitudes of some other Georgia freedpeople. For generations, masters forbade their slaves to read and write, and told them that they did not have the capability to learn. Some blacks understandably internalized those low expectations. Nelson's grandparents had been slaves who, she believed, "never had the vision to aspire further than domestics or servants in and around houses owned and occupied by white people." Financial imperatives also may have taken priority over "book learning," because in 1875, when her mother was only ten years old, an affluent white family offered her a job working as a maid in their home. Nelson placed the onus on the legacy of slavery when her grandparents, "not placing any value on education . . . readily agreed" that their daughter should leave school. They "pulled her right out of her fourth grade class," and the girl never returned to school.[73]

Freedmen's Bureau schools in Georgia lost their funding in 1870, and the Bureau itself passed out of existence in 1872. Reconstruction in the South limped along for another five years. But far more than did 1877—when Reconstruction officially ended and Rutherford B. Hayes became President, ordering the last federal troops withdrawn from the secessionist states—1879 marked the conclusion of one era and the beginning of another for the Hunts. Births, deaths, graduations, and departures were family landmarks that year. In the spring, Adella satisfactorily completed the course of study at the local school called Bass Academy, located just west of town, within walking distance of Hunt's Hill. The school was named for Hancock County's first superintendent of public education, W. H. Bass, who donated the land for the building. For many years Sparta's more privileged young people from the African-American community studied at Bass Academy. By 1880 more than one hundred students attended classes there. The school probably received no financial support from the county, but "the parents of school age children attending" paid its teacher's salary.[74] Richard Carter, an early graduate of Atlanta University who had completed its theological program a few years earlier, served as the head teacher at Bass in the late 1870s and early 1880s. The editor of Sparta's white-owned *Ishmaelite* considered him a superior teacher. Carter maintained close ties with Atlanta University while he lived in Sparta with his wife and children, and he also acted as local agent for the Athens *Blade,* the nearest newspaper published by and for African-Americans.[75]

Reconstruction Georgia urgently needed black teachers. From his vantage point near Augusta, Charles Stearns observed that it was "vastly important . . . that teachers should be furnished, who have full faith in the *natural* ability of the colored race . . . until the pure 'hard-pan' of intellectual strength is reached." Stearns identified three critical reasons for training and employing African-Americans. First, he thought black children would more readily accept teachers of their own race. Second, he believed that the black educator could better understand "the quality of the material he has to mold." Third, as role models, they set an excellent example for young people in particular and for the community as a whole.[76]

Stearns would have been pleased to read in the May 23, 1879, edition of the Sparta *Ishmaelite* that school superintendent W. H. Bass and three other white men "examined the applicants for license to teach in the public schools of Hancock county." The successful candidates included eight "colored" as well as four young white men and women. Adella Hunt was among the fledgling "colored" teachers. Newly certified, she accepted her first teaching job during that summer of 1879 when she was only sixteen years old and "very enthusiastic and anxious to do all that I could to help remove the cloud of ignorance that overhangs our Southern country people."[77]

Laura Mason from Greensboro also personified the young African-American teachers that Charles Stearns wanted to see. In 1876 Mason reported that "I am teaching now, have 25 scholars which are as many as I care to have for the present." She treasured her classroom assignment and recognized the importance of her work. "Last summer's teaching, and this term so far has been a great experience for me," she continued, "never in my life before have I thought so much of a teacher's responsibilities, troubles and trials as I do now." In addition to other problems she may have faced, the job was arduous. "Am also teaching night school and Sunday school so I am kept quite busy all the time," she said with no apparent complaint.[78]

Adella Hunt may have been a favorite of her teacher Richard Carter, and he must have recognized her capacity to benefit from more advanced education and anticipated her future as a teacher, because on May 3, 1879, he wrote W. J. Northen, Hancock's state representative, on her behalf. "I hereby recommend to you, Adella Hunt," he stated, "as in every way qualified to be appointed to free tuition in Atlanta University." Northen, in turn, endorsed Carter's request in a letter to Atlanta University president E. A. Ware. "As a member of the General Assembly," wrote Northen, "upon the certificate of her teacher, I recommend Adella Hunt to your instruction & free tuition."[79] Four years earlier, Rep. John Culver had nominated a young man named Congo Laughlin to "fill one of the free tuition schollarships in your University which Hancock County is entitle to." Like the Hunts, Laughlin and his family would have understood the importance of political support and the value of a well-connected white sponsor. Every state legislator could recommend one student to attend Atlanta University from each county in Georgia, but apparently only a few chose to do so. Sparta's newspaper even urged members of the African-American community to take advantage of these scholarship opportunities, commenting that "we have some very promising young colored people in this county, and by prompt action they may get the benefits proposed."[80] Adella Hunt's success in gaining admission to Atlanta University stemmed from a combination of fortuitous factors: her own abilities and assertiveness, her white family's status in the county, which would have ensured Northen's endorsement, her teacher's association with Atlanta University, and his recognition that she was academically worthy of his encouragement.

Only two years after the Civil War, the Superior Court of Fulton County had chartered Atlanta University "in accordance with the Laws of Georgia" to provide "an institution for the liberal and Christian education" of the freedpeople, and especially to train African-American teachers.[81] The cornerstone for the school's first dormitory and classroom building, North Hall, had been laid on a site known as Diamond Hill in the southwest quadrant of the city in June 1869, and the first students arrived that October. As the Board of Visitors—the school's oversight committee—stated to Gov. R. B. Bullock in 1871, Atlanta University was "designed to afford opportunities through education to members of a race only recently elevated to citizenship." The school was called a "university," but because of the needs and minimal educational preparation of the freedpeople, most of the early students enrolled at the preparatory level and in the normal school. A four-year college and theological program began in 1872. Six students who started that year, Adella Hunt's teacher and sponsor Richard Carter among them, graduated in 1876. The American Missionary Association sponsored Atlanta University, and the school received supplemental appropriations from the state, subject to the approval of the Board of Visitors. But state support was far from automatic. In the 1872 session of the legislature, "the appropriation was rejected with shouts of derision." The private philanthropic Peabody Fund also provided additional monies for the normal school program.[82]

Edmund Asa Ware, a Freedmen's Bureau official and a deeply religious Yankee committed to educating the freedpeople, became Atlanta University's first president. The other early teachers, all of them white as well, came from similar New England backgrounds. Ware personally believed that the school should be open to all races, but both law and tradition thwarted those aspirations. "The fact that teachers and scholars, white and colored, sat at the same tables at their meals seemed particularly distasteful to some," and when a local white woman asked Ware how he could live so intimately among African-Americans he responded, "Oh, I can easily explain that; I'm simply color blind." Ware adopted the motto of his own Yale University class of 1863 for Atlanta University: "I will find a way or make one." It reflected his personal philosophy as well as the determination of the students whom he would educate.[83]

People of color from Middle Georgia would have been denied admission to such schools as Franklin College in Athens, Greene County's Mercer University, and Oglethorpe, just outside of Milledgeville. Because no nearby all-white institutions would allow them access to the kind of quality education that they and their parents sought, during the school's first decade twenty young people of African descent from Hancock County went off to Atlanta University. The first was Ellen Moore, who attended preparatory classes in 1870. Most students enrolled in that program as well as in the "lower normal" division, which functioned as an elementary-level boarding facility. The first student from Sparta to receive any higher degree from Atlanta University was Adella Hunt, who graduated from the upper normal school (the equivalent of a two-year college program) in 1881.[84]

.Monetary problems delayed the arrival of some students from Middle Georgia and deterred the successful completion of their studies for others. From Milledgeville, a prospective student wrote President Ware in 1869 that "I have been laboring hard all this summer to come to Chool but my Farther has Bought a lot and it Coast $550 and he say if you let me work and pay for my Chooling I could come. I want to come bad." In 1876 a young man from Sparta explained that he had to drop out of school because he had not been able to work and pay his tuition expenses while he was ill and had accrued large medical bills. Another student, who hailed from the Camak railroad junction in Warren County, promised to take care of his outstanding obligations as soon as possible and begged the school's treasurer, "Please dont think no ways hard of me." From Greensboro, Laura Mason unhappily wrote her favorite teacher that she had to withdraw for a while because "father had his house reclaimed this summer which cost him a good deal, and thinks if I stay home this term that he will then be able to send me until I finish or as long as I want to go."[85]

Early Atlanta University students from Hancock County also included four members of the Dickson family, one of whom was Amanda America, daughter of Hancock's so-called "Prince of Farmers," David Dickson. Technically, Dickson had never manumitted his daughter, but he gave her elegant clothes, jewelry and every advantage his wealth could offer, and allowed her to live as if she were free. Amanda America Dickson attended Atlanta University when she was in her late twenties and had already been married and borne two children, but she left because she apparently did not like the austere dedication the school demanded.[86]

Atlanta University provided very stark dormitory facilities, and the Yankee administrators instituted compulsory Congregationalist church services plus twice-daily devotional prayers that seemed cold and impersonal to many of the students. Students could neither smoke nor drink, and the school forbade "the use of expensive and showy dresses," adding that "silks, velvets and jewelry worn by school girls are indicative neither of good taste nor good sense." "Prints, ginghams, and worsteds neatly made and colored underskirts are the most approved wear," the school's administrators directed.[87] The agricultural department raised vegetables, and its cows provided milk for the entire resident population. Many of the Southern students disliked much of the Yankee cuisine. They ate chicken, rice, sweet potatoes, and hominy, all of which were familiar, but had no pork, and the dining hall regularly offered such unaccustomed foods as Boston baked beans, New England boiled dinners, and steamed red snapper. University officials insisted that their young scholars must be "orderly in deportment, and serious in application" at all times as they pursued a demanding academic course of study plus "domestic instruction, in which the females are taught to cook and trained in the various arts of domestic economy." Before graduation, each girl had to know how to bake bread and sew "a small garment of calico." In addition to satisfying all other requirements, students had to fulfill supplemental daily work assignments. Understandably, this rigorous regime held little appeal for David Dickson's indulged daughter.[88]

Like Amanda Dickson and Adella Hunt, many of the students from Hancock and the surrounding counties who attended Atlanta University during the first decade or so of that school's existence either had been nominally free before emancipation or at least shared surnames and probably other connections with prominent white families from their home county. It is difficult to ascertain exactly how many were related, because slaves often took and kept their masters' names even when there was no actual kinship. One of the Hunts' cousins, Matilda Rogers, and Linton Stephens Ingram, the son of an affluent local planter who had willed the boy a considerable amount of money, also went to Atlanta University from Hancock County. Elsewhere in the eight-county region young people with similar backgrounds included Tolbert Bailey from the village of Barnett in Warren County, whom his white father had tried to man-umit and leave the body of his estate to; John Wesley Marlow (Marlor), from Milledgeville, whose grandfather had been freed by the state legislature to acknowledge his heroism in helping to save the state capitol from fire; and Crawfordville's Fannie and Quinnie Stephens, children of Alexander Stephens's so-called "free niggers."[89]

Following an 1878 visit the *American Missionary* magazine, report-ing on the progress of Atlanta University, recognized that the Yankee teachers had succeeded in eliminating much of the characteristic drawl from their students' speech and commented that "one blind-folded would never have guessed that he was listening to black stu-dents, all of whose parents were slaves." In fact, a disproportionate number of students from the eight-county region of Middle Georgia were not the children of slaves. Of the seventy-two students—twenty-two young women and fifty young men—from that area who attended Atlanta University in its first dozen years, twenty-seven or more were probably related to members of the small free African-American community that numbered only four hundred just before the war. Unlike the vast majority of people of color in Middle Georgia, many families of the Atlanta University students had also accumulated at least a small amount of personal or real property in the years following the war. Other students, though not free-born, had white kin. Of the seventy-two early students from Middle

Georgia, fewer than thirty did not clearly enjoy at least one or more of the combined advantages of antebellum freedom, money, and familial ties to influential whites. The parents of that minority would have been among the more than forty thousand slaves who lived in the eight-county region. Free status prior to the war, the accumulation of at least a small amount of money or property, and associations with prominent families in the white community combined to create an undeniable advantage in gaining access to a better education during Reconstruction.[90]

Illustrating the background and patronage of many early Atlanta University students, one affluent white man, possibly the girl's father, wrote to President Ware in 1869 explaining that Matilda Rogers, the prospective student, was "unfitted to make her living by hard work, . . . [but she] calculated to make herself useful as a teacher." He sent her off to Atlanta "with a full supply of clothing and everything essential to her comfort," where "a former servant" met her train and personally escorted her to Ware's residence. Matilda Rogers's sponsor further declared that "I can speak of her as a correct genteel girl and commend her for your kind care and protection." "I of course will be responsible for her support, tuition, etc," he concluded solicitously, "advise me at Sparta of her safe arrival . . . [and] should she require anything at all you will please furnish it and advise me."[91]

Hancock County's Matilda Rogers as well as a number of others were the daughters and sons of white men. Jennie Wynn—light-skinned and sandy-haired—a member of the class of 1881, came from nearby Augusta and went to teach in Milledgeville during her school holidays. She and her mother Louise had been nominally free, and her late father, a man of Scottish descent, had no white wife or children. Other men in the Wynn family had served as guardians of free people of color in the eight-county region. Photographs of several students from Middle Georgia who attended Atlanta University in its early years show young women who clearly had both black and white antecedents.[92]

The *American Missionary* also reported in 1878 that several of the new graduates "would pass for white anywhere" and rapturously declared that "the students . . . are, of course, the flower of the colored race." A white attendee at the school's 1877 graduation said that "proportioned as to complexion, the pupils of mixed blood largely predominate . . . [and] in one recitation room we counted thirty-eight mulattoes and one Albino out of forty-five girls." That same visitor also condescendingly suggested that "these poor things ought to be labelled white, and taken to the Black Hills, or California, where wives are in demand, there is no particular squeamishness on the part of the suitors, and their identity with the children of Ham can forever be extinguished." During Reconstruction those young people with lighter complexions had far greater access to such advantages as education. Though they had no greater intelligence or ability, mulattoes attended Atlanta University in numbers highly disproportionate to their percentages in the general population.[93]

The darker-skinned sons and daughters of slaves also attended Atlanta University, prompting the same observer to comment that blacks were "an intuitive race and seldom develop any regularity, or think for themselves." "Yet," he added, "here are many exceptions to the contrary, and there are not wanting instances of the full blooded, thick lipped and sooty descendants of Ham who can translate Greek and Latin, solve geometric problems, chop logic and recite rhetoric with surprising facility." These students, so derisively described, were equally as accomplished as the "pupils of mixed blood." "Some of our black friends," the visitor reluctantly concluded, were indeed "capable of receiving a high and polished education."[94]

As the mulatto daughter of a free family of color that had also acquired a little money and property, Adella Hunt was among a number of other young men and women from Middle Georgia with similar backgrounds who attended Atlanta University. Following her graduation from Bass Academy and her first summer working as a teacher, Adella left Sparta in the fall of 1879. Her cousin Susie, the younger Susan Hunt's oldest daughter, went off to school in Athens at the same time.[95] Adella would have boarded the new Macon and Augusta Railroad line in Sparta, traveled to Camak junction in Warren County, and transferred to a Georgia Railroad train that rattled past cotton fields, by white-columned mansions and sharecroppers' shacks, through the villages of Barnett, Crawfordville, Union Point, and Greensboro, on its way to the brash city of Atlanta—Georgia's new capital. Except for brief visits, Adella Hunt, the last of her family's free women of color born during the slave era, would not return home again.

Adella and Susie Hunt's departures concluded a series of transitional events for their family in 1879. Tom, the last of Henry and Mariah's eight children, had been born near the beginning of the year. Adella's white aunt Martha Ann Hunt, who reportedly had granted land in Hancock County to members of the African-American community, died of pneumonia that spring. In the early summer Adella's teacher from Bass Academy, Richard Carter, went to Atlanta to address a "colored school convention" on the subject: "Does it make any difference from what kind of textbooks the colored youth are instructed?" But, more than any other single incident, J. M. Hunt's death in July precipitated momentous changes and realignments in the family.

Not only was J. M. Adella's uncle, but her grandmother Susan had lived with him at Mount Zion for more than a quarter century. On July 18 the Sparta *Ishmaelite* tersely reported that "James M. Hunt, an old and well-known citizen of this county died the first of the week." A local physician certified "paralysis" as the cause of death.[96]

Old Sparta residents recall a somewhat macabre story about J. M. Hunt's funeral. The people of color in the family purchased a gravestone, had it inscribed to his memory, and transported it out to the family cemetery. Their white relatives, however, refused to allow them to place it on the grave. Profoundly disappointed, they brought the headstone back to Hunt's Hill and placed it under one of their homes, where it still remains.[97]

J. M. Hunt's will and inventory, however, provide far more revealing information than the *Ishmaelite*'s brief obituary. The will had been written eleven years previously, and it was filed for probate on August 4, 1879. J. M. first directed that "my past debts [are] to be paid, and that my body shall be decently buried." The itemized settlement of those debts shows that Susan Hunt clearly had an intimate relationship with him. Though the census listed no woman at all living at his residence during the postwar years, his executor reimbursed one local merchant for Hunt's purchases of trimming, braid, ribbons, ruffling, ladies' hose, a lace collar and shawl, yards of calico, lawn, gingham, and cambric, cologne, kid gloves, tuck combs, and corset bones. These many yards of fine fabric and other personal accoutrements bought by J. M. Hunt suggest that Susan sewed for her daughters and granddaughters who lived nearby as well as for herself. The estate also paid a local physician's bill for a house call that he made on Susan Hunt. In addition, J. M., who could not read or write himself, purchased two spelling books during the final months of his life, probably demonstrating the avuncular role he continued to play with brother Henry and Mariah's children, one of whom was even named for him.[98]

Susan could have returned to the Hunt homestead in 1853 as a former family retainer, Nathan Sayre's widow, and little more. At one time she may have served as J. M. Hunt's housekeeper and nurse, but, by the time of his death, she had passed more than a quarter century in his home at Mount Zion. The nature and number of the expenditures that J. M. made on Susan's behalf and the land he deeded to her demonstrate that she had become far more than simply a poor relation or a domestic. She was someone whose needs and desires he carefully attended to and whom he treated as a woman of substance.

As to the final disposition of his estate, J. M. Hunt stated that "I give and bequeath to Maria, Susan and James, children of Susan Hunt, a free woman of color in said county [Hancock], the sum of five hundred dollars each," then added, "I give bequeath and devise to Susan Hunt, a free woman of color in said county and state all the rest and residue of my estate, real and personal." To ensure that none of his property would revert to his white relatives, J. M. Hunt further declared that, at the elder Susan's death, all of his property should "be divided share and share alike between all the children of said Susan Hunt." Not satisfied to terminate this chain of inheritance with her children, he closed the will with the statement that "it is my intention in the case of the death of any one of her children before her death leaving a child or children, such child or children shall inherit in the place of its or their deceased parent." Whatever his precise relationship with Susan and her descendants may have been, they were intimately bound to one another. J. M. cared for them, and he felt obligated or at least morally committed to such an extent that he left them his total estate in a carefully crafted will and through that testamentary document sought to protect their future interests through two succeeding generations. J. M. Hunt made not even the smallest bequests to his surviving brothers, sisters-in-law, or white nieces and nephews.[99]

The Hunts who have remained closely tied to Hancock County over the years know few details about how the case unfolded, but they still recall the basic outlines of the story their parents told them. The older generation remembered that one of the white Hunt brothers left all of his money to his "colored family," and the disinherited white relatives tenaciously contested the will for more than a decade before it was finally settled. Those long years during which J. M.'s will remained unsettled extends the Hunts' saga beyond Reconstruction and the departure of Adella from Hancock County.[100]

Until the end of the Civil War, only a few people of African descent—one half of one percent of Middle Georgia's total population—were free. Although many African-Americans became bound to white employers with extended labor contracts and by disabling debt, general emancipation brought at least limited personal freedom to all people of color. But in the minds of most whites in the region, those people all remained part of an inherently inferior group. The Athens *Blade,* which probably reflected the views of many members of the black community, editorialized that "we do not complain of that part of slavery which is dead, but of that part of it which is living." "Now in the day of freedom," it continued, "all that is needed for peace in the South is for our white neighbors to come up fully to the law and spirit of freedom." The *Blade*'s publishers realized, however, that most whites in the region did not want to acknowledge that new "day of freedom."[101]

After the war, the few people of color who had been free in the antebellum years became integrated into the African-American community in its entirety and no longer belonged to a legally distinct caste. Nor did any number of white antecedents entitle them to a privileged position in Reconstruction society. The termination of slavery freed almost a half a million people in Georgia, and it also usurped many of the intimate relationships that plantation life had condoned and sometimes even nurtured between whites and people of color. This rift may have been especially wrenching for such free families as the Hunts who had been closely linked with the white community by both conjugal and blood relationships, but on occasion it applied as well to the complex and contradictory ties between slaves and masters, even when kinship was not involved.

Anglo-American Southerners treated everyone who was not white as their inferiors, and to some extent this scorn and adversity may have reinforced community solidarity among people of color. When whites demeaned everyone with any black antecedents at all, the all-inclusive African-American community bonded together for mutual support. Nonetheless, color and class distinctions remained. African-

Americans sometimes considered "lightness" or "whiteness" per se a desirable attribute and aspired to emulate the speech, manner, and dress of white people around them. In Milledgeville, Jennie Wynn from Atlanta University, herself the child of a white man, sadly told about one of her students at the Eddy school who was "not at all satisfied with nature's finishing touch, but wants to be a white boy; and to do this he keeps his face covered with flour or meal, and has come to the conclusion that if he could be boiled he would be white." In the 1870s one young woman in Hancock County reportedly "became a perfect imitator of madam and was often told that if she was heard and not seen she could easily be mistaken for the madam."[102] But such whites as plantation owner Frances Butler Leigh wanted to ensure that blacks remained securely "in their place." She insisted that women on her plantation must look and behave just as they had when they were her slaves, and condemned and demeaned "the absurd little hats they bought and stuck on in order to follow the fashion of their white sisters."[103]

Many African-Americans, however, left the confines of plantation life and the opprobrious surveillance of such women as Leigh. Within their newly structured community, a number of factors began to define and determine status; among them were financial standing, occupation, church affiliation, education, and freedom prior to the war. Although they remained fiercely loyal to their kin and honored their black forebears, the social standing of white antecedents as well as living relatives also could help to establish a mulatto family's status during the postwar years. The Hunts always respected their "inheritance of blood, tradition and history of which any American . . . might be proud," and that "history" included African and Cherokee as well as English antecedents. Though young Henry Hunt in particular had little affection for his father, the family as a whole considered its white colonial ancestry, Revolutionary war service, and antebellum affluence as at least one significant part of its diverse heritage. The absence of records and the priorities and values of a hegemonic white society meant that much of their African and Cherokee heritage either had been deliberately obliterated or simply forgotten. Other members of African-American society's "elite" mulatto segment in Middle Georgia had similar experiences.[104] Many of the old intimate ties of hearth and home—especially relationships with white men—began unravelling during Reconstruction, but African-Americans cherished and upheld traditional family values at least as intensely as whites and tenaciously maintained their kinship ties. A few literate women of color in the region praised the bonds of intergenerational love and enduring conjugal relationships. One poet described her eighty-year-old mother as a "precious old darling . . . so dear to our hearts" whom the family called "queen lamb"; while another, characterizing a woman as the "vine" and her husband an "oak," sentimentally lauded the satisfactions of enduring marriage:

> And what, though Life's burdens may whiten the hair,
>   And the furrows the roses may hide,
> Can the years rob the heart of its love, or make
>   The lover forget his bride?
> For e'en though the heart may forget its song,
>   When grief or earth-cares beguile,
> Yet we know that true love abideth for aye,
>   And beareth its fruit all the while!
>   So taking the years together, my dear,
>   We've had more of sun than of shade.[105]

A number of middle-class women of color became well educated, worked for a living, and were fully capable of supporting themselves and their children, yet divorce was considered a family embarrassment at best, or even a scandal. They cherished and nurtured all of the family's children, but looked disapprovingly on any evidence of indiscriminate sexual behavior such as out-of-wedlock pregnancies and births. Any aspersions or allegations of sexual promiscuity haunted them. Conjugal relationships which could not be legitimized between women of color and white men almost ceased, and African-Americans who belonged to the emerging middle class most often married within their social group and even within their own families. These endogamous marriages more closely paralleled patterns established by their Anglo-American antecedents than those adhered to by most people of African descent.[106] The Hunts and others like them maintained and established solid associations with the freedpeople but still used and manipulated relationships with their Anglo-American kin and other old acquaintances in the white community to best serve their own needs.

Members of the African-American community sometimes formed

patron/client relationships, in which those people of color—often mulattoes—who had a little more education, money, and influence than others served as employers, teachers, ministers, advisors, spokespersons, and sponsors for less affluent and less well-educated blacks. Most members of the more privileged class felt a compelling sense of obligation and committed themselves to work for the betterment of the African-American community in its entirety. Adella Hunt, her sister Sarah, and their brother Henry all chose to teach in "one of the darkest regions of the South," as did many other early Atlanta University graduates.[107] In 1875 Laura Mason told her favorite teacher that "it is my whole soul's desire to do all the good I can in the line of teaching, and I ask your prayers that I may do much good towards . . . the elevation of the poor race."[108]

Their dedication to helping the needier sectors of their black community and lingering ties with whites notwithstanding, these relatively privileged few focused their primary loyalties on a closely knit group of extended family and friends, most of whom shared similar racial, social, and financial backgrounds. The neighborhoods where they lived and their common church and school affiliations reinforced those bonds. Even in the relatively isolated towns and villages of Middle Georgia, these people began to coalesce into a small, newly identifiable African-American middle class. To some extent their status could be measured by economic standing, occupations, and education. But style, dress, physical appearance, speech, manners and mores, attitudes, associates, and avocations provided less measurable but equally important indicators of their position in society.

In a region where more than 99 percent of all people of color had been slaves, some members of this nascent middle class group naturally shared that common past with other, less comfortably situated African-Americans. On the other hand, many people of color who had been free prior to general emancipation never managed to acquire an education, accumulate any property, or extricate themselves from the most menial and unrewarding occupations. Nonetheless, a highly disproportionate segment of this new group did emerge from the small ranks of those who had lived in the shadowy and ambiguous world of free people of color prior to the Civil War. During Reconstruction, the Hunts and Dicksons in Hancock County, the Flaggs and Marlows from Milledgeville, the Wynns who turned up in a number of jurisdictions throughout the region, and a few other comparably situated women and men of color acquired a little property, some education, and the where-withal needed to forge successful lives and to meet challenging new circumstances that in some ways were more difficult than any they had faced before.

V

The Hunt and
Dickson Wills and More

One ever feels [her] two-ness,—an American, a
Negro, two souls, two thoughts, two unreconciled
strivings; two warring ideals in one dark body
whose dogged strength alone keeps it from being
torn asunder.

W. E. B. Du Bois
The Souls of Black Folk, 1903.

The plantation economy never fully recovered after the war, and
Middle Georgia was becoming a desolate backwater region of the
South. Although the state's mental institution remained in Milledgeville, the capital had been relocated to the burgeoning city of
Atlanta—the crossroads of Georgia's railway system about eighty
miles to the northwest—and most industrialization and economic
development bypassed the eight counties. Nonetheless, life stumbled
haltingly along, and in 1880 Hancock County began constructing a
new courthouse, financed in part by loans underwritten by its most
affluent citizen, David Dickson. Henry and Mariah Hunt's oldest
daughter Lula married a brick mason who had moved to Sparta to
help build that handsome Victorian building crowned with its imposing cupola and clock tower.[1]

Hancock County remained predominantly agricultural, although
the total acreage under cultivation as well as the numbers of horses,
mules, cattle, sheep, and swine all stayed well below the levels

attained in the antebellum years. The boll weevil had not yet attacked Georgia's cotton, but cotton production and most other commercial crops never again prospered as they formerly had. Most cotton processing had moved away from the plantations and into the larger public ginneries. New peach and pecan orchards countered the overall decline in agriculture and began flourishing throughout the region. Chickens, pigs, and even an occasional cow still meandered about the streets of the towns, but fencing laws enacted in 1883 began to curtail most of the wandering livestock. Sparta and the villages in the surrounding countryside included a number of small commercial ventures as well as several medical and legal practitioners. Except for agricultural enterprise, however, the textile factory in the town of Jewell's Mills that straddled the Ogeechee River between Hancock and Warren counties, was the single largest employer in both. Economic times were not good in Middle Georgia. Agricultural production was low, prices high, credit short. Labor, reportedly, was both discontent and inefficient.[2]

Black and white parishioners in the South became increasingly segregated during the final decades of the nineteenth century, and religious passions gripped both races. Members of the African-American community worshipped with their own AME, AME Zion, CME, and Baptist congregations, while the white Methodists developed a permanent campsite near the town of Culverton and all-white Baptist, Presbyterian, and even Episcopal churches thrived in Middle Georgia. Only the presence of two or three Catholic churches and one small synagogue in Milledgeville relieved the region's overwhelming Protestantism.

Although Hancock County residents professed a serious interest in education, both black and white children lacked adequate facilities. After 1872 public schools for blacks in the state of Georgia were only expected to be "equal so far as practicable." Sparta's "free colored school" stayed in session just three months per year during the 1880s, but African-American children did attend the elementary grades in numbers proportionate to the total population. White officials who controlled public funds thought that people of African descent should be trained only for agricultural or domestic work, and therefore needed but a few years of basic education. The county supported high schools for whites, however, and several private academies flourished as well.[3]

Most African-Americans in the eight-county region of Middle Georgia eked out meager existences as sharecroppers and tenant farmers, and many slipped into conditions of debt peonage. In 1880 they owned an average of only $5.36 worth of real and personal property. In Hancock County, that amount was even lower, and the total value of property held by people of color dropped to only half of what it had been just a few years before.[4]

The white Hunts did not prosper as they had before the war, but they managed well enough through the 1880s, and the family had its share of both satisfactions and misfortunes. Henry and J. M. Hunt's nephew Thomas, a young lawyer, received acclamation in the *Ishmaelite* for his part in preparing Hancock County's prize-winning exhibit at the state fair in Macon, and he was a community leader who tried to solicit support for a new Savannah-to-Atlanta rail link through the county. On the negative side, the shotgun blast that accidently injured "a negro boy by the name of Monroe Horton" on one of the Hunt plantations concerned the entire family.[5] Beyond that one disturbing incident and the overall slump in the area's economy, the decade following Adella's 1879 departure from Middle Georgia and the death of J. M., who left his entire estate to his longtime companion Susan and her descendants, was characterized by sharp realignments in relationships between white and nonwhite members of the family. This was certainly not a singular phenomenon that pertained to but one family, because death and the ensuing bitter wrangling over property distribution often strain the bonds of kinship and precipitate reordered alliances. Internal family squabbles hardly require interracial relationships as their prerequisites, but in this case race played a significant role, as did time and place.

Little concrete evidence documents the details of his white family's extended efforts to overturn the provisions of J. M. Hunt's will, but a better-known case that unfolded concurrently in Hancock County contained striking similarities in both the issues and circumstances involved, and even included some of the same participants. In the late 1840s David Dickson, soon to become Hancock County's wealthiest planter, sexually violated his young slave, Julia Frances Lewis, who subsequently became his long-standing mistress. David and Julia had one daughter named Amanda America, whom her father loved, pampered, and educated. Amanda entered into an arranged marriage with a relative of Dickson's, a white man named

Charles Eubanks, with whom she had two sons. That relationship foundered, and Amanda returned with her children to the Dickson plantation where the boys quickly became their grandfather's favorites. David Dickson married briefly when he was in his sixties, but he and his white wife had no children and she died two years later. When David died in 1885 his Anglo-American relatives expected to inherit his vast estate, but he left them only specific bequests amounting to about $30,000. He willed the bulk of his fortune, totalling perhaps $300,000, to his daughter Amanda, whom he accorded "unlimited discretion in managing the property . . . clear and discreet from the marital right, power, control or custody of any husband she may have." Following Amanda America Dickson's death, everything bequeathed to her was to be conveyed to her sons.[6]

Local attorney and former state representative Charles W. DuBose drew up Dickson's will and served as his executor. DuBose also performed similar legal functions for J. M. Hunt. With his lawyer's assistance, David Dickson carefully crafted his will to minimize the likelihood of a successful challenge by the white relatives. Dickson and DuBose both realized that if the property conveyed by any portion of the will could be considered a bequest given in return for Julia's sexual favors, or if it could in any way be interpreted to imply that either Julia or Amanda had unduly or improperly influenced David Dickson, the whole document might be invalidated under Georgia law. Similarly, J. M. Hunt's will revealed nothing about his personal relationship with Susan Hunt, referred to her only as "a free woman of color," and designated small bequests for "her children." When J. M. gave Susan a plot of land in 1878, he clearly stated that the gift was compensation for her services as a "nurse." Whether or not a sexual relationship ever developed between him and Susan during the quarter century they lived together, nothing in J. M.'s will could be construed to affirm or even imply that any sort of intimacy bound them to one another.[7]

As soon as David Dickson's white relatives discovered that he planned to deny them the body of his estate, they hired their own cadre of lawyers, including the firm of Harley and Hunt, to contest the will. Thomas M. Hunt, respectfully called "Colonel," a member of that partnership, began his practice after he passed his "law examinations" in 1882, and he quickly gained a "reputation as a formidable trial lawyer."[8] He was the nephew of both J. M. and Henry Hunt, and a politician who in 1886 was elected as Hancock County's representative to the Georgia legislature. Harley and Hunt became attorneys for David Dickson's white family, while Charles DuBose and several others served on behalf of Dickson's daughter Amanda. Handling the Dickson case familiarized "Colonel" Hunt with issues much like those involved in his own family's legal problems, and he probably advised his white relatives with respect to his late uncle's will.[9]

When David Dickson's executors filed his will, the probate court promptly upheld its validity. The white family's lawyers protested and demanded that the case be tried in Hancock County Superior Court. At that trial, which began in November 1885, Harley and Hunt first contended that Dickson must have been mentally incompetent when he drew up the will. Then they claimed that Amanda might not be David's daughter at all, but in a contradictory tactic, further asserted that as a result of their sexual relationship, his mistress, Julia, had exerted undue and improper influence over him. Since the state of Georgia forbade fornication—any sex outside of marriage—and also deemed interracial marriage a felony, the white family's lawyers argued that the document was "illegal and immoral" and violated public policy because it tolerated and even encouraged those crimes. David Dickson had subjected himself to local opprobrium during the years when he had lived openly with Amanda under conditions that most people interpreted as intimate in nature. Several witnesses testified that they had seen David kiss Julia and otherwise treat her affectionately. They remembered that she carried the keys to his plantation on her belt and essentially maintained full authority over his household. Others, however, disputed those recollections and that interpretation of David and Julia's relationship. The lawyers contended that condoning any sort of intimate union between a white man and a woman of African descent endangered the purity of the "Anglo-Saxon race"—they cited the dangers of "mingling of the blood"—and threatened all of the most fundamental and sacred Southern traditions and values. The superior court judge, however, instructed the jurors that they must first recognize the inviolability of private property rights. The jury disregarded the emotional pleadings of the lawyers for the white family, followed the judge's instructions, and decided in Amanda Dickson's favor.[10]

When they learned that they had lost, attorneys for the white

Dickson family immediately filed an appeal with the Georgia Supreme Court in Atlanta. The panel of presiding justices there decided that Hancock County's Superior Court had already found David Dickson to be of sound mind when he drafted his will. Amanda was clearly his child, she and Julia had not improperly influenced him, and he had every right to leave his daughter the body of his estate, race notwithstanding. The decision cited the Fourteenth Amendment, stating that the Constitution of the United States had abolished distinctions between the races concerning the basic rights of citizenship and had placed people of color on an equal footing with whites when it came to economic matters. It consequently found that the state of Georgia was legally obligated to comply with that authority. Much like the lower court, the supreme court based its decision on the widely accepted principle of the inviolability of private property rights. The justices concluded that property rights should be absolute and must be protected for everyone—in this case both the white man who chose to bequeath his property in a particular fashion and the woman of color whom he designated to receive it. No state law, the court argued, could take primacy over that fundamental principle. The Georgia Supreme Court did not hand down its opinion until June of 1887, but at that time the judges stated that because they had heard no new or extenuating evidence and found no misinterpretation of either law or procedure, their only option was to uphold the original decision in the controversial case of David Dickson's will.[11]

Amanda America Dickson became a very rich woman when she finally acquired her father's money. Once she received unquestioned access to her inheritance she stood on the Hancock County courthouse steps and, in a dramatic gesture of accommodation to Sparta's white community, officially forgave twenty-one thousand dollars in debts owed the estate of David Dickson. Amanda soon moved to an elegant house in nearby Augusta where her neighbors included many of that city's wealthier whites and a few prosperous men and women of African descent. Louise Wynn, a widowed woman of color whose mulatto daughter Jenny attended Atlanta University shortly after Amanda, lived just a few blocks away. Shortly thereafter, one of Amanda's sons married Julia Holsey, a graduate of the same school who was also the daughter of Ebenezer Memorial Church's Bishop Lucius Holsey.[12]

Amanda America Dickson's legal victory and her vast fortune notwithstanding, the wealth and resulting advantages that accrued to one single African-American woman and her family, as well as the success of a few others who lived more modestly but still in comfort, had little effect on the state's social, economic, or legal order. Most people of color remained poor and repressed, and no civil rights decisions in the state were ever based on precedents established in the Dickson case.[13] A few more prosperous people of color could call on a kind of private privilege to protect their families from some of the harsher realities that beset most other black Georgians, but nonetheless, segregation was becoming deeply entrenched, and with few exceptions African-Americans had limited economic opportunities, almost no political rights, and little access to equal accommodations in public transportation, housing, hospitals, public schools, hotels, restaurants, or places of entertainment.

Some people of color who had been free prior to the war prospered, but most of them also suffered from the overall economic underdevelopment in the region, which hindered the success of African-Americans even more than it did for whites. Through the 1880s most members of the interlocking Ross-Bellamy family, who had farmed so industriously in Hancock and Baldwin counties prior to the war, remained in Atlanta, where the women worked as cooks, dressmakers, and laundresses and the men as grocers, carpenters, brakemen for the railroad, and unskilled laborers. One was a teacher.[14] The clergyman Wilkes Flagg, who had owned so much land in Baldwin County, where a colony of his relatives once lived and farmed, disparaged the progress his people had made in the period since emancipation. White associates contended that Flagg "bankrupted himself and died poor, leaving his old widow who had lived in luxury for fifty years a pauper."[15]

African-Americans throughout Georgia faced difficult times, but, insofar as their opinion was reflected by the *Savannah Tribune*, members of that community applauded the Dickson decision, which, the paper argued, represented welcome progress for the race because David Dickson had formally acknowledged his mulatto daughter and treated her as he would a white child, and the courts of Georgia had upheld the rights of a woman of color.[16] But the *Ishmaelite*, owned and operated by whites in Sparta, was predictably appalled. "The *ISHMAELITE* reprobates David Dickson's methods of life as illustrated and brought to light in all this case as abhorrent to race, instincts, and to the proprieties of decent living," the local paper editorialized.[17] Popular response among whites in Hancock County notwithstanding, the decision set an important precedent for the Hunt family. It forced the white Hunts to examine the legal writing on the wall and abandon their struggle against Susan and her descendants.

The Hunts and Dicksons lived in the same small community, and these parallel cases concerning the two families unfolded during the same years. Amanda Dickson's lawyer, Charles DuBose, an old associate of Nathan Sayre's as well, had served as Nelly Watkins's executor a few years earlier. He did the same for J. M. Hunt's estate and steadfastly remained involved in the case on behalf of J. M.'s legatees. Although the value of the property involved in the Hunt will hardly compared to the amount in the Dickson case, it was easily sufficient to create an incentive for prolonged dispute. In many instances the two cases included similar issues. With no concrete evidence to the contrary, Harley and Hunt, represented by "Colonel" Thomas Hunt, had failed to prove that David Dickson was mentally incompetent simply because he chose to leave his money to a mulatto woman— whether or not she was his daughter. They also produced no evidence showing that his fortune had been bequeathed in exchange for sexual favors or as a result of improper influence on the part of Julia Dickson. Two courts upheld Dickson's right to dispose of his property as he pleased—other members of his family, the white race in its entirety, past traditions, and the state's presumed public policy interests notwithstanding. The precedents established in the Dickson case effectively undercut any legal foundation on which the white Hunts might have sought to build their own case to circumvent the obvious intent of J. M. Hunt's will. Attorney Thomas Hunt may well have advised his family that any further attempts to invalidate the will would be fruitless.

The dispute over J. M. Hunt's will never went to trial. Presumably, the white Hunts simply challenged, stalled, and obstructed final settlement as long as they retained any hope of defeating their nonwhite relatives. J. M. Hunt had died in late 1879, at which time Charles DuBose promptly petitioned the court to sell eighty-six shares of "the Capital Stock of the Georgia Rail Road and Banking Co., belonging to the estate of said deceased."[18] Objections from the white family, however, delayed that early attempt to liquidate the estate, and only in 1886, after the superior court upheld the claims of Amanda Dickson, did Susan Hunt start receiving stock dividends of more than two hundred dollars quarterly. Executor DuBose kept careful accounts of those allocations, each of which the recipient, Susan Hunt, acknowledged with her mark. Over the next four years, the estate of J. M. Hunt paid Susan a total of about four thousand dollars in dividends, enough income to support her in reasonable comfort.[19] By April of 1890 the legitimate heirs had fallen into a disagreement with attorney DuBose over legal fees and his final accounting of the estate, and this new dispute went to arbitration that month. Susan Hunt and her children then needed to acquire the services of a different lawyer to represent their interests. Paradoxically, "Colonel" Thomas Hunt, J. M.'s nephew who probably had previously advised his own white family as he had the white Dicksons, then entered the case on behalf of his nonwhite relatives and served as their designated arbitrator, selected by the elder Susan and her children. More than a decade after J. M. Hunt's death, apparently no one recognized the irony in the court's assertion that arbitration would "avoid the delay and expense of litigation."[20]

A month later, both the family and DuBose accepted the terms agreed to by the arbitrators. That settlement acknowledged that the elder Susan's daughters (Mariah and the younger Susan) had already received their legacy of five hundred dollars each. Their brother James Herbert was awarded the same five hundred plus interest, amounting to an additional one hundred and fifty dollars, which had accrued over the previous eleven years. The elder Susan, who was about eighty years old by 1890, acquired title to a "tract of land near Linton in said county of Hancock, that being all the real estate of said deceased." The tract included about a thousand acres of good farmland. In its major finding, the arbitration team concluded that Susan should also receive "the only other property belonging to said estate in the hands of said Executor." That property consisted of eighty-six shares of stock in the Georgia Rail Road Company. The market value at that time was $204 per share, amounting to a total of $17,544. The arbitrators further ordered some $650 paid to DuBose for his legal expenses, plus court and arbitration fees of another $75.[21]

Susan Hunt and her children had resided for over twenty years in the household of Nathan Sayre, a man who had lived and breathed the law and had collected one of the largest private law libraries in the South. Although they never became technically versed in law, things that they had heard and learned at Pomegranate Hall must have led them to believe that the legal system could be made to work for them. These women of color could not afford the luxury of behaving like the often ridiculed and stereotypically helpless "Southern belles." They did everything that they could to control their own fate, and they possessed the intelligence, perseverance, determination, and political connections that they needed to resist their influential white family, which attempted to deny them their rightful inheritance for more than a decade.

Nathan Sayre's inventory, compiled following his death in 1853, showed a diversified estate. His assets included real estate, outstanding loans, and personal property, as well as corporate stock—notably, a number of shares in the Georgia Rail Road Company. The Hunt family, on the other hand, held most of its assets in land and slaves and lost much of its former affluence as a result of the Civil War. J. M. Hunt gave Susan a plot of land on Hunt's Hill in 1878, and he may have transferred other real property to members of his white family during his lifetime. At the time of final settlement, J. M.'s estate included nothing more than a little cash, the railroad stock, and the tract in southern Hancock County near Linton. The stock, at least, probably had originally belonged to Nathan Sayre. More than a quarter century before J. M.'s death, Nathan and his executors, apparently fearing that the courts would not uphold the claims of an undocumented free woman of color, had transferred those shares to J. M. Hunt for safekeeping with the understanding that he would care for Susan during his lifetime and give her the stock when he died. J. M. honored that gentlemen's agreement and formally bequeathed the stock and his entire estate to Nathan's former consort Susan and the three children.[22]

The first Susan Hunt lived at least long enough to see the final satisfactory settlement of that estate in 1890. She died in the early years of that decade, though the exact date is not known. Her gravesite has never been found, but neither have markers been located for any white members of the family. Most of the Hunts were interred in the family cemetery near the old homestead by the banks of Fort Creek where reportedly "they buried the colored people . . . too." Susan may have been buried there as well, but that graveyard has now completely disappeared.[23]

Most of Susan's older daughter's children remained in the area for many years. Her second daughter Mariah's husband—J. M.'s youngest brother Henry—continued to farm in Hancock County through the 1880s. Although the region remained economically depressed, Henry's farm survived. He kept bees, made honey, and grew championship beans, onions, corn, turnips, apples, and tobacco, and his cotton seed was acclaimed as the most prolific in the state. Henry Hunt left no will or other record concerning disposition of his property when he died in 1889 after "a short and severe illness"—the same year that arson destroyed Bass Academy, where his and Mariah's children attended school. The Sparta *Ishmaelite* noted only that "he was the last of a family of [five] genial brothers, and was a quiet, peaceable and industrious citizen."[24]

During the winter of 1895, Henry's widow Mariah traveled to Tuskegee, Alabama, to visit her daughter. She fell asleep while rocking by the hearth holding her infant grandson on her lap, and their clothes caught fire. The baby soon died as a result of his extensive burns, and Mariah never recovered. She succumbed later that year. Bishop Lucius Holsey probably delivered the eulogy, and Mariah Hunt was buried in the cemetery of Sparta's Ebenezer Methodist Episcopal Church.[25]

The choices made by Mariah and Henry Hunt's children reveal the kaleidoscopic patterns of their lives. Their oldest son, Will, left Hancock in the 1880s and went to Marietta, Georgia, where he worked for a white family as their butler and carriage driver. He then moved to Tuskegee, Alabama, and married a dark-skinned woman, the daughter of a successful farmer, with whom he had one child. He returned to agricultural work as his father had before him, and managed the seven hundred–acre farm that belonged to his sister Adella. His friends among the local white farmers could not believe that Will was a Negro but thought instead that he was some kind of "peculiar" white man who had taken up with a black woman.[26]

Mariah and Henry's second son, known as Mac, remained in Hancock County, worked as a laborer, and probably died before 1900. Their oldest daughter, Lula, married a vigorous black man named Gilbert McLendon. The family lived on Hunt's Hill in a spacious, comfortable home built by Gilbert, who worked as a stone and brick mason. Lula kept house, tended the flower and vegetable garden, fed her chickens, sewed, worshipped regularly at Ebenezer

Methodist Episcopal Church, corresponded with her sisters, and raised seven children. Although the McLendons owned their home, a little surrounding land, and a horse and buggy, they had limited material wealth. The marriage was happy, and, though their surname was McLendon, Lula and Gilbert's children enjoyed a certain privileged status accorded them as Hunts in Hancock County.[27]

The second daughter, Adella, devoted much of her life to educating blacks in the South. After graduating from Atlanta University she taught in southwest Georgia and then at Tuskegee Institute, where she also worked with local farm women and children to improve their diet, health, and living conditions, participated in the colored women's club movement, and fought for the cause of woman's suffrage. Even before J. M. Hunt's will had been settled, she married Warren Logan, the treasurer of Tuskegee and a Hampton Institute graduate. Logan was a mulatto who looked almost as white as his wife. The couple had nine children. Adella Hunt Logan was a willful woman who rarely avoided controversy. On one occasion she raised the ire of conservative African-Americans as well as whites in the rigidly segregated town of Tuskegee, Alabama, when she attempted to have her son's hair cut at the local "white" barber shop. Gender and race notwithstanding, her upbringing and education led her to believe that she was, or should be, the social, political, and intellectual equal of anyone, and she vigorously challenged any curtailment of her personal or civil rights. She was beset by health problems and personal crises and became deeply depressed because she could not tolerate the racist and sexist society in which she lived and the people who refused to treat a woman of color as their equal. Her life spiraled downward, she became increasingly despondent, and in 1915 she took her own life. The magnitude of Adella's anguish, alienation, and isolation touched the family's friend W. E. B. Du Bois, and he memorialized her as the tragic and doomed "Princess of the Hither Isles," one of his "voices from within the veil."[28]

Henry A. Hunt, Jr., the fifth child, followed his sister Adella to Atlanta University, where he graduated in 1890. He too devoted most of his adult life to educating blacks in the rural South, first at Johnson C. Smith College in North Carolina and then as president of the Fort Valley, Georgia, industrial school. In the 1930s he went to work for the Farm Services Administration, where he became a member of President Franklin Delano Roosevelt's "black cabinet" in the nation's capital. In remembering Henry Hunt, W. E. B. Du Bois acknowledged that, because he looked white, Hunt "was continually facing a situation where, after having been treated as a man . . . he suddenly was subjected to ostracism when it was found that he openly identified himself with the Negro race." Nonetheless, Du Bois continued, "Henry Hunt was never unhappy at having chosen to identify himself with the race to which only one of his sixteen great [great] grandparents belonged." Like his sister Adella, Henry also married an educated person whose racial and social background resembled his own.[29]

Sarah Hunt, born in 1869, graduated from Atlanta University as her sister and brother had before her and taught for more than twenty years in schools for blacks throughout the South. At Tuskegee Institute in the early 1900s, she and the eminent botanist George Washington Carver "almost married," and, reportedly, she was his "only love." Although others vehemently deny it, a few Tuskegeans thought that some members of the Hunt family considered Carver "too black" for Sarah. If that difference in pigmentation did bother the Hunts, recent experience as well as older memories from Georgia may have stimulated concerns for the safety of their sister (who looked white) had she married a dark-skinned man in Alabama. In 1902 several unidentified white men attacked and almost killed Carver and terrorized his companion, a white female photographer, when he accompanied her around the school's environs as her official escort from the Institute. Sarah Hunt never bore children of her own but served as substitute mother for her sister's children following Adella's suicide. Then well into her middle years, Sarah moved to California, where she entered into an endogamous marriage with a relative from Sparta, Felix Rogers. Rogers was the widower of yet another cousin, his childhood sweetheart, Susie—the daughter of Mariah Hunt's sister Susan. Sarah helped to raise the widowed Rogers's children. Felix Rogers and his first and second wives, both of them Hunt women from Hancock County, lived in Los Angeles, where their ambiguous racial identity seems to have attracted less attention.[30]

Ella Hunt, Mariah and Henry's youngest daughter, finished her education at Barber-Scotia College in North Carolina. Ella was a tall, vibrant beauty who, during her young adulthood, lived in Savannah, where she managed a drug store and married a black laborer named

Berzilia Payne. In segregated Georgia, Berzilia Payne had difficulties contending with the daily problems engendered by his marriage to someone who looked white, and he took up with a dark-skinned woman. Ella would not tolerate his blatant indiscretion and soon left him. She moved to New York City, where on at least one occasion the police "almost arrested" her and admonished her for "going around with colored people."[31]

Tom Hunt, the family's youngest child by seven years, lived for some time with his sister Adella and graduated from Tuskegee Institute. Around 1897 he moved to Massachusetts, where he worked as a public gardener in a town near Boston, completed the agricultural program at the University of Massachusetts and then went west to settle in California, where he served for many years on the agricultural faculty of the state university at Berkeley. All of Mariah and Henry Hunt's children were as light-skinned as most Anglo-Americans, but the older children "were white only in complexion, [and] very colored inside." Tom alone elected to leave the black world and pass over into the white. As W. E. B. Du Bois explained, any member of the Hunt family "had a choice as to which race he would belong." Furthermore, Du Bois continued, "not many of us have any such choice; nor do we give adequate thought and sympathetic attention to the intricate problems which this involves." Blessed with good looks, an education, ambition, and opportunity, Tom Hunt succumbed to the obvious and seductive advantages of living as a white man in a racist society. His diverse heritage—Cherokee and Anglo-American as well as black—muddied his sense of racial identity, and the ties of kinship and his Southern roots apparently anchored him less securely than they did his older siblings. There is no telling, however, the anguish he may have known as he abandoned the family into which he had been born. James Weldon Johnson chronicled the life of a similarly successful individual who chose to live as a white man but ultimately discovered that he could not "repress the thought that, after all, I have taken the lesser part . . . [and] sold my birthright for a mess of pottage." In California Tom Hunt "narrowly escaped" the 1906 San Francisco earthquake, corresponded infrequently with his family, married a white woman, had two sons, both of whom died in World War II, and saw his sister Sarah Hunt Rogers "somewhere other than his home" by appointment only.[32]

A full century in the lives of the Hunts and other free people of color raises questions about how they initially established their limited and tenuous conditions of freedom. But it must always be remembered that even as they endured severely curtailed liberty over the years, experienced the perpetual insults of racism, and faced lifelong frustrations, free people of color nonetheless were far more fortunate than others of their race. They could always enjoy some few satisfactions denied the majority of cruelly and unjustly enslaved people among whom they lived. On infrequent occasions in the early nineteenth century, white owners chose to manumit one or more of their slaves for a number of reasons—meritorious service, familial attachments, and economic self-interest among them. Self-purchase also provided a few such Southern blacks as Wilkes and Lavinia Flagg with opportunities to free themselves. Through the first six decades of that century, however, Georgia legislators continued to shut down even those limited routes to freedom, making manumission almost an impossibility. Ellen Craft and a few other African-American women from Middle Georgia ingeniously effectuated their own freedom by escaping to the North, and Hancock County's Biddy Mason accompanied her master to California, but then successfully resisted his attempts to take her back to a slave state.[33] But the great majority of free people of color, like the Hunts, were born to that condition resulting from the status of their mothers and grandmothers. Their nonslave classification most often was not a result of their own doing but rather of circumstance alone. Most of those female progenitors were free women of African descent, a few were white, and in at least some cases they were Native Americans who had established intimate relationships with black men.

Some free women and men of color either lived on their own or with white guardians and fully complied with the law. They kept careful track of their mandated documentation, had legal guardians, and registered annually in the county courthouses as officially required. Others resisted complying with the restrictions imposed on them by a repressive and racist society. Still others remained outside of the rigid structure of Southern plantation life as a result of their close associations with white relatives. Although some whites did not want to label their own loved ones—consorts, siblings, children—as slaves, they also hesitated to openly declare them free, when without extensive documentation that precarious status might bring on unpleasant legal, social, and personal wrangling and upheavals. Inadequately documented people in this group were subject to fine, imprisonment, banishment from the state, and even enslavement. The nonwhite Hunts never appeared on any census or county records, and probably never possessed manumission papers or other documentation of free birth that would support their ambiguous status. Their experience suggests that a number of other free men and women of color may have assiduously avoided either categorization or official recognition of that status. In the plantation belt this small caste consisted of at least three separate sub-groups: one that appeared regularly in county registers and census schedules, who had stable families, and most of whom worked as farmers, artisans, or domestic servants; a second smaller minority who seemed to lead economically and socially marginal lives; and a third group that lived under the paternalistic and protective penumbra of respected and often influential white people. It is impossible to determine how many such "hidden" families as the Hunts may never have appeared in any official documentation at all until after the Civil War.

Those virtually "invisible" and often elusive people—a majority of whom may have been women—sometimes benefitted from unexpected economic privileges resulting from their sponsorship by affluent white men. The fact that they accepted and appreciated those privileges, however, does not imply that they were merely the passive recipients of largess from their white benefactors, and certainly these women maintained strong alliances and friendships and often had relatives in the slave community. Circumstances forced them into the interstices of plantation society, where they carved out meaningful lives for themselves and also influenced those around them. Their experiences incorporated elements from the lives of both white plantation mistresses and slave women.

So few free people of color lived in the plantation belt that no sizable support community existed. Nonetheless, by the late antebellum years, a fair number of them resided close to one another in neighborhood clusters, and they also developed extensive interrelated family networks through blood, marriage, and common residence. The tenuous nature of their existence—both economically and legally—required remarkable adaptability. Additionally, their small numbers and social isolation and the opprobrium of the majority of the white community demanded independence, endurance, and fortitude in dealing with their white, black, and racially heterogeneous families and neighbors.

The trauma of the Civil War disrupted plantation life and ended the oppressive reign of slavery. In its wake, all people of African descent sought new and better lives for themselves, while members of the former slaveholding class tried to replicate their old world as best they could. General emancipation meant that the "ole-time" free persons of color no longer enjoyed even the limited legal and social privileges that had once set them somewhat apart from the slave community. All African-Americans became bound together in one "inferior" class based on race alone.

Yet the termination of that intermediary caste of free people of color did not preclude social divisions in the new all-inclusive black community. Following emancipation, some lighter-skinned African-Americans who enjoyed greater economic advantages bonded together, sometimes to the exclusion of others. Some of them had been at least nominally free prior to the war. Family associations, financial status, occupation, neighborhood living patterns, as well as education and institutional associations, often set this sub-group apart, and endogamous marriages reinforced its internal cohesiveness. But those proscriptive links sometimes created fissures in the overall solidarity of the African-American community. Members of the more privileged class of African-Americans occasionally exhibited attitudes of superiority and even arrogance. But this very human frailty must not be overemphasized, and their more admirable behavior should be recognized, understood, and appreciated as well. Many people in this group still lived marginal economic lives themselves and of course they too suffered from the racist attitudes and actions of whites. Wealth is only relative, and, in spite of a few such notable exceptions as Amanda Dickson, the economic advantages that this nascent African-American middle class enjoyed were significant only by comparison with the majority of blacks, and not because their financial standing surpassed or even equalled that of any sizable portion of the white community. In addition, although this group—dominated in many instances by mulattoes—tended to be cohesive, its members also identified strongly with their less privileged black relatives and associates, and acted in accordance with their sense of moral commitment and responsibility toward the African-American community in its entirety. A number of them became the teachers, physicians, lawyers, and businessmen and -women who provided leadership and support for those with fewer material advantages.

In spite of loyalties to the African-American community as a whole and special ties with their own class, such people as the Hunts also used familial experience and alliances in the white community for their own economic and "political" advantage. They figured out how to employ both personal contacts and the law to obtain and keep their property and to acquire an education and the other tools necessary for survival in a racist society.

The end of the slave era hardly severed all interracial contacts, but it did terminate many intimate relationships between women of color and white men. The Hunts' experience is not atypical. After at least two and possibly three generations characterized by alliances with white men, the Hunt women of the generation that grew up in the decades following the Civil War had other options, and they all chose to marry men of color. In this family the only interracial union initiated after emancipation was one in which a young man married a white woman, passed over into her world, and abandoned his African-American heritage.

For the Hunts and for others as well, educational opportunities for the generation born during and after the Civil War were greater than for those born earlier. In their family, the last women born to non-white mothers and white men demonstrated their determination to succeed both educationally and professionally. They combined that determination with a devotion to family and a commitment to addressing their community's diverse needs.

This story of an admittedly atypical family, covering about a century in the lives of a small group of people in Middle Georgia, also illustrates the danger of compressing the "black experience" into a single picture characterized only by deprivation, confrontation, instability, and devastation. Over the years, societal upheavals and evolutions, as well as unique circumstances and familial rites of passage shaped the Hunt women. Their lives never remained static. As their world evolved, they too changed through several generations, from the post-Revolutionary frontier era, to the antebellum years, and on through the disruptions of the Civil War and the upheavals of Reconstruction.

Place as well as time also influenced their experiences. In other areas of the country free persons of color were more concentrated, and documentation of their lives has been more accessible. In the Middle Georgia plantation belt, however, members of this small group led vastly different lives from similarly designated people in the border states, around the port cities of the Deep South, or certainly north of slavery.

Finally, gender significantly molded and structured their lives as well. White men often victimized women of color, free and slave alike. But overgeneralizing about this exploitation distorts both fact and interpretation. Women of color could be, but were not always, exploited. Some, like the Hunt women, lived in physical comfort with their children and their white consorts. Such women as these often obtained some material advantages and a little education for those children as well. They managed their own households, had friends and family within and without the slave community, and often had fulfilling creative and religious lives as well. Whether or not they remained economically and legally dependent, the totality of their experience was neither defined nor circumscribed by the domination of white men. They faced different problems and difficult choices, but these women sometimes enjoyed privileges that most African-American men—slave or free—did not. The lives of these particular women differed in nature, in substance, and in degree from the experiences of men.

This story, which follows one family in depth and several others much like it in eight rural Georgia counties, is hardly definitive. Sources were diverse, hard to ferret out, and often perplexing to deal with. Small but precious jewels of information were mined from the shadowy and contradictory reminiscences of people whose memories were clouded by age, time, and distance. Oral accounts, bits of legal documentation and architectural evidence often corroborated stories that at first seemed scarcely believable. Shreds of material culture, newspaper and federal government reports, school, church, and county court records had to be compared and woven together.

Documenting the lives of women tends to be more difficult than it is for men. Similarly, it is harder to find information about people of color than about whites. Too often, their experiences have been disregarded, intentionally suppressed, and generally considered insignificant, but slavery and racism, as well as the pervasive injustices against women, should not be purged from the nation's memory. These people are still underrepresented in historical literature, and frequently when they do appear, as one provocative statement suggests, "all the women are white, all the blacks are men."[34]

Recreating the lives of free women of color—a little-known minority within the minority—is rarer and more difficult still. The most frustrating void has been the paucity of evidence preserved in their own words. Trying to discover and hear their "voices from within the veil" is critical. Mary Ross's testimony about life on her farm and the depredations of Sherman's army is extraordinary, but unique. Sarah Shuften, whose family also may have been free prior to emancipation, published but one poem about the heroism of black troops in the Civil War, and only a few of Laura Mason's poignant letters have been found. Adella Hunt Logan's words reflect on her childhood from a distance of many decades and miles removed from antebellum Middle Georgia. With the exception of those sparse observations, Susan Hunt, her children, grandchildren, and others like them are primarily seen and heard through the eyes and ears of others—often white, often male. But in spite of these problems, their story may help to contradict a few stereotypical images about the way that some people of color, especially women, once lived.

Historians need to reclaim and reconstruct the lives of many more women, free persons of color, and other nonwhite Americans. At least occasionally, these people have experienced in at least some ways the discomforting "two-ness" familiarized by W. E. B. Du Bois, but they always have contributed to the intricate mosaic of our national experience. Although their history has been bypassed, ignored, demeaned, and even obliterated, uncovering and elucidating these less visible subjects presents important and stimulating challenges. The contradictory and ambiguous lives of free women of color—and our other forgotten people—deserve broader and deeper investigation, and this story is but one small and imperfect fragment.

Notes

AME	African Methodist Episcopal Church.
AMEZ	African Methodist Episcopal Zion Church.
AU	Atlanta University, Special Collections and Archives.
BalCC	Baldwin County Courthouse, Milledgeville, Georgia.
CME	Colored Methodist Episcopal Church.
DAR	Daughters of the American Revolution.
GDAH	Georgia Department of Archives and History.
GPO	U.S. Government Printing Office.
GreCC	Greene County Courthouse, Greensboro, Georgia.
HanCC	Hancock County Courthouse, Sparta, Georgia.
NA	National Archives, Washington, D.C.
PutCC	Putnam County Courthouse, Eatonton, Georgia.
RG	Record Group.
TalCC	Taliaferro County Courthouse, Crawfordville, Georgia.
WarCC	Warren County Courthouse, Warrenton, Georgia.
WasCC	Washington County Courthouse, Sandersville, Georgia.
WPA	Works Progress Administration.

Prologue: Heredity

1. Atlanta University, *Social and Physical Condition of Negroes in Cities. Report of an Investigation under the Direction of Atlanta University: And Proceedings of the Second Conference for the Study of Problems Concerning Negro City Life,* convened at Atlanta University, May 25–26, 1897, Atlanta University Publications no. 2. (Atlanta: Atlanta University Press, 1897), 37–40; and Caroline Bond Day, *A Study of Some Negro-White Families in the United States* (Cambridge: Harvard University Press, 1932), 33. Pictures of Adella Hunt Logan in the possession of the author and from the Atlanta University Special Collections and Archives and Herndon Home photograph collection, Atlanta, Ga.

2. Atlanta University, *Social and Physical Conditions of Negroes in Cities*, 30, 37–40.

3. Adella Hunt Logan, "Prenatal and Hereditary Influences" in Atlanta University, *Social and Physical Condition of Negroes in Cities*, 37–40. Logan's interest in heredity and genetics may also have stemmed from a contemporary curiosity about evolution and eugenics, stimulated by the works of Charles Darwin and Sir Francis Galton, with which Logan was familiar.

4. Ibid.

5. Ibid.

6. D. W. Culp, ed., *Twentieth Century Negro Literature; or, A Cyclopedia of Thought on the Vital Topics Relating to the American Negro* (Atlanta: J. L. Nichols and Co., 1902), 198.

7. W. E. B. Du Bois, *Darkwater: Voices from within the Veil* (1920; reprint, New York: Schocken Books, 1969).

8. W. E. B. Du Bois, "The Significance of Henry Hunt," *The Fort Valley State College Bulletin: Founder's and Annual Report* 1 (October 1940): 6, 7.

9. Ibid., 7.

10. In this study, Middle Georgia has been defined as an eight-county region with Hancock County at its hub. Surrounding counties are Baldwin, Putnam, Greene, Taliaferro, Warren, Glascock, and Washington. The region was the core of the old plantation belt, also known as the black belt, about one third of the way between Atlanta and Savannah. Baldwin County's Milledgeville was Georgia's antebellum capital.

11. Pomegranate Hall was built in Sparta, Georgia, by Judge Nathan C. Sayre in 1830. Sayre was Adella Hunt Logan's maternal grandfather.

12. Day, *Study of Some Negro-White Families,* records the physical anthropology of families with black, Native American, and white antecedents. Barbara J. Fields, "Ideology and Race in American History," in *Region, Race and Reconstruction: Essays in Honor of C. Vann Woodward,* ed. J. Morgan Kousser and James M. McPherson (New York: Oxford University Press, 1982), 145, for example, warns of the "fallacy of regarding race as a physical fact."

13. W. E. B. Du Bois, *The Souls of Black Folk* (1903; reprint, Chicago: A. C. McClurg and Co, 1940), 2.

14. Logan, "Prenatal and Hereditary Influences," 38.

I. Pioneers on the Georgia Frontier

1. Elizabeth Wiley Smith, *The History of Hancock County* (Washington, Ga.: Wilkes Publishing Co., 1974), vol. 2, *Ancestors, Families and Genealogies,* 91. Mary Green Smith's account of the Hunts' migration to Georgia, in her 1926 application to the DAR, differs slightly and states that Judkins Hunt went to

Hancock County in 1794 with a "family" of nine children and thirteen black servants. Parke Rouse, Jr., *The Great Wagon Road from Philadelphia to the South* (New York: McGraw Hill, 1973), frontispiece map; and Henry DeLeon Southerland and Jerry Elijah Brown, *The Federal Road through Georgia, the Creek Nation, and Alabama, 1806–1836* (Tuscaloosa: University of Alabama Press, 1989), 103.

2. Daughters of the American Colonists, "Bible Genealogical Records, 1937–1939" (typescript, n.d.), 62.

3. Vance T. Little, *The Hunts of Tennessee* (Nashville: Vec El Ancestral Studies, 1969), 2. Mary Green Smith's DAR application states that Judkins Hunt's family was descended from Rev. Robert Hunt, who came to Jamestown from England in 1606 with Capt. John Smith but that version of the Hunt family's genesis seems less likely.

4. The genealogy of Martha Batte (variously spelled Batts and Betts) Hunt provided from the private papers of Sarah Milam Exum, Leslie, Ga.

5. Deeds and Mortgages, 1793–95, HanCC.

6. Smith, *History of Hancock County* 2: 91. Deeds and Mortgages, 1793–95, 88–90, HanCC.

7. Smith, *History of Hancock County* 2: 91.

8. Ibid.

9. Smith, *History of Hancock County* 2: 91; vol. 1, *History, Heritage and Records*, 53; and Julia Cherry Spruill, *Women's Life and Work in the Southern Colonies* (1938; reprint, New York: W. W. Norton and Co., 1972), 81.

10. Washington and Baldwin were among the original Georgia counties; Greene County was laid out in 1786, Hancock and Warren in 1793, Putnam in 1807, Taliaferro in 1826, and Glascock in 1857.

11. Augustus Smith Clayton, *A Compilation of the Laws of the State of Georgia, Passed by the Legislature Since the Political Year 1800, to the Year 1810, Inclusive* (Augusta: Adams and Duyckinck, 1813), 209.

12. Smith, *History of Hancock County* 1: 4, 5, 7; James C. Bonner, "Profile of a Late Ante-Bellum Community," *The American Historical Review* 49 (July 1944): 665; and Bonner, "Genesis of Agricultural Reform in the Cotton Belt," *Journal of Southern History* 3 (November 1943): 475. A discussion with Dr. Bonner shortly before his death provided valuable perspective about the history of Hancock and Baldwin counties.

13. Ridgely Torrence, *The Story of John Hope* (New York: Macmillan Co., 1948), 18. Torrence, for example, restates the rumor that a slave familiar with the problem of cleaning cotton came up with the idea for the gin. Marylou DiPietro, "Ms. Quiz," *Ms.*, 1, 4 (January–February 1991): 59, gives credit to plantation mistress Catherine Littlefield Green.

14. Smith, *History of Hancock County* 1: 3, 5, 6.

15. Smith, *History of Hancock County* 1: 5; and Absalom H. Chappell,

Miscellanies of Georgia: Historical, Biographical, Descriptive, Etc. (Atlanta: James F. Meegan, 1874), 8, 9.

16. Smith, *History of Hancock County* 1: 124; and Rebecca Latimer Felton, *Country Life in Georgia in the Days of My Youth* (1919; reprint, New York: Arno Press, 1980), 8. *Acts of the General Assembly of the State of Georgia* 1828: 87.

17. Smith, *History of Hancock County* 1: 5.

18. Chappell, *Miscellanies of Georgia,* 12, 13.

19. Rudi Halliburton, Jr., *Red over Black: Black Slavery among the Cherokee Indians* (Westport, Conn.: Greenwood Press, 1977), 51.

20. Daniel Littlefield, *Africans and Creeks* (Westport: Greenwood Press, 1979), 33–36, 87; Carl Mauelshagen and Gerald H. Davis, trans. and eds., *Partners in the Lord's Work: The Diaries of Two Moravian Missionaries in the Creek Indian Country, 1807–1813,* Research Paper no. 21 (Atlanta: Georgia State College, 1969), 52, 71; Clayton, *Compilation of the Laws of Georgia,* 679; and Halliburton, *Red over Black,* 11–13.

21. Chappell, *Miscellanies of Georgia,* 13–19.

22. Garnett Andrews, *Reminiscences of an Old Georgia Lawyer* (Atlanta: Franklin Printing House, 1870), 10; and John Brown, *Slave Life in Georgia,* ed. L. A. Chamerovzov (London: n.p., 1855), 198.

23. *The Missionary,* November 24, 1823, and October 14, 1824. Announcements of slave sales and rewards for returns of runaways appeared in every issue from 1823 to 1825.

24. Thomas Jefferson set forth these views in *Notes on the State of Virginia,* in 1880–82. Winthrop D. Jordan, *White over Black: American Attitudes toward the Negro, 1550–1812* (New York: W. W. Norton and Co., 1977), 168–69. The Jefferson-Hemings story is most thoroughly explored in Fawn M. Brodie, *Thomas Jefferson: An Intimate History* (New York: W. W. Norton, 1974).

25. Torrence, *The Story of John Hope,* 5.

26. Jordan, *White over Black,* 168, 169; and Joel Williamson, *New People: Miscegenation and Mulattoes in the United States* (New York: Free Press, 1980), xi, 96. The mulatto protagonist in Charles W. Chesnutt's novel *The House behind the Cedars* declares, "you must take us for ourselves alone we are new people." *Webster's New International Dictionary,* 2nd. ed., unabridged (Springfield, Mass.: G. and C. Merriam, 1960), defines mulatto: "[Pg. and Sp. *mulato,* masc. *mulata,* fem., of mixed breed, fr. *mulo,* mule, fr L. *mulus.* See MULE.] The first generation offspring of a pure negro and a white; in popular use, any person of mixed Caucasian and negro blood." "Mestizo" and "mustizo" are variant spellings in early Georgia records. Webster's defines mestizo: "Esp. in Spanish America . . . a person of mixed blood; esp., the offspring of a . . . person of European stock and an (East) Indian, Negro . . . or other person of dark, non-European stock . . . hence, loosely, any half-breed," and mustee: "[From MESTIZO.] Strictly, an octoroon; loosely, any half-breed."

27. John Rozier uses the term "no-nations" in *Black Boss: Political Revolution in a Georgia County* (Athens: University of Georgia Press, 1982). The term was handed down in the family of Rozier's black housekeeper in Hancock County.

28. Theda Perdue, *Slavery and the Evolution of Cherokee Society, 1540–1866* (Knoxville: University of Tennessee Press, 1979), 48, 57; Halliburton, *Red over Black*, 4, 37, 50; and Charles M. Hudson, ed., *Red, White and Black: Symposium on Indians in the Old South*, Southern Anthropological Society Proceedings no. 5, (Athens: University of Georgia Press, 1971), 99.

29. Littlefield, *Africans and Creeks*, 68; and John R. Swanton, *Social Organization and Social Usages of the Indians of the Creek Confederation*, Bureau of American Ethnology, 42nd Annual Report (Washington, D.C.: GPO, 1928), 223. Robert and George Watkins, *A Digest of the Laws of the State of Georgia from Its First Establishment as a British Province Down to the Year 1798 Inclusive* (Philadelphia: R. Aitken, 1800), 163.

30. Mauelshagen and Davis, *Partners in the Lord's Work*, 71. Battis herself might even have been the daughter of one of Martha Batte (or Batts) Hunt's slaves. The name is uncommon, and the distortion in the spelling is only slight. Mary Ann Battis is not identifiable in the census or any Baldwin County records.

31. James Hunt will, November 14, 1868, HanCC. *The Missionary*, April 4 and May 3, 1824. Other people having Cherokee and African-American heritage lived near Scull Shoals in Greene County. The reference to "Cherokee Mariah Lilly" appears in the baptismal records of the Mount Zion Presbyterian Church, February 1843, GDAH.

32. John Reed Swanton, *Indians of the South Eastern United States*, Smithsonian Institution, Bureau of American Ethnology, Bulletin no. 137 (Washington: GPO, 1946), 500; and Day, *Study of Some Negro-White Families*, 33, 34, and pl. 38. Day describes Susan's granddaughter Sarah Hunt, whose hair had "extraordinary length, extending to her knees, and is of a fine silky quality." Also oral accounts and observations by Houser Miller, Fort Valley, Ga., March 1983, and Mamie McLendon Thomas, Chester, Pa., November 1982.

33. James Mooney, "Myths of the Cherokee," in Bureau of American Ethnology, *Nineteenth Annual Report, 1897–98* (Washington, D.C.: GPO), 16; Perdue, *Slavery and the Evolution of Cherokee Society*, 33, 51, 44; Charles Hudson, *The Southeast Indians* (Knoxville: University of Tennessee Press, 1976), 313; Thomas M. N. Lewis, *Oconaluftee Indian Village: An Interpretation of a Cherokee Community of 1750* (Cherokee Historical Association, 1954), 42; William Harlen Gilbert, *The Eastern Cherokees*, Smithsonian Institution, Bureau of American Ethnology, Bulletin 133, (New York: AMS Press, 1948), 339; and Swanton, *Indians of the South Eastern United States*, 233.

34. James Adair, *History of the American Indians, Particularly Those Natives Adjoining to the Mississippi, East and West Florida, Georgia, South and North*

Carolina, and Virginia (London: Edward and Charles Dilly, 1775), 56, 22, 52, 18; Lewis *Oconaluftee Indian Village,* 8, 15, 28, 21; Paul B. Hamel and Mary U. Chiltoskey, *Cherokee Plants and Their Uses: A 400 Year History* (Sylva, N.C.: Herald Publishing Co., 1975), 20, 18, 16; Mooney, "Myths of the Cherokee," 82; Marion Lena Starkey, *The Cherokee Nation* (New York: Russell and Russell, 1946), 16; William Harlen Gilbert, *Eastern Cherokee Social Organization* (Chicago: University of Chicago Libraries, 1935), 341; and *The Missionary,* February 25, 1825.

35. Mooney, "Myths of the Cherokee," 419, 397.

36. Hudson, *Southeast Indians,* 321; Gilbert, *Eastern Cherokees,* 340, 345; Swanton *Indians of the South Eastern United States,* 713; and Hamel and Chiltoskey, *Cherokee Plants and Their Uses,* 23–58.

37. Oral accounts from Charles Hunt, Sparta, Ga., and members of the Logan family; also Culp, *Twentieth Century Negro Literature,* 198.

38. Alvin Mell Lunceford, Jr., *Taliaferro County Georgia, Records and Notes* (Spartanburg, S.C.: Reprint Co., 1988), 618–19. Bolton Newland Lunceford supplemented the revised edition of her husband's book with a compilation from county registries and a new chapter, "Free Persons of Color: Orphans of History," 601–31. Herbert Aptheker, *American Negro Slave Revolts* (1943.; reprint, New York: International Publishers, 1963), 246.

39. *Fifth Census, or Enumeration of the Inhabitants of the United States, 1830* (Washington, D.C.: Duff Green, 1832); and U.S. Census Office, *Statistical View of the United States,* Seventh Census, 1850 (Washington, D.C.: A.O.P. Nicholson, 1854), 65. U.S. Census records for Baldwin, Greene, Hancock, Putnam, Taliaferro, Warren, and Washington counties, Ga., 1830.

40. U.S. Census records for Greene, Hancock, and Washington counties, Ga., 1820 and 1830.

41. General Index of Warren County, 1811–36, GDAH. *Georgia Genealogical Magazine,* 1969, 2329, from Warren County, Minutes of the Inferior Court, 1807–14. U.S. Census records for Warren County, Ga., 1820 and 1830. The white Wynn(e) family in Middle Georgia became involved in many ways with people of color. Benjamin, Peter, Clement, and Thomas Wynn were guardians in Warren County in 1820 and 1840. Samuel Wynn established a lasting relationship with a woman of color, nominally free, named Louise. Their daughter Jennie attended Atlanta University in its earliest years. Anderson Wynn, a mulatto, was a successful Hancock County blacksmith and property owner in 1870.

42. Taliaferro County Registry of Free Persons of Color, 1829, GDAH; and Lunceford, *Taliaferro County,* 601–31. Among the eight counties of Middle Georgia, only Taliaferro's registers of free persons of color are available prior to 1830. *Digest of the Laws of the State of Georgia, 1755 to 1800, Inclusive* (Savannah: Seymour, Woolhopter and Stebbins, 1802), 204, states in reference to the will of

Daniel Grant, "the several negro slaves therein mentioned, are hereby declared to be freed and liberated, at the times and on the terms and conditions therein expressed; any law, usage or custom, to the contrary notwithstanding."

43. *Digest of the Laws of the State of Georgia, 1755 to 1800,* 205, 206. The name Going is alternatively spelled Goings, Goynes, Gowens, Gowins, and even Garnes in different records. U.S. Census records for Greene, Taliaferro, and Baldwin counties, Ga., 1820–50.

44. *Fifth Census; Acts of the General Assembly* 1823: 146; and U.S. Census records for Greene County, Ga., 1820–50. In 1870 an elderly farmer named Nelson Perry appears as one of the propertied people of color in Greene County. Although the name is not common in the region, there is no proof of any relationship between him and Betsy Perry.

45. Virginia Hill Wilhoit, *History of Warren County* (WPA Project no. 4341, 1939), 258; and Crooked Creek Primitive Baptist Church records, GDAH, 30, 33.

46. September 1822, Inferior Court Records, Trials of Slaves, Putnam County, Ga., GDAH. Nothing else is known about John Brown or any of his relatives who may have lived in the region. In the only other appearance of the name, in association with free people of color, a white man named Reuben Brown from adjoining Greene County had a free person of color—a fourteen-year-old boy—living with him in 1820.

47 Baldwin County, Trials of Slaves, 1812–1826, November 16, 1812, and April 18, 1815, GDAH; and James C. Bonner, *Milledgeville: Georgia's Antebellum Capital* (Athens: University of Georgia Press, 1978), 115.

48. Oliver Prince, *A Digest of the Laws of the State of Georgia* (Milledgeville: Grantland and Orne, 1822), 456–57.

49. *Acts of the General Assembly* 1806: 53.

50. Watkins, *Digest of the Laws of the State of Georgia,* 164, 167, 42. The 1801 law limiting manumissions to those granted through legislative act was eased in 1815 but fully reinstated in 1818.

51. Clayton, *Compilation of the Laws of Georgia,* 369; and Prince, *Digest of the Laws of the State of Georgia ,* 465–67. *Acts of the General Assembly* 1810. 117.

52. *Acts of the General Assembly* 1828: 177, and 1829: 170 and 175.

53. *Acts of the General Assembly* 1818: 130.

54. In *Slaves without Masters: The Free Negro in the Antebellum South* (New York: Pantheon Books, 1972), Ira Berlin argues that in the early 1800s free people of color were not generally seen as a threat to the rigid color and caste system in the South. Paranoia over free people of color increased as years passed, but the actions of the legislature and reports from the local branches of the American Colonization Society indicate that even before 1830 whites in Georgia had unreasonable concerns about the disruptive potential of that very small group. See also, James Maurice Gifford, "The African Colonization

Movement in Georgia, 1817–1860," Ph.D. diss., University of Georgia, 1977, 32, 33.

55. U.S. Census records for Hancock County, 1830–70.

56. In *Free Negro Heads of Families in the United States in 1830, Together with a Brief Treatment of the Free Negro* (Washington, D.C.: Association for the Study of Negro Life and History, 1925), 21, Carter G. Woodson includes twenty free people of color in west Georgia's Carroll County who bore Indian names. They too may have been the children of Indian women and black men, who acquired their free status through the condition of their mothers. Others elsewhere in the state probably had similar parentage, but they are not identifiable by name.

57. Will of James Hunt, HanCC. The DAR application of Mary Greene Smith of Atlanta mentions Judkins Hunt's burial on the "old Hunt plantation." That story is corroborated by Katherine Neal Hunt, who was born in 1891 and remembers the Hunt family cemetery from her youth. No records give the name of James Hunt's wife. Andrews, *Reminiscences of an Old Georgia Lawyer,* 13.

58. Will and inventory of James Hunt, HanCC. A supplemental inventory in 1819 showed six additional slaves: three women, Jehita, Dinah, and Lithia, and three unnamed "boys."

59. Exum Papers; and will of Judkins Hunt, January 1818, Book F., 177; Deeds and Mortgages, 1793–95; and Tax Digest, 1794, HanCC. The first Judkins Hunt died in 1817, but his will was written around 1810, following the death of his wife. Smith, *History of Hancock County* 2: 91, states that the Hunts owned five hundred slaves. That is an exaggeration, but a precise number is hard to come by. The 1860 census shows that James Hunt's five sons—James, Jr., Thomas, Judkins, Henry, and William—plus William's wife, owned over two hundred. That total would not have included slaves belonging to the first Judkins's four married daughters or other peripheral relatives. Forrest Shivers has generously shared information about Hancock County.

60. Will of James Hunt, HanCC; Daughters of the American Colonists, *Bible Genealogical Records,* 62; and Berlin, *Slaves without Masters,* 48.

61. *Georgia Genealogical Magazine,* 1968, 2169, will of John Finley, June 22, 1801, and 1966, 1313; and will of John Browne, in WarCC, Will Book A.

62. Will of Thomas Cobb, January 31, 1830, Will Book F, 147, GreCC.

63. The *Augusta Chronicle,* February 7 and November 14, 1807, and November 4, 1809. Prince, *Digest of the Laws of the State of Georgia,* 460. Discussion of journalistic commentary about free people of color appears in Berlin, *Slaves without Masters,* 31, 87, 96.

64. Milledgeville, *Southern Recorder,* June 19, 1830; and Gifford, "The African Colonization Movement," 32, 33.

65. The narrative of Henry Rogers discussed in chapter three attests to the generally kind and paternalistic treatment of the Hunt slaves.

66. *Second Annual Report of the Putnam Auxiliary Society for Colonizing the Free*

Persons of Color of the United States (Milledgeville, Ga.: Camak and Hines, 1821). The following information is taken from this pamphlet. Other auxiliaries in Georgia had been established in Jackson County and in the cities of Milledgeville, Augusta, and Savannah.

67. Ibid.; and Prince, *Digest of the Laws of the State of Georgia,* 463. Ruth Scarborough, *The Opposition to Slavery in Georgia Prior to 1860* (Nashville: George Peabody College for Teachers, 1933), 214. The Milledgeville (Baldwin County) and Putnam County branches drew their membership from Hancock, Greene, and Washington counties as well. The local organizations had no female members of record.

68. *Second Annual Report of the Putnam Auxiliary Society,* 3–52; and *The Missionary,* September 8, 1823.

69. *Second Annual Report of the Putnam Auxiliary Society ,* 3–52.

70. Ibid.

71. Ibid.

72. Ibid.; and *The Missionary,* November 29, 1824.

73. Scarborough, *Opposition to Slavery in Georgia,* 203.

74. African-American Family History Association, "Slave Bill of Sales Project," 1: 16. This transaction had no listed date.

75. *Second Annual Report of the Putnam Auxiliary Society.* These affluent white men were primarily interested only in controlling the black population, not in granting them freedom. With one possible exception—and that not until 1860—none of the original members emancipated any slaves so that they might emigrate to Africa under the society's auspices. Names of members of the society in Middle Georgia were cross-checked against the names and former owners of people of color who went to Africa compiled by Tom W. Shick in *Emigrants to Liberia 1820–1843: An Alphabetical Listing* (Newark: Dept. of Anthropology, University of Delaware, 1971); and the files of Debra Newman supplementing her Ph.D. dissertation, "The Emergence of Liberian Women in the 19th Century," Howard University, 1985.

76. U.S. Census records for Baldwin County, 1840. Wilhoit, *History of Warren County.* U.S. Census records for Taliaferro County, Ga., 1830–40. The 1830 census says Winslow Bird, but the 1840 census lists the name Williamson Bird.

77. E. Merton Coulter, *Old Petersburg and the Broad River Valley of Georgia: Their Rise and Decline* (Athens: University of Georgia Press, 1965), 39, 127; Theodore M. Banta, *Sayre Family: Lineage of Thomas Sayre, a Founder of Southhampton* (New York: De Vinne Press, 1901), 16; and records of the Mount Zion Presbyterian Church, 1813–59, GDAH. Although several sources corroborate the Sayres' presence in Hancock County during the mid-1820s, their names do not appear in the 1830 census.

II. Pomegranate Hall

1. Mary Moragne, *The Neglected Thread: A Journal from the Calhoun Community, 1836–1842,* ed. Delle Mullen Craven (Columbia: University of South Carolina Press, 1951), 146.

2. U.S. Census records for Hancock County, Ga., 1830–50. Scarborough, *Opposition to Slavery in Georgia,* 210. John Rozier, "Joseph Bryan, 1768–1861," Sparta *Ishmaelite,* August 13, 1981.

3. Aptheker, *American Negro Slave Revolts,* chap. 12, "The Turner Cataclysm," 293–324.

4. Bonner, *Milledgeville,* 117.

5. *Acts of the General Assembly* 1831: 223; 1832: 179; 1833: 202, 207, and 228; 1834: 228; 1835: 264–65, and 268; and 1838: 117.

6. *Acts of the General Assembly* 1841: 139; 1847: 105; and 1849–50: 405. Peter Wallenstein, *Slave South to New South* (Chapel Hill: University of North Carolina Press, 1987), 88–95, discusses the detrimental effects of prejudicial taxes on free people of color in Georgia.

7. *Acts of the General Assembly* 1843: 59.

8. Cooper and Worsham v. Mayor and Aldermen of Savannah, *Reports of Cases in Law and Equity Argued and Defended in the Supreme Court of the State of Georgia* 4: 68–75.

9. Lessie Brannen Brinson, "A Study of the Life and Works of Richard Malcolm Johnston," Ph.D. diss., George Peabody College for Teachers, Nashville, Tenn., 1937 (abstract); and Smith, *History of Hancock County* 1: 25.

10. Moragne, *Neglected Thread,* 144.

11. Richard Malcolm Johnston, *Autobiography of Richard Malcolm Johnston* (Washington, D.C.: Neale Co., 1900), 81.

12. Johnston, *Autobiography,* 81; and Paul M. Cousins, *Joel Chandler Harris* (Baton Rouge: Louisiana State University Press, 1968), 53. Also see Richard Malcolm Johnston, *Old Mark Langston, a Tale of Duke's Creek* (New York: Harper and Brothers, 1884).

13. Johnston, *Autobiography,* 80–83; and Andrews, *Reminiscences of an Old Georgia Lawyer,* 49.

14. Johnston, *Autobiography,* 85; Catherine Clinton, *The Plantation Mistress: Woman's World in the Old South* (New York: Pantheon Books, 1982), 80–85; and Suzanne Lebsock, *The Free Women of Petersburg: Status and Culture in a Southern Town, 1784–1860* (New York: W. W. Norton and Co., 1984), 68–72. Odom v. Odom, *Reports of Cases in Law and Equity* 36: 286–321.

15. Andrews, *Reminiscences of an Old Georgia Lawyer,* 39; and Forrest Shivers, *The Land Between: A History of Hancock County, Georgia to 1940* (Spartanburg, S.C.: Reprint Co., 1990), 111.

16. Johnston, *Autobiography,* 82, 83. Jean E. Friedman, *The Enclosed Garden,*

Woman and Community in the Evangelical South, 1830–1900 (Chapel Hill: University of North Carolina Press, 1985), addresses the centrality of the church in the lives of antebellum Southern white women.

17. Historic marker, Mount Zion Presbyterian Church. Records of Mount Zion Presbyterian Church, 1813–59, and Sparta Presbyterian Church, 1841–91, both GDAH; and Smith, *History of Hancock County* 1: 72, 124.

18. Smith, *History of Hancock County* 1: 24, 37; and Johnston, *Autobiography*, 80. Shivers, *Land Between*, 104.

19. *The Missionary*, February 2, 1824.

20. Felton, *Country Life in Georgia*, 249.

21. U.S. Census records for Hancock County, Ga., 1830–70; and Milledgeville *Southern Recorder*, July 30, 1834, List of Free Persons of Color in Hancock County Georgia, GDAH.

22. Ibid.; Deed book P, 609, and Deed book Q, 624, HanCC.

23. U.S. Census records for Hancock County, Ga., 1840 and 1850; Deed Book P, 213, Deed Book Q, 364, HanCC; and U.S. Southern Claims Commission, Mary Frazier, Claim no. 17402.

24. U.S. Census records for Warren County, Ga., 1840 and 1850. Mercy Joiner is listed as a single woman aged forty-one in 1840, and the children were four to six. In 1860 the group appears in newly formed Glascock County. There her age is given as fifty-eight, making it less likely but certainly possible that the teenaged children were hers.

25. U.S. Census records for Taliaferro County, Ga., 1840; and Registries of Free Persons of Color, 1829–64, Taliaferro County, Ga., GDAH.

26. Ibid.; and "Interview with Georgia Baker," in Martha F. Norwood, *Liberty Hall: Taliaferro County, Georgia* (Atlanta: Georgia Department of Natural Resources, 1977), 257. U.S. Census records for Taliaferro County, Ga., 1850.

27. Scarborough, *Opposition to Slavery in Georgia*, 184; U.S. Census records for Taliaferro County, Ga., 1860; and Norwood, *Liberty Hall*, 127–32, 257.

28. U.S. Census records for Greene County, Ga., 1850 and 1860; and October 1868, will of Ned Parks, Sr., Will Book G, 362, GreCC.

29. U.S. Census records for Putnam County, Ga., 1840 and 1850.

30. Milledgeville, *Southern Recorder*, March 15, 1832; Registries of Free Persons of Color, 1832–64; and U.S. Census records for Baldwin County, Ga., 1840 and 1850.

31. U.S. Census records for Baldwin County, Ga., 1850; Registries of Free Persons of Color, Baldwin County, 1833–1863, GDAH. George Rawick, *The American Slave: A Composite Autobiography* (Westport: Greenwood Press, 1972), vol. 13, *Georgia Narratives*, pt. 3, testimony of Ferebe Rogers, 209.

32. U.S. Census records for Baldwin County, Ga., 1840, 1850, and 1860. Milledgeville *Southern Recorder*, January 6, 1846; Lois W. Lane, "A History of Flagg Chapel Baptist Church, Milledgeville, Georgia" (photocopy), 1–3; Kate

Haynes Fort, *Memoirs of the Fort and Fannin Families* (Chattanooga: MacGowan and Cooke, Co., 1903), 221–23, 25; State v. Lavinia and Wilkes, *Reports of Cases in Law and Equity* (1858): 311–16. This case treats the two as slaves and cites the applicability of slave law. In the antebellum years, people of color apparently could not marry, according to law. Wilkes Flagg and Lavinia Robinson were married by a county official in September of 1865, immediately after the Civil War. Some sources argue that Flagg was born in Virginia, but the censuses list Georgia as his birthplace.

33. Baldwin County, Register of Free Persons of Color, 1833–63. *Acts of the General Assembly* 1834: 229; and Bonner, *Milledgeville,* 108. The name is alternatively spelled Marler, Marlor, and then Marlow.

34. *Acts of the General Assembly* 1833: 289.

35. U.S. Census records for Washington County, Ga., 1840 and 1850; Inferior Court Minutes, 1843–62; and Inferior Court Minutes, Book A, 1849–69, WasCC.

36. Sandersville *Central Georgian,* June 1, 1852.

37. Andrews, *Reminiscences of an Old Georgia Lawyer,* 62.

38. Store accounts of Rhodes and Rogers, and records of Mount Zion Presbyterian Church, GDAH. Savannah *Georgian,* July 8, 1826; and U.S. Census records for Hancock County, Ga., 1830.

39. John Linley, *Architecture of Middle Georgia: The Oconee Region* (Athens: University of Georgia Press, 1972), 80; Lane Mills, *Architecture of the Old South: Georgia* (Savannah: Beehive Press, 1986), 186; Frederick Doveton Nichols, *The Architecture of Georgia* (Savannah: Beehive Press, 1976), 244; Moragne, *Neglected Thread,* 144–51; Mrs. Terrell Moore, "Pomegranate Hall or Oliver House," *Sparta Ishmaelite,* May 9, 1963; Sparta-Hancock County Chamber of Commerce, "Landmarks of Historic Sparta," (n.d.); and U.S. Census records for Hancock County, Ga., 1830 and 1840.

40. U.S. Census records for Hancock County, Ga., 1830 and 1840; Free and Slave Schedules, 1850; and will of Nathan C. Sayre. Wills are filed alphabetically in HanCC and also appear in chronological books. Because the proceedings pursuant to final settlement were so complex and appear in dozens of locations in the chronological books, references herein are only given as "Will and Inventory" where the Sayre material is packaged all together. Nathan Sayre's will was executed in February 1850 and filed for probate February 1853.

41. Clinton, *Plantation Mistress,* 87, 111; and also addressed in Deborah Gray White, *Ar'n't I a Woman? Female Slaves in the Plantation South* (New York: W. W. Norton and Co., 1985), chap. 1, "Jezebel and Mammy."

42. Bishop Lucius Henry Holsey, D.D., *Autobiography, Sermons, Addresses and Essays of Bishop Lucius Henry Holsey, DD.* (Atlanta: Franklin Printing and Publishing Co., 1898), 9; Virginia Kent Anderson Leslie, "Woman of Color, Daughter of Privilege: Amanda America Dickson, 1849–1893," Ph.D. diss., Emory University, 1990, 143; and supplemental conversations with Leslie.

43. George Rawick, Jan Hillegas, and Ken Lawrence, eds., *The American Slave: A Composite Autobiography,* suppl., ser. 1 (Westport: Greenwood Press, 1978), vol. 4, *Georgia Narratives,* 372. John W. Blassingame, "Using the Testimony of Ex-Slaves: Approaches and Problems," *Journal of Southern History* 41 (Nov. 1975): 473–92, provides helpful guidelines and lays out potential pitfalls in using this material. Blassingame asserts that "the Georgia collection is one of the most reliable of the WPA volumes."

44. Rawick et al., *American Slave,* suppl., ser. 1, 4: 420; Felton, *Country Life in Georgia,* 79.

45. Odom v. Odom, *Reports of Cases in Law and Equity* 36: 296–97.

46. "Faithful concubinage" is used by Kenneth Little, "Some Aspects of Color, Class and Culture in Britain," in John Hope Franklin, ed., *Color and Race* (Boston: Beacon Press, 1968), 237.

47. Pomegranate Hall still stands at 322 Adams Street in Sparta. Descriptions are culled from personal observations; notes and photographs by Virginia Kent Anderson Leslie; oral accounts from Tony Poss, James Hight, John Gaissert, John Rozier, and Forrest Shivers. Unless otherwise indicated, descriptions and published photographs of the mansion and its furnishings and reports of activities there are culled from: Mills, *Architecture of the Old South,* 186; Linley, *Architecture of Middle Georgia,* 80, 81; Nichols, *Architecture of Georgia,* 244–45; Moragne, *Neglected Thread,* 144, 145; Moore, "Pomegranate Hall or Oliver House"; and Will and Inventory of Nathan Sayre, HanCC.

48. In another version of the designation of Pomegranate Hall as the "half house," sources argue that Nathan Sayre and his relatives quarreled over a house they inherited in New Jersey. Local legend has it that Nathan had his half of the house dismantled, loaded on a cargo boat, and shipped to Savannah, where the pieces were strapped onto ox carts and transported more than one hundred miles overland to Sparta. Since the granite foundations, bricks, and other construction materials of Pomegranate Hall are of local origin, the story seems unlikely in its entirety. However, Nathan and the other Sayres who went to Georgia *were* children of their father's second marriage to Margaret Stone, who died in 1814. Prolonged quarreling over the estate between the children of a first and second marriage could have led to the dismantling of the family house. In that case, Nathan may well have shipped mahogany doors, marble fireplace façades, and other architectural features from New Jersey, fueling the persistent legend of the "half-house."

49. Inventory of Nathan C. Sayre, HanCC, itemizes the titles of many of his books, including Alexander Walker's *Intermarriage; or, The Mode in Which and the Causes Why, Beauty, Health and Intellect, Result from Certain Unions, and Deformity, Disease and Insanity, from Others* (New York: J. and H. G. Langley, 1839) iii, 316, 320.

50. Moore, "Pomegranate Hall or Oliver House."

51. Pendleton billed Nathan Sayre's estate for attending several members of

Sayre's nonwhite family. Gladys-Marie Fry, "Harriet Powers: Portrait of a Black Quilter," in *Missing Pieces, Georgia Folk Art, 1770–1976* (Georgia Council for the Arts and Humanities, 1976), 16–22, 79; and Rawick et al., *American Slave,* suppl., ser. 1, 4: 674.

52. Milledgeville *Southern Recorder,* March 7, 1854.

53. Moragne, *Neglected Thread,* 89.

54. Ibid., 150.

55. Will and Inventory of Nathan C. Sayre, and Index to Deeds and Mortgages, Book B, 1838–78, HanCC. Elizabeth Garnes appears in Hancock County's registry of free people of color, GDAH. Also, oral accounts from John Gaissert, Sparta.

56. Shivers, *Land Between,* 64.

57. *Journal of the Senate of the State of Georgia* (Milledgeville: Polhill and Fort, 1829, 1830, 1838, 1842, and 1843); *Journal of the House of Representatives for the State of Georgia* (Milledgeville: Polhill and Fort, 1833). Nathan C. Sayre to Gov. George M. Troup, August 19, 1826; George R. Clayton to Nathan C. Sayre, August 26, 1826; Nathan C. Sayre to Governor George R. Gilmer, November 18, 1829 and February 17, 1831, Governors' Correspondence, GDAH. Andrews, *Reminiscences of an Old Georgia Lawyer ,* 104.

58. *Journal of the Senate,* 1830, 28, 61, 80, 109, 117, 338, 349, 375; 1838, 281; 1842, 74, 79, 211; and *Journal of the House of Representatives,* 1833, 154, 412.

59. *Journal of the Senate,* 1843, 258–59.

60. Charles Lyall, *A Second Visit to the United States of North America* (London: John Murray, 1849), 2: 18.

61. Andrews, *Reminiscences of an Old Georgia Lawyer,* 20, 24.

62. James C. Bonner, *A History of Georgia Agriculture, 1732–1860* (Athens: University of Georgia Press, 1964), 63, 67, 98, 112–14, 189, 193–94; Bonner, "Genesis of Agricultural Reform in the Cotton Belt," 475–500; Bonner, "A Georgia County's Historical Assets," *Emory University Quarterly* 9 (March 1953): 24–30; and Bonner, "Profile of a Late Ante-Bellum Community," 633–80.

63. Bonner, "Genesis of Agricultural Reform," 476–77.

64. Ibid.; and Smith, *History of Hancock County* 1: 70.

65. Milledgeville *Southern Recorder,* August 3, 1841; Bonner, "Genesis of Agricultural Reform," 478; Hancock County Manuscripts, Planters' Club of Hancock County, Ga., 1837–48, Folders 2, 3, 5, 7, GDAH.

66. John Gaissert, "Down the Road Some Things That Certain People Did," Sparta *Ishmaelite,* December 17, 1981; catalogue, Sparta Female Model School, 1838, GDAH; and WPA, *Georgia: A Guide to Its Towns and Countryside* (Athens: University of Georgia Press, 1940), 492. Lithograph of the Sparta Female Model School, from the Hargrett Rare Book and Manuscript Library, University of Georgia Libraries, Athens.

67. Gaissert, "Down the Road"; catalog, Sparta Female Model School, GDAH; and Smith, *History of Hancock County* 1: 23, 49.

68. Moragne, *Neglected Thread,* 145–50.

69. Ibid.

70. Ibid.

71. Felton, *Country Life in Georgia,* 32; and will of Nathan C. Sayre, HanCC. The census of 1870, the first in which the "free colored" Hunts appear at all, shows that the younger Susan stated she could read and write, while her sister Mariah said that she could not. However, documentation accompanying James Hunt's will in 1879 and an 1873 land purchase both show Mariah's signature. Mariah's daughters Adella, Sarah, and Lula all were accomplished musicians.

72. John Dollard, *Caste and Class in a Southern Town* (Garden City, N.Y.: Doubleday Anchor Books, 1957), 150.

73. Torrence, *The Story of John Hope,* 6–8; and oral accounts from Virginia Kent Anderson Leslie.

74. Moragne, *Neglected Thread,* 143–51; and will of Nathan C. Sayre, HanCC.

75. A. C. Sterling, "Sewing Up Hearts, Dr. Myra Logan Wins Them, Too," New York *Compass,* September 17, 1952; and private papers of Arthur Silvers, Santa Fe, N.M.

76. U.S. Census records for Hancock County, Ga., 1840; and oral accounts from Charles Hunt, Sparta, Ga., 1983.

77. Nathan Sayre's will, executed in 1850, indicates that he was planning an extended trip out of the country at that time. Nothing about that trip has been found to indicate whether or not Susan or his children accompanied him. None of them appear in the federal census compiled that summer in Hancock County.

78. Warrenton *Rural Cabinet* (n.d.), GDAH.

79. E. Franklin Frazier, *The Negro Family in the United States* (1939; reprint, New York: Dryden Press, 1951), 50.

80. Clinton, *Plantation Mistress,* 18, 21–22; also see Ann Firor Scott, *The Southern Lady: From Pedestal to Politics, 1830–1930* (Chicago: University of Chicago Press, 1970), 31. Susan Hunt is assumed to have been illiterate because she signed her mark "X" on papers pursuant to James Hunt's 1879 will.

81. U.S. Census records for Hancock County, Ga., 1840 and 1850.

82. These items are specifically reported in the inventory of Nathan Sayre's belongings, HanCC.

83. The younger Susan was described by her great-granddaughter Romie Turner of Sparta, Ga.

84. Inventory of Nathan C. Sayre, HanCC; and Moragne, *Neglected Thread,* 150.

85. Friedman, *Enclosed Garden,* 33; and Moragne, *Neglected Thread,* 149.

86. Oral accounts from Tony Poss and Linda Snead.

87. Records, Court of Ordinary, 1838–1853, January 7, 1839, HanCC.

88. Herbert G. Gutman, *The Black Family in Slavery and Freedom, 1750–1925* (New York: Pantheon Books, 1976), pt. 1, "The Birthpangs of a World"; and

Barbara Jeanne Fields, *Slavery and Freedom on the Middle Ground: Maryland during the Nineteenth Century* (New Haven: Yale University Press, 1985), 28.

89. Frazier, *Negro Family in the United States,* 50; and Ralph B. Flanders, "The Free Negro in Ante-Bellum Georgia," *North Carolina Historical Review* 9 (July 1932): 277.

90. Oral accounts from Hunt family members consistently confirm the legality of Mariah's "marriage" to Henry Hunt. The approximate time when they initiated that relationship is assumed from the date of birth of their first child, about 1854.

91. Oral account from Wanda Hunt McLean; "Henry Alexander Hunt" in *The National Cyclopaedia of American Biography* 27: 31–32; and Day, *Study of Some Negro-White Families,* Hunt-Logan, pl. 38, 33–34.

92. Holsey, *Autobiography,* 233, 238.

93. *Acts of the General Assembly* 1851–52: 262.

94. Will and Inventory of Nathan C. Sayre, HanCC.

95. Will and Inventory of Nathan C. Sayre, HanCC; George Barton Cutten, *The Silversmiths of Georgia: 1733–1850* (Savannah: Pigeonhole Press, 1958); the Milledgeville *Southern Recorder,* November 1, 1853; and information provided by Georgie Packwood, an authority on American antiques. The spoon bearing the hallmark "O. Childs" belongs to the author. It was engraved at a later date with the name "Adella." Presumably, each of Mariah and Henry Hunt's eight children was given a similar engraved spoon.

96. Milledgeville *Southern Recorder,* "Death Loves a Shining Mark," February 8, 1853; Sandersville *Central Georgian,* February 8, 1853; and Macon *Messenger,* February 9, 1853. Rev. Carlisle Beman was the son of Rev. Nathan Beman. Will and Inventory of Nathan C. Sayre, HanCC. The gravestone stands in Sparta's town cemetery.

97. Will Book B, 1829–68, 71–74, May 1839, BalCC.

98. Will of Robert Bledsoe, Will Book B, 252, PutCC; Hunter v. Bass, *Reports of Cases in Law and Equity* 18 (1855): 127–29; and Adams et al. v. Bass, 137–70.

99. Helen Tunnicliff Caterall, *Judicial Cases Concerning American Slavery and the Negro,* vol. 3, *Judicial Cases Concerning Slavery in Georgia* (Washington, D.C.: Carnegie Institution, 1932), 53, 54.

100. Will of Nathan C. Sayre, HanCC.

101. Will and Inventory of Nathan C. Sayre, HanCC. The previously mentioned case of Moses, the slave freed by Judkins Hunt, is an example of a slave granted his independence as a reward for long and faithful service.

102. Caterall, *Judicial Cases Concerning American Slavery and the Negro* 3: 86; and Will and Inventory of Nathan C. Sayre, HanCC. U.S. Census records for Richmond County, Ga., 1860.

103. Debra Newman graciously checked her private files for information about manumitted slaves who emigrated to Liberia.

104. Will of Nathan Sayre, HanCC; and U.S. Census records for Baldwin and Hancock counties, Ga., 1850 and 1860. Will and Inventory of Nelly Watkins, March 1874, Will Book FF, 203, 297, HanCC. Records of the Mount Zion and Sparta Presbyterian Church, 1813–59, GDAH.

105. Edward Forrest Sweat, "The Free Negro in Antebellum Georgia," Ph.D. diss., University of Indiana, 1957, 43.

106. Romie Turner from the Hunt family in Sparta explained the appellation "J. M."

107. Minutes of Superior Court, Hancock County, October 13, 1848, 498, GDAH.

108. U.S. Census records for Hancock County, 1850 and 1860; Will and Inventory of Nathan C. Sayre; will of James M. Hunt, 1879; and auxiliary documents, HanCC.

III. Plantation Life through the Civil War

1. No firm documentation proves that Mariah and Susan resided with Henry and J. M. Hunt, but no other explanation seems likely. The brothers lived with or near each other for decades, but no nonslave women, of any racial designation, are listed at their residences in the 1850 or 1860 censuses. In 1870 no adult male lived with Mariah. Henry A. Hunt lived elsewhere in the county but she bore Henry's children from 1854 through 1879. According to the 1860 census, J. M. owned a sixty-year-old female mulatto slave who had not been with him in 1850. Susan was probably at least ten years younger, judging from the ages of her children and the fact that she was alive in 1890. Since she had not been Nathan Sayre's slave, it would be surprising to find her considered J. M. Hunt's slave. Nonetheless, the mulatto slave reported as living on his plantation might have been Susan. Her age may have been incorrectly recorded, and the census marshal might have assumed that any woman of color was a slave.

2. Harriet Beecher Stowe, *Uncle Tom's Cabin; or, Life among the Lowly*, ed. Kenneth S. Lynn (Cambridge: Belknap Press, Harvard University Press, 1962) was serialized in 1851 and came out as a book in 1852. Mary H. Eastman, *Aunt Phillis's Cabin; or, Southern Life as It Is* (1852; reprint, New York: Negro Universities Press, 1960) was a typical pro-slavery novel.

3. *Acts of the General Assembly* 1851–52: 102, 262, 287, 436. J. William Harris, *Plain Folk and Gentry in a Slave Society: White Liberty and Black Slavery in Augusta's Hinterlands* (Middletown, Conn.: Wesleyan University Press, 1985), 56–57.

4. *Acts of the General Assembly* 1853–54: 104–5; 1857: 320, 199, 144; 1859: 68, 146; and Wallenstein, *Slave South to New South*, 93.

5. Bryan v. Walton, *Reports of Cases in Law and Equity* 20 (1856): 480. State

v. Lavinia and Wilkes, *Reports of Cases in Law and Equity* 25 (1858): 311. The court was ambivalent in this case as to whether laws applying to free people of color or to slaves should apply.

6. *Acts of the General Assembly* 1853–54: 104, 105; 1857: 199, 320; 1859: 68, 146; and U.S. Census records for Middle Georgia in 1850 and 1860.

7. Debra Newman's files list female emigrants to Liberia, 1843–65, to supplement "The Emergence of Liberian Women in the Nineteenth Century." The 1850–53 registries of free people of color in Baldwin County show that Richard Fo[a]rd and Elizabeth and Virginia Bugg lived together. Hunter v. Bass, The American Colonization Society v. Bass, and Adams v. Bass, *Reports of Cases in Law and Equity* 18 (1855): 127. Cuthbert's name appears in the *Second Annual Report of the Putnam Auxiliary Society,* 39.

8. Milledgeville *Southern Recorder,* March 15, 1853. Inventory of Nathan C. Sayre, HanCC.

9. U.S. Census records for Hancock County, Ga., 1830–60; agricultural and slave schedules, 1850 and 1860; Smith, *History of Hancock County,* 184.

10. U.S. Census records for Hancock County, Ga., 1830–70; and Smith, *History of Hancock County* 1: 184.

11. U.S. Census records for Hancock County, Ga., 1830–70. Oral tradition corroborates the suspicion that William fathered at least some of these children.

12. U.S. Census records for Hancock County, Ga., free and slave schedules 1860, 1870, and 1880; Hancock County Manuscripts, ledger books of T. J. Little, 1855–61; G. G. Morris, 1860; and Pharmacy, 1854, GDAH. The decreased number of J. M.'s slaves, combined with Henry's new ownership of them, might indicate that J. M. gave his youngest brother slaves when Henry married Mariah and became head of his own household.

13. U.S. Census records for Hancock County, Ga., 1840 and 1850; and Smith, *History of Hancock County* 2: 91.

14. Cluster analysis is derived from examination of the U.S. Census schedules in the eight-county region, 1850 and 1860.

15. U.S. Census records for Warren County, Ga., 1850 and 1860.

16. Identification of interlinked families combines census data with information from county registers of free persons of color; from the claims of Mary Frazier, no. 17,402, and John Ross, no. 9,136, to the Southern Claims Commission, NA; and from the wills of Nathan C. Sayre and Nelly Watkins, HanCC.

17. U.S. Census records for Bibb (Macon), Clarke (Athens), and Richmond (Augusta) counties, Ga., 1860.

18. Wills of Nathan C. Sayre and Nelly Watkins, HanCC. Nelly Watkins does not appear in the 1860 census, but she lived in Sparta before the Civil War and at least between 1862 and her death in 1874. U.S. Census records for Hancock County, Ga., 1860 and 1870, Warren County, Ga., 1860.

19. U.S. Census records for Baldwin County, Ga., 1850 and 1860. Will of Nathan C. Sayre, HanCC.

20. Elmcroft, from Jones County photographs in the Vanishing Georgia collection, GDAH. This description of the Hunt family plantation derives from those photographs.

21. Ibid.; Smith, *History of Hancock County* 1: 105. Photographs of similar baskets appear in the Georgia Writer's Project, *Drums and Shadows: Survival Studies among the Georgia Coastal Negroes,* introduction by Charles Joyner, (Athens: Brown Thrasher Books, University of Georgia Press, 1986), pl. XVc.

22. Except where otherwise cited as corroborating evidence, the information in the succeeding paragraphs comes from Rawick, *American Slave* 13, pt. 3, "Henry Rogers of Washington-Wilkes," 218–28.

23. U.S. Census records for Hancock County, Ga., 1860, agricultural and slave schedules.

24. "Down the Road: The Blind Hog Found Another Acorn," Sparta *Ishmaelite,* January 19, 1984.

25. Manuscript Collection, Hancock County, E. S. Ray ledgers, (n.d.), GDAH, show that Judkins Hunt purchased violin strings.

26. Rawick, *American Slave* 13, pt. 3, p. 222.

27. Rawick, *American Slave* 12, pt. 1, p. 127. The presence of brush arbors used by slaves in Hancock County has been confirmed by oral accounts from Charles Hunt.

28. Smith, *History of Hancock County* 1: 184, 40.

29. Presbyterian Church Records, Hancock County, GDAH.

30. Fort Valley State College Library, Founders' File, Fort Valley *Message,* November 1934; and Henry D. Spalding, ed., *Encyclopedia of Black Folklore and Humor* (Middle Valley, N.Y.: Jonathon David Publishers, 1972), 33. Many of the African-American Hunts from Sparta who went to Chester, Pennsylvania, early in the twentieth century affiliated themselves with the Presbyterian church there.

31. Index to Deeds and Mortgages, Book B, 1838–78, 366, HanCC; oral accounts from Charity Hunt, Katherine Neal Hunt, and Mae Harper Lucas; Hancock County Manuscripts, Pharmacist's Ledger, (n.d.), GDAH; and U.S. Census records for Hancock County, Ga., 1850 (slave schedule), 1860, and 1870.

32. Male ex-slaves whose narratives are included in Rawick, *American Slave* 12 and 13; and Rawick et al., *American Slave,* suppl., ser. 1, vol. 4, are Jasper Battle from Taliaferro County; Pierce Cody and Bryant Huff, Warren County; Isiah Green and William McWhorter, Greene County; and David Goodman Gullins, Putnam County. The women are Rachel Adams and Della Briscoe, Putnam County; Georgia Baker and Fannie Jones, Taliaferro County; Minnie Davis, Dosia Harris, Emmaline Kilpatrick, and Emeline Stepney, Greene

County; Edie Dennis and Mollie Kinsey, Hancock County; Amanda Jackson, Glascock County; and Snovey Jackson, Carrie Mason, and Ferebe Rogers, Baldwin County.

33. Rawick, *American Slave* 12, pt. 1, pp. 3, 39, 254, and pt. 2, p. 106.

34. Rawick et al., *American Slave*, suppl., ser. 1, 4: 372; Rawick, *American Slave* 12, pt. 1, p. 252, and pt. 2, p. 289.

35. Rawick, *American Slave* 12, pt. 1, p. 125, and pt. 2, p. 304; and Felice Swados, "Negro Health on the Antebellum Plantation," *Bulletin of the History of Medicine* 10 (1941): 465. Robert N. Fogel and Stanley L. Engerman, *Time on the Cross. The Economics of American Negro Slavery* (Boston: Little, Brown and Co., 1974), 109–26.

36. Rawick, *American Slave* 12, pt. 2, p. 104; and Scott, *Southern Lady*, 36.

37. Rawick et al., *American Slave*, suppl., ser. 1, 4: 420; E. M. Pendleton, "On the Susceptibility of the Caucasian and African Races to Different Causes of Disease," *Southern Medical Reports*, 1856, 336–42.

38. Rawick, *American Slave* 13, pt. 3, p. 209; and vol. 12, pt. 2, p. 304.

39. Ibid., vol. 12, pt. 1, pp. 127, 3, 257; pt. 2, p. 405.

40. U.S. Census records for Hancock, Greene, Taliaferro, Warren, Baldwin, and Glascock counties, Ga., and Hancock agricultural census, 1860. The fact that she was known by the appellation "Free Creecy" was shared by Lucretia Ruff's descendant, Edna Ruff Mayweather, Hancock County, Ga., 1990.

41. U.S. Census records for Baldwin County, Ga., 1860; Registry of Free Persons of Color; and Will Book B, 210, August, 1853, BalCC.

42. James Silk Buckingham, *The Slave States of America* (London: Fisher, Son and Co., 1842) 1: 199–200; Orland Kay Armstrong, *Old Massa's People: The Old Slaves Tell Their Story* (Indianapolis: Bobbs Merrill Publishing Co., 1931), 115. Discussions about household servants appear in Eugene D. Genovese, "Life in the Big House" in *A Heritage of Her Own*, Nancy F. Cott and Elizabeth H. Pleck, eds., (New York: Simon and Schuster, 1979), 290–97; and Jesse W. Parkhurst, "The Role of the Black Mammy in the Plantation Household," *Journal of Negro History* 23 (July 1938): 349–69.

43. U.S. Census records for the eight counties, 1850 and 1860. Registers of free people of color in Baldwin, Glascock, Hancock, Taliaferro, and Warren counties, GDAH. "List of Free Persons of Color Registered for the Year 1860," *Central Georgian*, August 8, 1860, Sandersville, Ga.

44. Edward A. Pollard, *Black Diamonds Gathered in the Darkey Homes of the South* (1859; reprint, New York: Negro Universities Press, 1968), 28; and Milledgeville *Southern Recorder*, June 20, 1844.

45. Harris, *Plain Folk and Gentry in a Slave Society*, 55; and Milledgeville *Southern Recorder*, September 27, 1832, November 13, 1833, February 12, 1834, April 26, 1836, March 8, 1837, March 19, 1839, January 8, 1840, February 9, 1841, February 6, 1844, December 1, 1846, August 5, 1851, January 3, 1854,

September 5, 1854, June 26, 1860, July 31, 1860, and March 19, 1861, GDAH.

46. WPA, *Georgia,* 494; and Milledgeville *Southern Recorder,* January 26, 1841, and July 11, 1865, GDAH.

47. Charles Ball, *Slavery in the United States: A Narrative of the Life and Adventures of Charles Ball, a Black Man* (1837; reprint, New York: Negro Universities Press, 1969), 489; *Acts of the General Assembly* 1853–54: 103.

48. *Acts of the General Assembly* 1855–56: 589.

49. Taliaferro County Ordinary, Register of Free People of Color, and Hutchinson family Bible records, GDAH. U.S. Census records for Taliaferro and Glascock counties, Ga., 1850 and 1860.

50. Free Persons of Color, 1855–62, Hancock County, GDAH.

51. GDAH, Free Registers, Baldwin, Glascock, Hancock, and Warren counties; U.S. Census records for Baldwin, Glascock, Hancock, Warren, and Washington counties, Ga., 1820, 1830, 1850, and 1860. Sandersville *Central Georgian,* August 8, 1860, GDAH. Bonner, "Profile of a Late Ante-Bellum Community," 674, 676.

52. Taliaferro County, Trials of Free Persons of Color, 1857–1858, GDAH.

53. Berlin also makes this suggestion in *Slaves without Masters,* 49.

54. July De Saussure testified on behalf of John Ross, Claim no. 9,136, before the Southern Claims Commission. He appears in the 1870 census for Baldwin County as a successful farmer. Bonner in *Milledgeville,* 236, claims that "July De Sauseaure" was a slave, but De Saussure's own testimony that he bought and sold cattle prior to the war argues that he was at least nominally free.

55. Sayre supervised the 1840 Hancock County census, and his signature is affixed to the document.

56. Frazier, *Negro Family in the United States,* 158; and White, *Ar'n't I a Woman?,* 35–37.

57. Berlin, *Slaves without Masters,* 163; Flanders, "The Free Negro in Ante-Bellum Georgia," 259; and Caterall, *Judicial Cases Concerning American Slavery and the Negro* 3: 88. The applicability of Georgia's "one-eighth" rule to Henry and Mariah Hunt's children cannot be accurately determined. Such designations are biologically indefensible as well as offensive, but if they were judged one-eighth black, the Hunt children would legally have been categorized as "Negroes," and if they were one-sixteenth black, they would not.

58. Flanders, "The Free Negro in Ante-Bellum Georgia," 264; and Joel Chandler Harris, *Free Joe and Other Georgia Sketches* (New York: Charles Scribner's Sons, 1881), 1, 8. *Acts of the General Assembly* 1861: 121.

59. Pollard, *Black Diamonds,* 55–58.

60. Oral accounts from Beulah Cooper and Rowena Hunt Bracken, Tuskegee, Ala.; Mamie McLendon Thomas; and Magnolia Hunt, Sparta.

61. Joel Chandler Harris, *Daddy Jake the Runaway and Short Stories Told after*

Dark (New York: Century Co., 1885), 119; and Frances Butler Leigh, *Ten Years on a Georgia Plantation since the War* (1883; reprint, New York: Negro Universities Press, 1969), 94.

62. Mary Karasch, "Anastacia and the Slave Women of Rio de Janeiro," in *Africans in Bondage: Studies in Slavery and the Slave Trade,* ed. Paul E. Lovejoy (Madison: University of Wisconsin Press, 1986), 84. Oral accounts from Rowena Hunt Bracken and Bess Bolden Walcott, Tuskegee, Ala.; and Rawick, *American Slave* 12, pt. 1, p. 256.

63. Eugene D. Genovese, *The World the Slaveholders Made: Two Essays in Interpretation* (New York: Random House, 1969), 45.

64. Oral accounts from Kate Dickson Lee, Jimmy Hight, Sparta, and Mamie McLendon Thomas, and private collection of the author.

65. Oral account from Kate Dickson Lee. The Old Paris porcelain cup is in the possession of the author.

66. James Weldon Johnson, *The Autobiography of an Ex-Colored Man,* 1927, reprint in *Three Negro Classics* (New York: Avon Books, 1965), 393, 394.

67. T. I. Little Ledgers, Hancock County Manuscripts, GDAH.

68. Deeds, Book S, 42, and Book FF, 203, HanCC.

69. Department of Commerce, Bureau of the Census, *Negro Population of the United States, 1790–1915* (Washington, D.C.: GPO, 1918), 57. Fields, *Slavery and Freedom on the Middle Ground,* chaps. 1–4.

70. Flanders, "The Free Negro in Ante-Bellum Georgia," 260.

71. Inferior Court Minutes, Book A, 1849–69, 191, WasCC.

72. U.S. Census records for Hancock County, Ga., 1870 and 1880; and Culp, *Twentieth Century Negro Literature,* 198. Della or Adella Hunt was probably named for her grandfather Nathan Sayre's sister Delia Sayre Watkins. The Sayre family also included the more unusual name "Adelia."

73. U.S. Census records for Taliaferro County, Ga., 1860. Caterall, *Judicial Cases Concerning American Slavery and the Negro* 3: 72. Ralph Betts Flanders, *Plantation Slavery in Georgia* (Chapel Hill: University of North Carolina Press, 1933), 272; Day, *Study of Some Negro-White Families,* 22, and pl. 15; and Leslie, "Woman of Color, Daughter of Privilege," 142. U.S. Census records for Richmond County, Ga., 1880, show Louise Wynn, a forty-nine-year-old widow living with her twenty-two-year-old daughter Jennie.

74. Oral account from Mamie McLendon Thomas. Lula Hunt's daughter Mamie remembers her mother's flower garden and the beautiful clothes she made. Adella and Sarah Hunt both played the piano and wrote music. Adella Hunt Logan, "Letters from Graduates," *Bulletin of Atlanta University,* December 1895.

75. Harris, *Plain Folk and Gentry in a Slave Society,* 64–65.

76. Smith, *History of Hancock County* 1: 129, 141; Harris, *Plain Folk and Gentry,* chap. 5, "The Strains of War."

77. Estelle W. Wilcox, *The Dixie Cook-Book* (Atlanta: L. A. Clarkson, 1883), 78.

78. Holsey, *Autobiography*, 11, 12.

79. Smith, *History of Hancock County* 1: 64 and 2: 91.

80. William and Harriet Sayre to James Thomas, 1863 and 1864, James Thomas Correspondence, GDAH; and oral account from Linda Snead, a descendant of William Handy Horton.

81. Southern Claims Commission, Claims of Mary Frazier, no. 17,402, Fulton County, Ga.

82. Harris, *Plain Folk and Gentry in a Slave Society*, 171; *Acts of the General Assembly* 1861: 69; Milledgeville *Southern Recorder,* October 6 and 13, 1863.

83. Milledgeville *Southern Recorder,* October 6 and 13, 1863; Atlanta *Daily Intelligencer,* October 17, 1863; and Superior Court Records, 1863, HanCC.

84. Harris, *Plain Folk and Gentry,* 169.

85. Milledgeville *Southern Recorder,* October 13 and December 15, 1863.

86. Atlanta *Daily Intelligencer,* October 17, 1863. A letter from Forrest Shivers to the author, October 26, 1983, provided information from HanCC records concerning the slave insurrection. Harris, *Plain Folk and Gentry in a Slave Society,* 167–69.

87. David P. Conyngham, *Sherman's March through the South with Strategies and Incidents of the Campaign* (New York: Sheldon and Co., 1865), 250; Arthur F. Raper, *Tenants of the Almighty* (New York: Macmillan Co., 1943), 70.

88. Conyngham, *Sherman's March,* 264–68.

89. Corydon Edward Foote and Olive Deane Hormel, *With Sherman to the Sea: A Drummer's Story of the Civil War* (New York: John Day Co., 1960), 216; Rawick, *American Slave* 12, pt. 1, p. 256; and George W. Nichols, *The Story of the Great March from the Diary of a Staff Officer* (New York: Harper and Brothers Publishers, 1865), 56, 62, 211.

90. Foote and Hormel, *With Sherman to the Sea,* 222. Marion Alexander Boggs, *The Alexander Letters, 1787–1900* (Savannah: privately printed for George J. Baldwin, 1910), 283.

91. Smith, *History of Hancock County* 1: 61; oral account from Kate Dickson Lee; and Fort, *Memoirs of the Fort and Fannin Families,* 222.

92. Southern Claims Commission, Claims of Mary Frazier, no. 17,402; John Ross, no. 9,136; and Currell Ross, no. 10,702.

93. Ibid.; and Fort, *Memoirs of the Fort and Fannin Families,* 222.

94. Smith, *History of Hancock County,* 1: 57.

95. Rawick, *American Slave* 13, pt. 3, p. 221.

96. Smith, *History of Hancock County* 1: 56.

97. Eliza Frances Andrews, *The War–Time Journal of a Georgia Girl, 1864–1865,* ed. Spencer B. King (1870; reprint, Macon: Ardivan Press, 1960), 347.

98. Sarah E. Shuften, Augusta *Colored American,* December 30, 1865. A male relative, Thomas Shuften, published that journal. The U.S. Census listed a free barber named Thomas Shuftel in Richmond County (Augusta) in 1860. This is probably the same family.

IV. On Hunt's Hill

1. Rawick, *American Slave* 12, pt. 1, p. 3.

2. Ibid.; and Rawick et al., *American Slave,* suppl., ser. 1, 4: 421.

3. Rawick, *American Slave* 12, pt. 1, p. 262.

4. Joel Chandler Harris, *Plantation Pageants* (Boston: Houghton, Mifflin and Co., 1899), 7–8; Rawick et al., *American Slave,* suppl., ser. 1, 4: 374; and Sidney Andrews, *The South Since the War: As Shown by Fourteen Weeks of Travel and Observation in Georgia and the Carolinas* (1866; reprint, Boston: Houghton, Mifflin Co., 1971), 352.

5. Andrews, *War-Time Journal of a Georgia Girl,* 223, 267, and 306.

6. J. T. Trowbridge, *The South: A Tour of Its Battlefields and Ruined Cities* (1866; reprint, New York: Arno Press, 1969), 486; and Ulrich Bonnell Phillips, ed., *The Correspondence of Robert Toombs, Alexander Stephens and Howell Cobb* (1913; reprint, New York: DaCapo Press, 1970), 692; Alexander Stephens to Howell Cobb, September 8, 1866.

7. Leigh, *Ten Years on a Georgia Plantation,* 238–39. C. Mildred Thompson, *Reconstruction in Georgia: Economic, Social, Political 1865–1872* (New York: Columbia University Press, 1915), 83; and Milledgeville *Southern Recorder,* January 2, 1866.

8. Macon *American Union,* October 29, 1869, quoted in Edmund L. Drago, "Militancy and Black Women in Reconstruction Georgia," *Journal of American Culture* 1 (Winter 1978): 841.

9. Andrews, *South Since the War,* 345–48.

10. Mary L. Edgeworth, *The Southern Gardener and Receipt Book* (Philadelphia: J. B. Lippincott, 1859), 157, 171, 240; Mrs. M. E. Porter, *Mrs. Porter's New Southern Cookery Book* (1871; reprint, New York: Arno Press, 1973), 144, 145, 220, 316, 397; Mrs. A. P. Hill, *Housekeeping Made Easy: Mrs. Hill's New Family Receipt Book for the Kitchen* (New York: James O'Kane, 1867), 21, 41, 144, 189, 194, 196, 235, 239, 288, 321; Wilcox, *Dixie Cook-Book,* 166, 170, 517; Jessica B. Harris, *Iron Pots and Wooden Spoons. Africa's Gifts to New World Cooking* (New York: Atheneum, 1989), xii–xiii, 75, 115; Waverly Root, *Food* (New York: Simon and Schuster, 1980), 278, 294, 582; and Hunt family traditions.

11. Dorothy Sterling, ed., *The Trouble They Seen: Black People Tell the Story of Reconstruction* (Garden City, N.Y.: Doubleday and Co., 1976), 77.

12. Andrews, *War-Time Journal of a Georgia Girl*, 341; and Myrta Lockett Avery, *Dixie after the War* (Boston: Houghton-Mifflin, 1937), 209.

13. American Colonization Society, *Annual Reports*, vols. 44–53, 1861–70 (1911; reprint, New York: Negro Universities Press, 1969), 51: 9; and Milledgeville *Union and Recorder*, June 11, 1873.

14. Smith, *History of Hancock County* 1: 57; United States Congress, *Testimony Taken by the Joint Select Committee to Inquire into the Condition of Affairs in the Late Insurrectionary States*, Georgia Sub-Committee (Washington, D.C.: GPO, 1872), 927. Also see Alan Conway, *The Reconstruction of Georgia* (Minneapolis: University of Minnesota Press, 1966); Elizabeth Studley Nathans, *Losing the Peace: Georgia Republicans and Reconstruction, 1865–1871* (Baton Rouge: Louisiana State University Press, 1968); and Edmund L. Drago, *Black Politicians and Reconstruction in Georgia: A Splendid Failure* (Baton Rouge: Louisiana State University Press, 1982).

15. Frank Watkins to W. H. Harrison, April 25, 1870, Incoming Legislative Correspondence, GDAH. No evidence links this Watkins family to Nelly Watkins and her kin.

16. Affidavits of Luke and Green Rhodes, February 27, 1866. Letters Received, Georgia Assistant Commissioner, Freedmen's Bureau, RG 105, NA.

17. Affidavit by Peter Storey, Letters Received, Georgia Assistant Commissioner, Freedmen's Bureau, RG 105, NA.

18. U.S. Congress, *Testimony Taken by the Joint Select Committee*, Georgia Sub-Committee, 923–33.

19. Ibid., 982–85.

20. Freedmen and Southern Society Research Project, University of Maryland, file A-5845, Washington County, July 1867.

21. Allen W. Trelease, *White Terror: The Ku Klux Klan Conspiracy and Southern Reconstruction* (New York: Harper and Row, 1976), chap. 14, "Georgia and Florida: Warren County and the Conservative Conquest of Georgia," 226–41.

22. Smith, *History of Hancock County* 1: 56.

23. Isabel Howland to Susan B. Anthony, September 28, 1897, Anthony-Avery Papers, University of Rochester.

24. U.S. Census records for Hancock County, Ga., 1870 and 1880.

25. *Acts of the General Assembly* 1866: 156, 239, 254, 146.

26. U.S. Census records for the eight-county region, 1870. Propertied families in the African-American community are defined here as those in which someone in the household had accumulated two hundred dollars or more in real and/or personal property. More than twenty residents of property-holding families residing in at least three separate households with more than two different surnames living in close proximity with one another satisfy the requirements for a neighborhood cluster. Only the larger clusters are included here.

27. HanCC, *Deeds,* Book S, December 3, 1869, 389.

28. U.S. Census records for Baldwin County, Ga., 1860 and 1870; and Agricultural schedule, 1870. The family name was given as "Ferrell" in the census reports prior to the Civil War.

29. Southern Claims Commission, Claims no. 9136, 10,702, and 17,402; BalCC, Deeds and Mortgages, Book N, 1867–71, 86; and Atlanta, Ga., City Directories 1875–85.

30. Fort, *Memoirs of the Fort and Fannin Families,* 222.

31. U.S. Census records for Baldwin County, Ga., 1870. There is a disparity between the main census schedule where Flagg's real property is valued at five hundred dollars and his personal estate at twelve hundred dollars, and the agricultural schedule which valued his land at five thousand dollars, plus improvements.

32. Phillips, *Correspondence,* 684; U.S. Census records for Baldwin County, Ga., 1870; Fort, *Memoirs of the Fort and Fannin Families,* 223; and Lane, "History of Flagg Chapel Baptist Church," 10, 21.

33. U.S. Census records for Hancock County, Ga., 1870; and Milledgeville, *Southern Recorder,* February 26, 1873.

34. U.S. Census records for eight-county region of Middle Georgia, 1870.

35. Frank Horne, "Henry A. Hunt, Sixteenth Spingarn Medalist," *Crisis* 20 (August 1930): 261; oral accounts from Katherine, Charles, Mae, and Charity Hunt, Mamie McLendon Thomas, John Gaissert, Tony Poss, and James Hight. Mamie McLendon Thomas to Donnie Bellamy, June 19, 1976. Index to Deeds and Mortgages, Book B, 1838–78, HanCC. Martha Ann Hunt was a party to six real estate transactions between 1861 and 1876, but none involved anyone else named Hunt.

36. HanCC, *Deeds,* Book S, June 23, 1866, 47. Lester F. Russell, *Profile of a Black Heritage* (Franklin Square, N.Y.: Graphicopy, 1977). Russell states, 53, that in 1876, "Zach Hubert and his brothers became the first black property owners of record in Hancock County, Georgia," but he is mistaken. Several free people of color owned property before the war, and even after emancipation other African-Americans in the county purchased property prior to the Huberts.

37. *Deeds,* Book FF, March 12, 1872, 143, HanCC.

38. February 25, 1873, Index to Deeds and Mortgages, Book B., 1838–78, 414, HanCC. Photograph of Louisa Horton, private papers, and family Bible from Arthur Silvers, Santa Fe, N.M. U.S. Census records for Hancock County 1870.

39. HanCC, *Deeds,* Book U, December 25, 1878, 630.

40. Watkins will and inventory, HanCC, 1874.

41. Oral accounts from Mamie McLendon Thomas, Rowena Hunt Bracken, and Katherine, Charity, and Charles Hunt; and U.S. Census records for Hancock County, Ga., 1870 and 1880.

42. Oral accounts from Mamie McLendon Thomas, Rowena Hunt Bracken, and Kate Dickson Lee. Thomas recalled that during her childhood (c. 1900) she and her sisters tried on clothes in the local stores, a privilege rarely extended to other people of color. Kate Dickson Lee, David Dickson's great-granddaughter, reported that she was served ice cream at the Sparta drug store, accompanied by her nurse, when she was a small girl.

43. Willie Snow Ethridge, "Spingarn Medal to Georgia Negro," Macon *Telegraph,* July 6, 1930; and oral accounts from Charles Hunt and Mamie McLendon Thomas.

44. Culp, *Twentieth Century Negro Literature,* 198; oral accounts from Mamie McLendon Thomas, Gladys Hunt Galamison, and Kate Dickson Lee.

45. Oral accounts from Charles Hunt, Romie Turner, and Mamie McLendon Thomas. List of Hancock County cemeteries, HanCC, and a visit to Hunt's Chapel. Sparta *Ishmaelite,* September 5, 1879.

46. Oral accounts from Mamie McLendon Thomas and Katherine Neal Hunt.

47. Drago, *Black Politicians and Reconstruction in Georgia,* 19–22; and Clarence A. Walker, "The A.M.E. Church and Reconstruction," *Negro History Bulletin* 48, no. 1 (Winter 1985): 10–12. Atticus G. Haygood, *Our Brother in Black: His Freedom and His Future* (1889; reprint, Miami: Mnemosyne Publishing, 1969), 233. During Reconstruction, Haygood estimated CME membership at 112,000, AMEs at 215,000, AMEZs at 190,000, and Baptists at 500,000. Sparta *Ishmaelite,* May 2 and 9, 1879. Bonner, *Milledgeville,* 210.

48. Holsey, *Autobiography,* 11; C. H. Phillips, *The History of the Colored Methodist Episcopal Church in America* (Jackson, Tenn.: CME Church Publishing House, 1898), 32; and Leslie, "Woman of Color, Daughter of Privilege," 131.

49. Holsey, *Autobiography,* 10, 22.

50. Ibid., 217–18, 238; and Haygood, *Our Brother in Black,* 240.

51. George M. Fredrickson, *The Black Image in the White Mind: The Debate on Afro-American Character and Destiny, 1817–1914* (1971; reprint, Middletown, Conn.: Wesleyan University Press, 1987), chap. 6, "Race and Reconstruction," and chap. 7, "The New South and Paternalism, 1877–1890." Williamson, *New People,* chap. 2, "Changeover, 1850–1915."

52. Writings by Jesse Kimbrough in the private papers of Arthur Silvers, Santa Fe, N.M.; and Holsey, *Autobiography,* 22, 217–18.

53. Oral account from Katherine Neal Hunt and Charity Hunt.

54. Mariah's name has no "h" on her headstone, but she signed her name "Mariah" and must have preferred that spelling. That tombstone gives 1837 as her birthdate, but 1833 has been used here because it has more corroborative evidence behind it. Mariah's stone, dated 1895, is the oldest one found at Ebenezer cemetery, but others must have been overgrown or rotted—or perhaps another earlier cemetery existed elsewhere. Nelly Watkins's 1874 will

clearly directs that she wanted to be buried next to her brother in the Ebenezer graveyard. No other cemeteries with any older stones marking the graves of people of color have been found in Sparta.

55. The Fort Valley High School *Herald*, October 1943. Oral accounts from Mamie McLendon Thomas and Wenonah Logan.

56. Oral accounts from Mamie McLendon Thomas and Rowena Hunt Bracken. Thomas is the child of Mariah's oldest daughter, Lula Hunt McLendon, and Bracken is the daughter of her oldest son, Will.

57. Rawick, *American Slave* 12, pt. 2, p. 113; and the Athens *Blade,* January 10, 1880.

58. Renee Cooper, "A Volunteer Looks at Black Education in Post–Civil War Georgia," *National Archives Bulletin,* June–July 1983. The American Missionary Association schools in Georgia and the Northern white women who taught in them are the subjects of Jacqueline Jones's *Soldiers of Light and Love: Northern Teachers and Georgia Blacks, 1865–1873* (Chapel Hill: University of North Carolina Press, 1980). Rawick et al., *American Slave,* suppl., ser. 1, 4: 420.

59. July 27, 1869, J. S. W. Johnson to E. A. Ware; December 6, 1869, J. R. Lewis to J. S. W. Johnson; May 24 and July 15, 1870, E. A. Ware to J. S. W. Johnson; and other similar correspondence, Records of the Superintendent of Education for the State of Georgia, Bureau of Refugees, Freedmen and Abandoned Lands, 1865–70, RG 105, NA.

60. "Guillville" appears only in these Freedman's Bureau records. It is not on any map of Hancock County.

61. U.S. Census records for 1860 and 1870. Reel 4, 1868–70 Freedmen's Bureau Supt. of Educ., Ga., school reports, Hancock County, RG 105, NA. Accounts from all over the South indicate that not only children but also adults came to the new schools seeking to learn how to read and write.

62. Annual Report, Supt. of Educ., Ga., Bureau of Refugees and Freedmen, September 30, 1866; and correspondence of James R. Smith, March 23, 1867. Augusta *Loyal Georgian,* May 9, 1867.

63. James R. Smith to G. L. Eberhart, Freedmen's Bureau Educational Records, Annual Report, Supt. of Educ., Ga., September 30, 1866, and March 23, 1867, RG 105, NA.

64. July 15, 1870, E. A. Ware to J. S. W. Johnson, Reel 5, and other correspondence in Reels 22 and 24, Supt. of Educ., Ga., RG 105, NA. U.S. Census records for 1870.

65. *Acts of the General Assembly* 1866: 59; and *Acts and Resolutions of the General Assembly of the State of Georgia* 1871–72: 281.

66. Charles Stearns, *The Black Man of the South and the Rebels; or, The Characteristics of the Former, and the Recent Outrages of the Latter* (reprint, New York: Negro Universities Press, 1969), 481–84.

67. October 9, 1869, R. M. Gladding to E. A. Ware, 20-B-1-a, E. A. Ware Papers, AU; Letters Received, ser. 631, Asst. Comm., RG 105, NA; *American*

Missionary, May, 1868, 101; and Katherine Du Pre Lumpkin, *The Making of a Southerner* (New York: Alfred A. Knopf, 1947), 98. There is some confusion in these sources as to whether Gladding taught in Greene or Warren County, or both.

68. Russell, *Profile of Black Heritage*, 57–59.

69. Milledgeville *Southern Recorder*, August 6, 1873 and July 8, 1874; Bonner, *Milledgeville*, 209; and *American Missionary*, May, 1871, 119.

70. Culp, *Twentieth Century Negro Literature*, 198; and oral accounts from Mamie McLendon Thomas and Rowena Hunt Bracken. These "aunts" would have been the wives of her white uncles.

71. Ethridge, "Spingarn Medal to Georgia Negro."

72. Culp, *Twentieth Century Negro Literature*, 198; and Henry A. Hunt, "Letters from Graduates," Atlanta University *Bulletin*, November 1895.

73. Trena Threatt Nelson, *Scramble (Sunshine, Rainfall, Sunshine—Such Is Life)* (Hicksville, N.Y.: Exposition Press, 1979), 13.

74. Oral accounts from Mamie McLendon Thomas, Katherine Neal Hunt, and Forrest Shivers. Shivers reports that the original Bass school building burned down in a fire of suspicious origin in 1889, but a new building, attended by Thomas and remembered by Hunt, was constructed on the same site. Mamie Hunt McLendon to Donnie Bellamy, June 10, 1976.

75. *Catalogue of the Officers and Students of Atlanta University*, 1870–85; and U.S. Census records for Hancock County, Ga., 1880, Sparta *Ishmaelite*, June 25, 1880; and Athens *Blade*, February 6, 1880.

76. Stearns, *Black Man of the South and the Rebels*, 484.

77. Sparta *Ishmaelite*, May 23, 1879. The "colored" teachers were included in the same article as the whites, but listed separately with no honorific included before their names. But these new young "colored" teachers were not ignored, nor was there any indication that the county applied inferior standards for them.

78. Laura A. Mason to Mary F. Chase, March 1, 1876, 20-B-3-c, E. A. Ware Papers, AU.

79. Richard Carter to W. J. Northen, May 3, 1879, and W. J. Northen to E. A. Ware, May 24, 1879, E. A. Ware Papers, AU. The misspelling and grammatical errors appear in the original Northen letter.

80. December 31, 1875, John L. Culver to President, Atlanta University, 20-B-3-g, E. A. Ware Papers, AU. *Acts and Resolutions of the General Assembly* 1874: 32–33. The state legislature approved an eight thousand–dollar appropriation for Atlanta University, provided that each member of the house of representatives was entitled to nominate one student for admittance and free tuition. Sparta *Ishmaelite*, October 3, 1879.

81. Minutes of the Superior Court of Fulton County, Ga., Book E, October term, 1867, 566. Four of the eight "colored" teachers certified by Hancock County in 1879 attended Atlanta University.

82. Clarence A. Bacote, *The Story of Atlanta University, A Century of Service,*

1865–1965 (Princeton: Princeton University Press, 1969), chaps. 1 and 2; and *American Missionary*, March 1872, 27.

83. In 1875 Ware reportedly stated that the time was not yet "ripe" to hire a nonwhite teacher. *American Missionary*, April 1874, 74. Atlanta University's first black teacher was Charles Rice from the class of 1881. who taught during the year following his graduation. Ware tried to persuade Adella Hunt to teach at Atlanta University in 1883, but she chose to go to Tuskegee Institute instead.

84. *Bulletins* of Atlanta University, 1869–81. Female students were only admitted to the four-year college program after 1880.

85. Jesse B. Loften to E. A. Ware, October 1, 1869; O. D. Robbins to E. A. Ware, January 25, 1876; A. M. Hill to Thomas Chase, May 20, 1876; and Laura Mason to Mary F. Chase, October 10, 1875, all 20-B-3-c, E. A. Ware papers, AU.

86. Leslie, "Woman of Color, Daughter of Privilege," 133.

87. *Catalogue of the Officers and Students of Atlanta University*, 1885.

88. Bacote, *Story of Atlanta University*, chap. 9, "Student Life: 1869–1929," 236–55; and *American Missionary*, November 1879, 338.

89. *Catalogue of the Officers and Students of Atlanta University*, 1869–80. Bailey attended Atlanta University from 1872–74, Ingraham from 1876–81, Marlow from 1869–71, and the Stephenses from 1876–80. *Reports of Cases in Law and Equity* 29 (1861): 553; *Acts of the General Assembly* 1834: 229. Norwood, *Liberty Hall*, "Georgia Baker," 257. Stephens did not formally manumit any of his slaves according to law, but apparently allowed them to live on their own with considerable independence. Spelling of the Marlow name was changed from Marlor.

90. *Catalogues of the Officers and Students of Atlanta University*, 1869–81, AU. This analysis is based on free people of color found in the U.S. censuses for the eight-county region 1830–60, supplemental information about the Hunt, Dickson, and Holsey families, material from the E. A. Ware papers, AU, and identification of people of color in the 1870 census who had accumulated over two hundred dollars in real or personal property.

91. E. B. Long to E. A. Ware, May 13, 1869, 20-B-3-c, E. A. Ware Papers, AU.

92. Day, *Study of Some Negro-White Families*, 22; Athens *Blade*, April 4, 1880; and U.S. Census records for Richmond County, Ga., 1880.

93. Pictures of Individuals Files, AU; *American Missionary*, 1878; and "H. H. J.," *Atlanta Republican*, July 24, 1877.

94. *Atlanta Republican*, July 24, 1877.

95. Athens *Blade*, January 10, 1880.

96. U.S. Census records for Hancock County, Ga., 1880; Mortality Schedule, 1879; and Sparta *Ishmaelite*, May 30, and July 18, 1879. The Mortality Schedule states that James Hunt died at seventy. Other census records indicate that he would have been sixty-eight, but the difference is insignificant.

97. Charles, Katherine, and Louie Hunt all recount the story of the grave-stone under the house.

98. Will and inventory of James M. Hunt, 78–84, Book FF, HanCC.

99. Ibid.

100. Oral accounts from Charles and Louis Hunt.

101. Athens *Blade,* October 31, 1879.

102. Athens *Blade,* April 22, 1880; and Nelson, *Scramble,* 14.

103. Leigh, *Ten Years on a Georgia Plantation,* 160.

104. John G. Mencke, *Mulattoes and Race Mixture: American Attitudes and Images, 1865–1918* (Ann Arbor, Mich.: UMI Research Press, 1976), 3; Culp, *Twentieth Century Negro Literature,* 198; and oral account from Houser Miller.

105. Josephine Pollard, "A Wonderful Baby," February 20, 1880; and Louise S. Upham, "More of Sun Than of Shade," October 31, 1879, both in the Athens *Blade.*

106. Gutman, *Black Family in Slavery and Freedom,* 87–93. This section addresses the dominant exogamous practices of people of African descent.

107. *Bulletin* of Atlanta University, December 1895.

108. Laura Mason to Mrs. Thomas Chase, October 18, 1875, 20-B-3-c (pt. 2), E. A. Ware Papers, AU.

V. The Hunt and Dickson Wills and More

1. Leslie, "Woman of Color, Daughter of Privilege," 170–71. Oral account from Mamie McLendon Thomas. The courthouse, finished in 1883, still dominates the town.

2. U.S. Census records for Hancock County, Ga., 1880. Sparta *Ishmaelite,* November 28, 1883. Leslie, "Woman of Color, Daughter of Privilege," describes life in Hancock County in the 1880s, chap. 3, "The Dickson Will," 156–204, as does Forrest Shivers, "The Land Between: A History of Hancock County, Georgia to 1940," manuscript, chap. 13, "The Rebirth of Agriculture," 339–60, chap. 14, "Transportation and Industry after the Civil War," 361–80, chap. 15, "The Churches after Emancipation," 381–95, and chap. 16, "The Schools and the Introduction of Public Education," 396–416.

3. Georgia, Dept. of Educ. Reports, 1880–90. Forrest Shivers, "The Land Between," 399, 401, 408.

4. Compiled from W. E. B. Du Bois, *The Negro Landholder of Georgia,* Bulletin 35, Department of Labor (Washington, D.C.: GPO, 1901), 660, 684–85, 726.

5. Sparta *Ishmaelite,* September 6, 1882, October 28, 1887, and June 1, 1888.

6. Information concerning the case of David Dickson's will is garnered from Leslie, "Woman of Color, Daughter of Privilege"; and Jonathan M. Bryant, "Race, Class and Law in Bourbon Georgia: The Case of David Dickson's Will," *Georgia Historical Quarterly* 71 (Summer 1987): 226–42. Will of David Dickson, Probate Court Records, HanCC, March 3, 1885.

7. Leslie, "Woman of Color, Daughter of Privilege"; Bryant, "Race, Class and Law in Bourbon Georgia," 233; and will of James M. Hunt, 78–84, Book FF, HanCC.

8. Sparta *Ishmaelite,* December 6, 1882; and Forrest Shivers to the author, March 21, 1983.

9. Both Thomas M. Hunt and his son, who bore the same name, were lawyers, but the senior Thomas died around 1880. Bryant, "Race, Class and Law in Bourbon Georgia," 234. Forrest Shivers to the author, March 21, 1983, states concerning the designation "Colonel" Hunt that "all members of the Georgia bar in that era were honorary members of the governor's staff and hence entitled to the honorific."

10. Bryant, "Race, Class and Law in Bourbon Georgia," 235–36; and Leslie, "Woman of Color, Daughter of Privilege," 176, 191–97.

11. Leslie, "Woman of Color, Daughter of Privilege," 200.

12. Ibid., 203, 233, 243; Catalogue of Atlanta University, 1881; and U.S. Census records for Richmond County, Ga., 1880.

13. Ibid., 199–203; and Bryant, "Race, Class and Law in Bourbon Georgia," 242.

14. Atlanta, Ga., City Directories, 1880–90.

15. Fort, *Memoirs of the Fort and Fannin Families,* 223.

16. *Savannah Tribune,* August 6, 1887.

17. Bryant, "Race, Class and Law in Bourbon Georgia," 242.

18. Sparta *Ishmaelite,* March 26, 1880.

19. James M. Hunt Inventory, HanCC. A number of these receipts dated between 1886 and 1889 remain in the support documentation for J. M. Hunt's will. Susan's one thousand dollars in annual dividends can be compared, for example, with the annual salary of fifteen hundred dollars paid Atlanta University's president in 1880.

20. Arbitration proceedings pursuant to the will of James M. Hunt, April 8 and 16, 1890, HanCC.

21. Most financial experts allow for a multiplier factor of at least fifteen between 1890 and today's dollars, suggesting that Susan's inheritance of $17,544 for the stock alone is equivalent to over a quarter of a million dollars today. Some of the older Susan Hunt's children and grandchildren joined in the suit. They were her daughter Susan, her son James Herbert, and their children Aleck, Henry, James, Mark, and Oscar Hunt, Mariah Hunt Miller, Susie Hunt Rogers, and Mary Hunt Bacon. Nothing has been discovered concerning the absence of

Mariah and her children from this suit. Perhaps her marriage to Henry Hunt tied her more securely to the white branch of the family. It has been impossible to discover if the land in Linton originally came from Sayre or the white Hunt family. Shivers, *The Land Between,* 339–40, accounts for almost one thousand acres of land belonging to the older Susan's grandchildren in 1892. In the 1980s Oscar Hunt's son Louie still lived on the land near Linton that Susan Hunt inherited. Charles DuBose had been ill since that spring and died in October 1890, just a few months after the final settlement of J. M. Hunt's estate.

22. Will, inventory, and accounting of the estate of Nathan C. Sayre, 1850–68, and will of James Hunt, HanCC.

23. Oral account from Katherine Neal Hunt.

24. Agricultural census for Hancock County, 1880. Sparta *Ishmaelite,* June–November 1881, April 26, 1889, and May 24, 1895. Shivers informed the author about the arson at Bass Academy.

25. Oral account from Beulah Cooper, Tuskegee, Alabama.

26. Rowena Hunt Bracken to Donnie Bellamy, April 9, 1976; and oral accounts from Bracken.

27. Mamie McLendon Thomas to Donnie Bellamy, June 10, 1976; and oral accounts from Thomas.

28. Adele Logan Alexander, "Grandmother, Grandfather, W. E. B. Du Bois and Booker T. Washington," *Crisis* 73, February 1983, 8–11; and "How I Discovered My Grandmother, and the Truth about Black Women and the Suffrage Movement," *Ms.,* November 1983, 29–33. Oral accounts from Edward Taylor, Beulah Cooper, and Louise Logan. W. E. B. Du Bois, "The Princess of the Hither Isles" in *Darkwater,* 75. The "princess" in Du Bois's fable, first conceived by him about 1916, lived in an alien and remote land, under the domination of an evil king. Ultimately her emotional distress prompted her to leap to her death from a precipice. Adella Hunt Logan killed herself when she jumped from a high window in late 1915.

29. *General Catalogue of Atlanta University, 1867 1929,* 88; W. E. B. Du Bois, "The Significance of Henry Hunt."

30. Oral accounts from Rowena Hunt Bracken, Mamie McLendon Thomas, and Arthur Silvers. Linda O. McMurry, *George Washington Carver, Scientist and Symbol* (New York: Oxford University Press, 1981), 48, 120–21.

31. Oral accounts from Mamie McLendon Thomas; and city directories, Savannah, Georgia, 1900–10.

32. Oral accounts from Mamie McLendon Thomas; Du Bois, "The Significance of Henry Hunt," 6. Johnson, *Autobiography of an Ex-Colored Man,* 511. Adella Hunt Logan to Emily Howland, April 23, 1906, Emily Howland Collection, Cornell University.

33. Hallie Q. Brown, *Homespun Heroines and Other Women of Distinction* (1926; reprint, New York: Oxford University Press, 1988), 233–34.

34. Gloria T. Hull, Patricia Bell Scott, and Barbara Smith, eds., *All the Women Are White, All the Blacks Are Men, But Some of Us Are Brave: Black Women's Studies* (Old Westbury, N.Y.: Feminist Press, 1981).

Selected Bibliography and Sources

Primary Sources: Books

Adair, James. *History of the American Indians, Particularly Those Natives Adjoining to the Mississippi, East and West Florida, Georgia, South and North Carolina, and Virginia.* London: Edward and Charles Dilly, 1775.

Allen, William Francis, Charles Pickard Ware, and Lucy McKim Garrison, eds. *Slave Songs of the United States.* New York: A. Simpson and Co., 1867.

American Colonization Society. *Annual Reports 1818–1910.* 1911. Reprint, New York: Negro Universities Press, 1969.

Andrews, Eliza Frances. *The War-Time Journal of a Georgia Girl, 1864–1865* Ed. Spencer B. King. 1870. Reprint, Macon: Ardivan Press, 1960.

Andrews, Garnett. *Reminiscences of an Old Georgia Lawyer.* Atlanta: Franklin Printing House, 1870.

Andrews, Sidney. *The South Since the War: As Shown by Fourteen Weeks of Travel and Observation in Georgia and the Carolinas.* 1866. Reprint, Boston: Houghton Mifflin Co., 1971.

Armstrong, Orland Kay. *Old Massa's People: The Old Slaves Tell Their Story.* Indianapolis: Bobbs Merrill Publishing Co., 1931.

Atlanta University. *Social and Physical Condition of Negroes in Cities. Report of an Investigation under the Direction of Atlanta University: And Proceedings of the Second Conference for the Study of Problems Concerning Negro City Life.* Atlanta University Publications no. 2. Atlanta: Atlanta University Press, 1897.

Ball, Charles. *Slavery in the United States: A Narrative of the Life and Adventures of Charles Ball, a Black Man.* 1837. Reprint, New York: Negro Universities Press, 1969.

Blassingame, John W., ed. *Slave Testimony: Two Centuries of Letters, Speeches, Interviews and Autobiographies.* Baton Rouge: Louisiana State University Press, 1977.

Boggs, Marion Alexander. *The Alexander Letters, 1787–1900.* Savannah: privately printed for George J. Baldwin, 1910.

Brown, Hallie Q. *Homespun Heroines and Other Women of Distinction.* 1926. Reprint, New York: Oxford University Press, 1988.

Brown, John. *Slave Life in Georgia*. Ed. L. A. Chamerovzov. London, 1855.

Buckingham, James Silk. *The Slave States of America*. London: Fisher, Son and Co., 1842.

Burge, Dolly Sumner Lunt. *The Diary of Dolly Sumner Lunt Burge*. Ed. James I. Robertson, Jr. Athens: University of Georgia Press, 1902.

Caterall, Helen Tunnicliff. *Judicial Cases Concerning American Slavery and the Negro*. Vol. 3, *Judicial Cases Concerning Slavery in Georgia*. Washington, D.C.: Carnegie Institution, 1932.

Chappell, Absalom H. *Miscellanies of Georgia: Historical, Biographical, Descriptive, Etc*. Atlanta: James F. Meegan, 1874.

Cook, Anna Maria Green. *Journal of a Milledgeville Girl, 1861–1867*. Ed. James C. Bonner. Athens: University of Georgia Press, 1964.

Conyngham, David P. *Sherman's March through the South with Strategies and Incidents of the Campaign*. New York: Sheldon and Co., 1865.

Culp, D. W., ed. *Twentieth Century Negro Literature; or, A Cyclopedia of Thought on the Vital Topics Relating to the American Negro*. Atlanta: J. L. Nichols and Co., 1902.

Du Bois, W. E. B. *Darkwater: Voices from within the Veil*. 1920. Reprint, New York: Schocken Books, 1969.

———. *The Souls of Black Folk*. 1903. Reprint, Chicago: A. C. McClurg and Co., 1940.

Edgeworth, Mary L. *The Southern Gardener and Receipt Book*. Philadelphia: J. B. Lippincott, 1859.

Felton, Rebecca Latimer. *Country Life in Georgia in the Days of My Youth*. 1919. Reprint, New York: Arno Press, 1980.

Foote, Corydon Edward, and Olive Deane Hormel. *With Sherman to the Sea: A Drummer's Story of the Civil War*. New York: John Day Co., 1960.

Hill, Mrs. A. P. *Housekeeping Made Easy: Mrs. Hill's New Family Receipt Book for the Kitchen*. New York: James O'Kane, 1867.

Haygood, Atticus G. *Our Brother in Black: His Freedom and His Future*. 1889. Reprint, Miami: Mnemosyne Publishing, 1969.

Holsey, Lucius Henry. *Autobiography, Sermons, Addresses and Essays of Bishop Lucius Henry Holsey, D.D*. Atlanta: Franklin Printing and Publishing Co., 1898.

Johnston, Richard Malcolm. *Autobiography of Richard Malcolm Johnston*. Washington, D.C.: Neale Co., 1900.

Kemble, Fanny. *Journal of Residence on a Georgia Plantation*. Ed. John A. Scott. New York: Knopf Publishers, 1961.

Leigh, Frances Butler. *Ten Years on a Georgia Plantation since the War*. 1883. Reprint, New York: Negro Universities Press, 1969.

Lerner, Gerda, ed. *Black Women in White America, a Documentary History*. New York: Random House, 1972.

Logan, Adella Hunt. "Prenatal and Hereditary Influences." In Atlanta University Publications no. 2, *Social and Physical Condition of Negroes in Cities.* Atlanta: Atlanta University Press, 1897.

Lyall, Charles. *A Second Visit to the United States of North America.* Vol. 2. London: John Murray, 1849.

Mauelshagen, Carl, and Gerald H. Davis, trans. and eds. *Partners in the Lord's Work: The Diaries of Two Moravian Missionaries in the Creek Indian Country, 1807–1813.* Research Paper no. 21. Atlanta: Georgia State College, 1969.

Moragne (Davis), Mary. *The Neglected Thread: A Journal from the Calhoun Community, 1836–1842.* Ed. Delle Mullen Craven. Columbia: University of South Carolina Press, 1951.

Nelson, Trena Threatt. *Scramble (Sunshine, Rainfall, Sunshine—Such Is Life).* Hicksville, N.Y.: Exposition Press, 1979.

Nichols, George W. *The Story of the Great March from the Diary of a Staff Officer.* New York: Harper and Brothers Publishers, 1865.

Pendleton, E. M. "On the Susceptibility of the Caucasian and African Races to Different Causes of Disease." In *Southern Medical Reports.* Atlanta, 1856.

Phillips, C. H. *The History of the Colored Methodist Episcopal Church in America.* Jackson, Tenn.: C.M.E. Church Publishing House, 1898.

Phillips, Ulrich Bonnell, ed. *The Correspondence of Robert Toombs, Alexander Stephens and Howell Cobb.* 1913. Reprint, New York: DaCapo Press, 1970.

Pollard, Edward A. *Black Diamonds Gathered in the Darkey Homes of the South.* 1859. Reprint, New York: Negro Universities Press, 1968.

Porter, Mrs. M. E. *Mrs. Porter's New Southern Cookery Book.* 1871. Reprint, New York: Arno Press, 1973.

Rawick, George, ed. *The American Slave: A Composite Autobiography.* Vols. 12 and 13, *Georgia Narratives.* Westport: Greenwood Press, 1972.

Rawick, George, Jan Hillegas, and Ken Lawrence, eds. *The American Slave: A Composite Autobiography.* Supplement. Series 1, vol. 4, *Georgia Narratives.* Westport: Greenwood Press, 1978.

Second Annual Report of the Putnam Auxiliary Society for Colonizing the Free Persons of Color of the United States. Milledgeville, Ga.: Camak and Hines, 1821.

Stearns, Charles. *The Black Man of the South and the Rebels; or, The Characteristics of the Former, and the Recent Outrages of the Latter.* Reprint. New York: Negro Universities Press, 1969.

Sterling, Dorothy, ed. *The Trouble They Seen: Black People Tell the Story of Reconstruction.* Garden City, N.Y.: Doubleday and Co. 1976.

———. *We Are Your Sisters: Black Women in the Nineteenth Century.* New York: W. W. Norton and Co., 1984.

Trowbridge, J. T. *The South: A Tour of Its Battlefields and Ruined Cities.* 1866. Reprint, New York: Arno Press, 1969.

Walker, Alexander. *Intermarriage; or, The Mode in Which and the Causes Why,*

Beauty, Health and Intellect, Result from Certain Unions, and Deformity, Disease and Insanity, from Others. New York: J. and H. G. Langley, 1839.

Wilcox, Estelle W. *The Dixie Cook-Book.* Atlanta: L. A. Clarkson, 1883.

Secondary Sources: Books

Aptheker, Herbert. *American Negro Slave Revolts.* 1943. Reprint, New York: International Publishers, 1963.

Bacote, Clarence A. *The Story of Atlanta University: A Century of Service, 1865–1965.* Princeton: Princeton University Press, 1969.

Banta, Theodore M. *Sayre Family: Lineage of Thomas Sayre, a Founder of Southampton.* New York: De Vinne Press, 1901.

Berlin, Ira. *Slaves without Masters: The Free Negro in the Antebellum South.* New York: Pantheon Books, 1972.

Blassingame, John W. *The Slave Community: Plantation Life in the Antebellum South.* Rev. and enl. ed. New York: Oxford University Press, 1979.

Bonner, James C. *A History of Georgia Agriculture, 1732–1860.* Athens: University of Georgia Press, 1964.

———. *Milledgeville: Georgia's Antebellum Capital.* Athens: University of Georgia Press, 1978.

Botkin, B. A. *A Treasury of Southern Folklore.* New York: Bonanza Books, 1980.

Brodie, Fawn. *Thomas Jefferson: An Intimate History.* New York: W. W. Norton, 1974.

Clinton, Catherine. *The Plantation Mistress: Woman's World in the Old South.* New York: Pantheon Books, 1982.

Conway, Alan. *The Reconstruction of Georgia.* Minneapolis: University of Minnesota Press, 1966.

Coulter, E. Merton. *Old Petersburg and the Broad River Valley of Georgia: Their Rise and Decline.* Athens: University of Georgia Press, 1965.

Cousins, Paul M. *Joel Chandler Harris.* Baton Rouge: Lousiana State University Press, 1968.

Curry, Leonard P. *The Free Black in Urban America, 1800–1850: The Shadow of the Dream.* Chicago: University of Chicago Press, 1981.

Cutten, George Barton. *The Silversmiths of Georgia, 1733–1850.* Savannah: Pigeonhole Press, 1958.

Davis, Angela. *Women, Race and Class.* New York: Random House, 1981.

Day, Caroline Bond. *A Study of Some Negro-White Families in the United States.* Cambridge: Harvard University Press, 1932.

Dollard, John. *Caste and Class in a Southern Town.* Garden City, N.Y.: Doubleday Anchor Press, 1957.

Drago, Edmund L. *Black Politicians and Reconstruction in Georgia: A Splendid Failure.* Baton Rouge: Louisiana State University Press, 1982.

Du Bois, W. E. Burghardt. *Black Reconstruction, 1860–1880*. New York: Harcourt, Brace and Co., 1935.

———. *The Negro Landholder of Georgia*. Bulletin 35, Department of Labor. Washington, D.C.: Government Printing Office, 1901.

Engelman, G. J. *Labor Among Primitive Peoples*. St. Louis: J. H. Chambers. 1882.

Fields, Barbara J. "Ideology and Race in American History." In *Region, Race and Reconstruction: Essays in Honor of C. Vann Woodward*, ed. J. Morgan Kousser and James M. McPherson. New York: Oxford University Press, 1982.

———. *Slavery and Freedom on the Middle Ground: Maryland during the Nineteenth Century*. New Haven: Yale University Press, 1985.

Flanders, Ralph Betts. *Plantation Slavery in Georgia*. Chapel Hill: University of North Carolina Press, 1933.

Flynn, Charles L., Jr. *White Land, Black Labor: Caste and Class in Late Nineteenth-Century Georgia*. Baton Rouge: Louisiana State University Press, 1983.

Fogel, Robert N., and Stanley L. Engerman. *Time on the Cross: The Economics of American Negro Slavery*. Boston: Little, Brown and Co., 1974.

Fort, Kate Haynes. *Memoirs of the Fort and Fannin Families*. Chattanooga: MacGowan and Cooke, Co., 1903.

Fox-Genovese, Elizabeth. *Within the Plantation Household. Black and White Women of the Old South*. Chapel Hill: University of North Carolina Press, 1988.

Franklin, John Hope, ed. *Color and Race*. Boston: Beacon Press, 1968.

Frazier, E. Franklin. *The Negro Family in the United States*. 1939. Rev. and abr. ed. New York: Dryden Press, 1951.

Fredrickson, George M. *The Black Image in the White Mind: The Debate on Afro-American Character and Destiny, 1817–1914*. Middletown, Conn.: Wesleyan University Press, 1971.

Friedman, Jean E. *The Enclosed Garden: Woman and Community in the Evangelical South, 1830–1900*. Chapel Hill: University of North Carolina Press, 1985.

Fry, Gladys-Marie. "Harriet Powers: Portrait of a Black Quilter." In *Missing Pieces, Georgia Folk Art, 1770–1976*, 16–22. Georgia Council for the Arts and Humanities, 1976.

Genovese, Eugene D. "Life in the Big House." In *A Heritage of Her Own*, ed. Nancy F. Cott and Elizabeth H. Pleck. New York: Simon and Schuster, 1979.

———. *Roll, Jordan, Roll: The World the Slaves Made*. New York: Pantheon Books, 1972.

———. *The World the Slaveholders Made: Two Essays in Interpretation*. New York: Random House, 1969.

Gilbert, William Harlen. *Eastern Cherokee Social Organization*. Chicago: University of Chicago Libraries, 1935.

———. *The Eastern Cherokees*. Smithsonian Institution, Bureau of American Ethnology, Bulletin 133. New York: AMS Press, 1948.

Gutman, Herbert G. *The Black Family in Slavery and Freedom, 1750–1925*. New York: Pantheon Books, 1976.

————. "Marital and Sexual Norms among Slave Women." In *A Heritage of Her Own*, Ed. Nancy F. Cott and Elizabeth H. Pleck, 298–310. New York: Simon and Schuster, 1979.

Gwin, Minrose C. *Black and White Women of the Old South: The Peculiar Sisterhood in American Literature*. Knoxville: University of Tennessee Press, 1985.

Halliburton, Rudi, Jr. *Red over Black: Black Slavery among the Cherokee Indians*. Westport, Conn.: Greenwood Press, 1977.

Hamel, Paul B., and Mary U. Chiltoskey. *Cherokee Plants and Their Uses: A 400 Year History*. Sylva, N.C.: Herald Publishing Co., 1975.

Harris, J. William. *Plain Folk and Gentry in a Slave Society: White Liberty and Black Slavery in Augusta's Hinterlands*. Middletown, Conn.: Wesleyan University Press, 1985.

Harris, Jessica B. *Iron Pots and Wooden Spoons. Africa's Gifts to New World Cooking*. New York: Atheneum, 1989.

Harris, Joel Chandler. *Daddy Jake the Runaway and Short Stories Told after Dark*. New York: Century Co., 1885.

————. *Free Joe and Other Georgia Sketches*. New York: Charles Scribner's Sons, 1881.

————. *Plantation Pageants*. Boston: Houghton, Mifflin and Co., 1899.

Houston, Martha Lou. *Marriages and Land Lottery Records in Hancock County, Georgia, 1806–1850*. Ann Arbor: Edwards Brothers, 1947.

Hudson, Charles M., ed. *Red, White and Black: Symposium on Indians in the Old South*. Southern Anthropological Society Proceedings no. 5. Athens: University of Georgia Press, 1971.

————. *The Southeast Indians*. Knoxville: University of Tennessee Press, 1976.

Hull, Gloria T., Patricia Bell Scott, and Barbara Smith, eds. *All the Women Are White, All the Blacks Are Men, But Some of Us Are Brave: Black Women's Studies*. Old Westbury, N.Y.: Feminist Press, 1981.

Johnson, James Weldon. *The Autobiography of an Ex-Colored Man*. 1927. In *Three Negro Classics*, ed. Arna Bontemps. New York: Avon Books, 1965.

Johnson, Michael P., and Roark, James L. *Black Masters: A Free Family of Color in the Old South*. New York: W. W. Norton and Co., 1984.

Johnston, Richard Malcolm. *Dukesborough Tales*. New York: Harper and Brothers, 1883.

————. *Old Mark Langston, a Tale of Duke's Creek*. New York: Harper and Brothers, 1884.

————. *Old Times in Middle Georgia*. New York: Macmillan Co., 1897.

Jones, Jacqueline. *Labor of Love, Labor of Sorrow: Black Women, Work and the Family, from Slavery to the Present*. New York: Pantheon Books, 1985.

———. *Soldiers of Light and Love: Northern Teachers and Georgia Blacks, 1865–1873*. Chapel Hill: University of North Carolina Press, 1980.

Jordan, Winthrop D. *White over Black: American Attitudes toward the Negro: 1550–1812*. Chapel Hill: University of North Carolina Press, 1968.

Karasch, Mary. "Anastacia and the Slave Women of Rio de Janeiro." In *Africans in Bondage: Studies in Slavery and the Slave Trade*, ed. Paul E. Lovejoy. Madison: University of Wisconsin Press, 1986.

Knight, Lucian Lamar. *Georgia's Landmarks, Memorials and Legends*. Atlanta: Byrd Printing Co., 1913.

Lebsock, Suzanne. *The Free Women of Petersburg: Status and Culture in a Southern Town, 1784–1860*. New York: W. W. Norton and Co., 1984.

Lewis, Thomas M. N. *Oconaluftee Indian Village: An Interpretation of a Cherokee Community of 1750*. Cherokee Historical Association, 1954.

Linley, John. *Architecture of Middle Georgia: The Oconee Region*. Athens: University of Georgia Press, 1972.

Little, Vance T. *The Hunts of Tennessee*. Nashville: Vec El Ancestral Studies, 1969.

Littlefield, Daniel. *Africans and Creeks*. Westport: Greenwood Press, 1979.

Lumpkin, Katherine Du Pre. *The Making of a Southerner*. New York: Alfred A. Knopf, 1947.

Lunceford, Alvin Mell, Jr. *Taliaferro County Georgia, Records and Notes*. Spartanburg, S.C.: Reprint Co., 1988.

McMurry, Linda O. *George Washington Carver, Scientist and Symbol*. New York: Oxford University Press, 1981.

Mencke, John G. *Mulattoes and Race Mixture: American Attitudes and Images, 1865–1918*. Ann Arbor, Mich.: UMI Research Press, 1976.

Mills, Lane. *Architecture of the Old South: Georgia*. Savannah: Beehive Press, 1986.

Mohr, Clarence L. *On the Threshold of Freedom: Masters and Slaves in Civil War Georgia*. Athens: University of Georgia Press, 1986.

Mooney, James. "Myths of the Cherokee." In Bureau of American Ethnology, *Nineteenth Annual Report, 1897–98*. Washington, D.C.: Government Printing Office.

Nathans, Elizabeth Studley. *Losing the Peace: Georgia Republicans and Reconstruction, 1865–1871*. Baton Rouge: Louisiana State University Press, 1968.

Nichols, Frederick Doveton. *The Architecture of Georgia*. Savannah: Beehive Press, 1976.

Norwood, Martha F. *Liberty Hall: Taliaferro County, Georgia*. Atlanta: Georgia Department of Natural Resources, 1977.

Owsley, Frank. *Plain Folk of the Old South*. Baton Rouge: Louisiana State University Press, 1949.

Perdue, Theda. *Slavery and the Evolution of Cherokee Society, 1540–1866*. Knoxville: University of Tennessee Press, 1979.

Raboteau, Albert. *Slave Religion: The Invisible Institution in the Antebellum South.* New York: Oxford University Press, 1978.

Raper, Arthur F. *Tenants of the Almighty.* New York: Macmillan Co., 1943.

Root, Waverly. *Food.* New York: Simon and Schuster, 1980.

Rouse, Parke, Jr. *The Great Wagon Road from Philadelphia to the South.* New York: McGraw Hill, 1973.

Rozier, John. *Black Boss: Political Revolution in a Georgia County.* Athens: University of Georgia Press, 1982.

Russell, Lester F. *Profile of a Black Heritage.* Franklin Square, N.Y.: Graphicopy, 1977.

Scarborough, Ruth. *The Opposition to Slavery in Georgia Prior to 1860.* Nashville: George Peabody College for Teachers, 1933.

Scott, Ann Firor. *The Southern Lady: From Pedestal to Politics, 1830–1930.* Chicago: University of Chicago Press, 1970.

Shick, Tom W. *Emigrants to Liberia 1820–1843: An Alphabetical Listing.* Newark: Department of Anthropology, University of Delaware, 1971.

Shivers, Forrest. *The Land Between: A History of Hancock County, Georgia to 1940.* Spartanburg, S.C.: Reprint Co., 1990.

Smith, Elizabeth Wiley. *The History of Hancock County.* 2 Vols. Washington, Ga.: Wilkes Publishing Co., 1974.

Southerland, Henry DeLeon, and Jerry Elijah Brown. *The Federal Road through Georgia, the Creek Nation, and Alabama, 1806–1836.* Tuscaloosa: University of Alabama Press, 1989.

Spalding, Henry D., ed. *Encyclopedia of Black Folklore and Humor.* Middle Valley, N.Y.: Jonathan David Publishers, 1972.

Spruill, Julia Cherry. *Women's Life and Work in the Southern Colonies.* 1938. Reprint, New York: W. W. Norton and Co., 1972.

Starkey, Marion Lena. *The Cherokee Nation.* New York: Russell and Russell, 1946.

Swanton, John Reed. *Indians of the South Eastern United States.* Bulletin no. 137, Smithsonian Institution, Bureau of American Ethnology. Washington, D.C.: Government Printing Office, 1946.

————. *Social Organization and Social Usages of the Indians of the Creek Confederation.* Smithsonian Institution, Bureau of American Ethnology, 42nd Annual Report. Washington, D.C.: Government Printing Office, 1928.

Thompson, C. Mildred. *Reconstruction in Georgia: Economic, Social, Political 1865–1872.* New York: Columbia University Press, 1915.

Torrence, Ridgely. *The Story of John Hope.* New York: Macmillan Co., 1948.

Trelease, Allen W. *White Terror: The Ku Klux Klan Conspiracy and Southern Reconstruction.* New York: Harper and Row, 1976.

Wallenstein, Peter. *Slave South to New South.* Chapel Hill: University of North Carolina Press, 1987.

White, Deborah Gray. *Ar'n't I a Woman? Female Slaves in the Plantation South.* New York: W. W. Norton and Co., 1985.

Wilhoit, Virginia Hill. *History of Warren County.* WPA Project no. 4341, 1939.

Williamson, Joel. *New People: Miscegenation and Mulattoes in the United States.* New York: Free Press, 1980.

Woodson, Carter G. *Free Negro Heads of Families in the United States 1830, Together with a Brief Treatment of the Free Negro.* Washington, D.C.: Association for the Study of Negro Life and History, 1925.

———. *Free Negro Owners of Slaves in 1830.* 1925. Westport: Negro Universities Press, 1968.

Works Progress Administration. *Georgia: A Guide to Its Towns and Countryside.* American Guide Series. Athens: University of Georgia Press, 1940.

Secondary Sources: Articles from Journals and Periodicals

Alexander, Adele Logan. "Grandmother, Grandfather, W. E. B. Du Bois and Booker T. Washington." *Crisis* 73 (February 1983): 8–11.

———. "How I Discovered My Grandmother, and theTruth about Black Women and the Suffrage Movement." *Ms.* (November 1983): 29–33.

Blassingame, John W. "Using the Testimony of Ex-Slaves: Approaches and Problems." *Journal of Southern History* 41 (November 1975): 473–92.

Bonner, James C. "Genesis of Agricultural Reform in the Cotton Belt." *Journal of Southern History* 9 (Fall 1943): 475–500.

———. "A Georgia County's Historical Assets." *Emory University Quarterly* 9 (March 1953): 24–30.

———. "Profile of a Late Ante-Bellum Community." *The American Historical Review* 49 (July 1944)

Bryant, Jonathan M. "Race, Class and Law in Bourbon Georgia: The Case of David Dickson's Will." *Georgia Historical Quarterly* 71 (Summer 1987): 226–42.

Drago, Edmund L. "Militancy and Black Women in Reconstruction Georgia." *Journal of American Culture* 1 (Winter 1978): 840–50.

Du Bois, W. E. B. "The Significance of Henry Hunt." *The Fort Valley State College Bulletin: Founder's and Annual Report* 1 (October 1940): 5–16.

Flanders, Ralph B. "The Free Negro in Ante-Bellum Georgia." *North Carolina Historical Review* 9 (July 1932): 250–72.

Hagler, D. Harland. "The Ideal Woman in the Antebellum South: Lady or Farmwife?" *Journal of Southern History* 46 (August 1980): 405–18.

Horne, Frank. "Henry A. Hunt, Sixteenth Spingarn Medalist." *Crisis* 20 (August 1930): 261.

Horton, James Oliver. "Gender Conventions among Antebellum Free Blacks." *Feminist Studies* 12 (Spring 1986): 51–75.

Parkhurst, Jesse W. "The Role of the Black Mammy in the Plantation Household." *Journal of Negro History* 23 (July 1938): 349–69.

Pendleton, E. M. "On the Vital Statistics of Hancock County, Georgia." *Journal of Southern Medicine.* 1850.

Sterling, A. C. "Sewing Up Hearts, Dr. Myra Logan Wins Them, Too." New York *Compass,* September 17, 1952.

Swados, Felice. "Negro Health on the Antebellum Plantation." *Bulletin of the History of Medicine* 10 (1941): 460–72.

Toplin, Robert Brent. "Between Black and White: Attitudes toward Southern Mulattoes, 1830–1861." *Journal of Southern History* 45 (May 1979): 179.

Walker, Clarence A. "The A.M.E. Church and Reconstruction." *Negro History Bulletin* 48, no. 1 (Winter 1985): 10–12.

Federal Government Documents, Proceedings and Reports

Fifth Census, or Enumeration of the Inhabitants of the United States, 1830. Washington, D.C.: Duff Green, 1832.

U.S. Bureau of Freedmen and Abandoned Lands, Record Group 105, 1865–1870. Files of the Superintendent of Education for the State of Georgia. National Archives.

U.S. Census Office, *Statistical View of the United States,* Seventh Census. Washington D.C.: A.O.P. Nicholson, 1854.

U.S. Congress. *Testimony Taken by the Joint Select Committee to Inquire into the Condition of Affairs in the Late Insurrectionary States.* Washington, D.C.: Government Printing Office, 1872.

U.S. Department of Commerce, Bureau of the Census. Fourth Census (1820) for Greene, Hancock, Warren, and Washington counties, Georgia. Fifth (1830), Sixth, (1840), and Seventh (1850) Censuses for Baldwin, Greene, Hancock, Putnam, Taliaferro, Warren, and Washington counties, Georgia. Eighth (1860), Ninth (1870) and Tenth (1880) Censuses, for Baldwin, Bibb, Clarke, Glascock, Greene, Hancock, Putnam, Richmond, Taliaferro, Warren, and Washington counties, Georgia. Also slave schedules, 1850 and 1860; agricultural schedules, 1850, 1860, and 1870; and mortaliity schedules, 1870 and 1880.

———. *Negro Population of the United States, 1790–1915.* Washington, D.C.: Government Printing Office, 1918.

U.S. Southern Claims Commission Files for Georgia. Claims of Mary Frazier and Currell and John Ross.

Georgia Records and Documents

Acts and Resolutions of the General Assembly of the State of Georgia. 1871–79.

Acts of the General Assembly of the State of Georgia. 1799–1870.

Atlanta. City Directories, 1875–90.

Charlton, T. U. P. *Georgia Reports.* Atlanta: Franklin Turner Co., 1907.

Clayton, Augustus Smith. *A Compilation of the Laws of the State of Georgia, Passed by the Legislature Since the Political Year 1800, to the Year 1810, Inclusive.* Augusta: Adams and Duyckinck, 1813.

Digest of the Laws of the State of Georgia, 1755 to 1800, Inclusive. Savannah: Seymour, Woolhopter and Stebbins, 1802.

Governors' Correspondence, GDAH.

Journals of the House of Representatitives for the State of Georgia. Milledgeville: Polhill and Fort, 1833.

Journals of the Senate of the State of Georgia. Milledgeville: Polhill and Fort, 1829, 1830, 1838, 1842, 1843.

Lamar, Lucius Q. C. *A Compilation of the Laws of the State of Georgia, Passed by the Legislature Since the Year 1810 to the Year 1819, Inclusive.* Augusta. T. S. Hannon, 1821.

Legislative Correspondence, Incoming, 1870, GDAH.

Prince, Oliver. *A Digest of the Laws of the State of Georgia.* Milledgeville: Grantland and Orne, 1822.

Reports of Cases in Law and Equity Argued and Defended in the Supreme Court of the State of Georgia. Vols. 4–73 (1848–84).

Vanishing Georgia Collection, Baldwin, Greene, Hancock, Jones, Putnam, Taliaferro, Warren, and Washington Counties. GDAH.

Watkins, George and Robert. *A Digest of the Laws of the State of Georgia from Its First Establishment as a British Province Down to the Year 1798 Inclusive.* Philadelphia: R. Aitken, 1800.

County Records

BALDWIN COUNTY RECORDS, GDAH

Registries of Free Persons of Color, 1833–63

Trials of Slaves, 1812–26.

Will Books.

Deeds and Mortgages.

GREENE COUNTY RECORDS, GDAH

Will Books.

Hancock County Manuscripts, GDAH

Free Persons of Color, 1855–62.
Inferior Court Records, 1843–50.
Planters' Club Records.
Presbyterian Church Records.
Sparta Female Model School, catalogue, 1838.
Store Accounts.
Superior Court Records and Minutes, 1846–63.
Tax Digests, 1794, 1853, 1882.
Thomas, James. Correspondence.

Hancock County Courthouse Records

Cemetery Records
Deeds and Mortgages Books.
Probate Court Records re David Dickson's Will, March 1885
Will, inventory, and other documents pursuant to final settlement, James M.
     Hunt, 1879–90.
Will and Inventory of Judkins Hunt, 1810–19.
Will and Inventory of Nathan C. Sayre, 1850–68.
Will and Inventory of Nelly (Sayre) Watkins, 1874.

Putnam County Records, GDAH and Courthouse

Inferior Court Records, Trials of Slaves.
Will Books.

Taliaferro County Records, GDAH

Registry of Free Persons of Color, 1829–57
Trials of Free Persons of Color, 1857–58.

Warren County Records, GDAH

Crooked Creek Primitive Baptist Church Records.
General Index of Warren County.
Rural Cabinet, selected undated issues.

Washington County Records, County Courthouse

Inferior Court Minutes.

Unpublished Materials

African-American Family History Association. "Slave Bill of Sales Project."
N.d., n.p.

Brinson, Lessie Brannen. "A Study of the Life and Works of Richard Malcolm
Johnston." Ph.D. diss., George Peabody College for Teachers, Nashville,
Tenn., 1937.

Burnham, Margaret A. "An Impossible Marriage: Slave Law and Family Law."
The Mary Bunting Insitute of Radcliffe College, Cambridge, Mass., August
1986.

Daughters of the American Colonists. "Bible Genealogical Records,
1937–1939."

Gaissert, Margarette Goldsby. "Some Church Members and Records and Some
History of Some Hancock County Georgia Churches." Sparta, Ga., 1982.

Gifford, James Maurice. "The African Colonization Movement in Georgia,
1817–1860." Ph.D. diss., University of Georgia, 1977.

Lane, Lois W. "A History of Flagg Chapel Baptist Church, Milledgeville,
Georgia." Photocopy.

Leslie, Kent Anderson. "Amanda America Dickson." Seminar paper, Emory
University, 1984.

———. "Woman of Color, Daughter of Privilege: Amanda America Dickson,
1849–1893." Ph.D. diss., Emory University, 1990.

Otto, Rhea Cumming. "1850 Census of Georgia, Hancock County." N.d.

Shivers, Forrest. "The Land Between: A History of Hancock County, Georgia
to 1940." Manuscript, 1988.

Sweat, Edward Forrest. "The Free Negro in Antebellum Georgia." Ph.D. diss.,
University of Indiana, 1957.

Newspapers and Periodicals, Selected Issues

American Missionary.
Blade, The. Athens, Ga.
Central Georgian. Sandersville, Ga.
Chronicle. Augusta, Ga.
Colored American. Augusta, Ga.
Daily Intelligencer. Atlanta, Ga.
Georgian. Savannah, Ga.
Hancock Advertiser. Mount Zion, Ga.
Ishmaelite. Sparta, Ga.

Loyal Georgian. Augusta, Ga.
Messsenger, The. Macon, Ga.
Missionary, The. Mount Zion, Ga.
Southern Recorder. Milledgeville, Ga.
Times and Planter. Sparta, Ga.
Union and Recorder. Milledgeville, Ga.

Archives and Personal Papers

Alexander, Adele Logan. Private photographs and papers.

Anthony, Susan B., and Rachel Avery Papers. University of Rochester. Rochester, N.Y.

Catalogs and Bulletins of Atlanta University. Atlanta University Department of Archives and Special Collections, Woodruff Library, Atlanta, Ga.

Daughters of the American Revolution, Archives. Membership Papers for Descendents of Capt. Judkins Hunt. Washington, D.C.

Exum, Sarah Milam. Private papers. Leslie, Ga.

Freedmen and Southern Society Research Project, University of Maryland, College Park, Md.

Silvers, Arthur. Private photographs and papers. Santa Fe, N.M..

Ware, E. A. Papers. Atlanta University Department of Archives and Special Collections, Woodruff Library. Atlanta, Ga.

Oral Accounts

Bonner, James C. March 1983. Milledgeville, Ga.

Bracken, Rowena Hunt. December 1983. Tuskegee, Ala.

Gaissert, John. March 1983. Sparta, Ga.

Hight, Jimmy. June 1987. Sparta, Ga.

Hunt, Charity. April 1983 and July 1987. Washington, D.C.

Hunt, Charles. March 1983. Sparta, Ga.

Hunt, Katherine Neal. April 1983 and July 1987. Washington, D.C.

Hunt, Louie. March, 1983. Sparta, Ga

Hunt, Magnolia. March 1983. Sparta, Ga.

Ingram, Ann. October 1984. College Park, Md.

Kimbrough, Jesse. June 1983. Los Angeles, Cal.

Lee, Kate Dickson. March 1983. Tallahassee, Fla.

Leslie, Virginia Kent Anderson. April 1984 through October 1987. Atlanta, Ga.

Logan, Wenonah Bond. Extended. New York City and Alexandria, Va.

Logan, Louise. Extended. New York City.
Logan, Myra Adele. Extended. New York City.
Lucas, Mae Harper. July 1984. Columbia, Md.
Mayweather, Edna Ruff. June 1990. Sparta, Ga.
McLean, Wanda Hunt. August 1985. Elizabeth City, N.C.
Miller, Houser. March 1983. Fort Valley, Ga.
Poss, Tony. June 1987. Sparta, Ga.
Rozier, John. June 1985, July 1987. Atlanta, Ga.
Shivers, Forrest. June 1985, July 1987. Opelika, Ala.
Silvers, Arthur. February 1983. Santa Fe, N.M.
Snead, Linda. June 1989. East Orange, N.J.
Thomas, Mamie McLendon. November 1982 through September 1987. Chester, Pa.
Turner, Romie. July, 1990. Sparta, Ga.
Walcott, Bess Bolden. December 1983 and June 1985. Tuskegee, Ala.

Index

fathers, 59; as guardians, 80; sexual
behavior of, 26, 53, 64–66; and
women of color, 59, 64–67, 82, 83,
114, 157, 180, 185–88, 190
Anglo-Americans, 4, 6; class distinctions
among, 51; and colonization, 43;
defined, 12; diet of, 145–46; education for, 51, 54, 184; and free people
of color, 36, 45, 57–58, 59, 60, 61,
62, 106, 118, 120–23, 128, 129, 134,
197, 198; gender relations among,
52–53, 83; heritage of, 197; and
Native Americans, 23, 24; and Nat
Turner rebellion, 48; and people of
color, 24, 51, 52, 145, 164–67, 178,
200; racial attitudes of, 28; and slaves,
167-68
Anglo-American women: abuse of, 53;
as "belles," 192; during Civil War,
131, 135–36, 139; complexions of,
79; and domestic sphere, 52, 152;
education of, 54, 74, 76–77; and free
children of color, 57–58, 118, 197;
hair of, 124; of planter class, 8, 84,
86, 115; political exclusion of, 152;
property rights of, 126; during
Reconstruction, 143-44, 145; sexual
behavior of, 64; subordinated, 52–53;
wives' roles among, 83
Antimiscegenation. See Miscegenation
Arson during Civil War, 132, 136
Artisans: free people of color as, 127,
198. See also individual occupations
Ashton, Frances, 55
Athens, Ga., 105, 171, 175
Atlanta, Ga., 134, 154, 175, 176, 183,
189
Atlanta University, 163, 168–75, 188,
194, 195; graduates of, 5, 181; and
Negro Life conferences, 3–5, 13; as
source for African-American history,
11
Augusta, Ga., 18, 41, 80, 165, 168, 174,
188; free people of color in, 32, 105,
127, 128
Autobiography of an Ex-Colored Man, The
(J. W. Johnson), 125, 196
Auxiliary Society for Colonizing the
Free Persons of Color. See American
Colonization Society

Bailey, Tolbert, 173
Baldwin County, Ga., 16, 20, 28, 90, 91,
94, 142, 147, 189; African-American
churches in, 160; African-American
neighborhoods in 153, 154; during
Civil War, 134–37; Freedmen's
Bureau schools in, 164, 166–67; free
people of color in, 34, 35–36, 59–61,
106, 114, 118–19, 120, 132; slaves in
65, 112, 113
Baptists, 53, 60, 110, 159, 184. *See also*
Churches
Barber-Scotia College (North Carolina),
195
Barbers, free people of color as, 56, 59
Barnes, Eli, 147–50
Barnett (Warren County), 173, 175
Bass Academy (Sparta), 168, 175, 176,
193
Bass, W. H., 168, 169
Batte, Henry, 18
Batte, Martha. *See* Hunt, Martha Batte
Battis, Mary Ann, 28, 38
Beall, Thomas E., 91
Beasley, Spencer, 133
Bellamy family, 55, 119, 136, 153. *See
also* Ross family
Bellamy, Mary Ross. *See* Ross, Mary
Bellamy, Robert, 56, 154
Bellamy-Ross family, 56
Bellamy, Valentine, 55, 76,
Beman, Carlisle, 90, 109
Beman, Nathan S. S., 25, 54
Benefield family, 105
Bentley family, 21
Berkeley, University of California at,
196
Biracial: unions, 5; use of term, 12. *See
also* "Indians of the half blood";
Mestizoes; Miscegenation;
Mulattoes; "No-nations"
Bird, Thompson, 45
Bird, Williamson, 45
Black: accurate use of term, 11–12
Black cabinet: Roosevelt's, 194
Blacks. *See* African-Americans, Slaves,
Women of color
Blacksmiths: African-Americans as 155;
free people of color as, 58, 59, 60,
104, 116

Methodist Church, South, 159–61, 164–65, 184

Methodists: African-American, 110, 154; Anglo-American, 53. *See also* African Methodist Episcopal Church; African Methodist Episcopal Zion Church; Methodist Church, South

Middle Class: African-American, 153–54, 181, 199

Middle Georgia, 11, 200, 27, 47–48, 130, 142, 183–85; American Colonization Society in, 41–45; economy of, 21, 74; education in, 171; free people of color in, 33–36, 55–62, 197; Native Americans in, 21–25, 27–29, 31; people of color in, 12, 153–57, 200–01; during Reconstruction, 149; religion in, 53, 184; slaves in, 65, 115. *See also* individual counties

Midwives, 57

Milledgeville (Baldwin County), 42, 74, 153, 155, 171, 181, 183; Atlanta University students from, 173, 174; during Civil War, 135–38; free people of color in, 60–61, 100, 105; Moravian mission near, 28; and Nat Turner rebellion, 49; during Reconstruction, 144–45, 147, 155; Sayre property in, 73; school for freedpeople in, 164, 166–67; as state capital, 20

Milledgeville and Eatonton Railway, 154

Millie (free woman of color), 40

Milly (slave of Thomas Cobb), 40

Mims, David, 33

Ministers: African-American, 4, 49, 60, 154, 155, 181, 189; free people of color as, 198; and interracial marriages, 87; moral positions of, 53. *See also* Churches; Clergy

Miscegenation, 64, 88, 89, 123–24, 174–75, 187; American Colonization Society opposes, 44; Jefferson's views on, 26; prohibited, 99, 103, 121, 152–53; Union soldiers comment on, 134

Missionary (Mount Zion), 25, 29, 30, 42, 44, 47, 54

Missions, 24, 28, 29

Missouri, 99

Mistresses: women of color as, 80, 82–83, 86–87, 93. *See also* Concubinage; *Plaçage*

Montgomery (freighter), 44

Moore, Ellen, 171

Moragne, Mary, 68, 73, 77–80, 85

Moravian missions, 24, 28

Moses (slave of the first Judkins and Martha Batte Hunt), 19, 39–40

Moss family, 33, 56, 59, 104

Moss, Mary, 114

Mount Zion (Hancock County), 16, 23, 98, 151, 176, 177; church at, 53–54, 162; free people of color at, 56; Hunts at, 28–29, 38, 45, 63, 95, 107, 109–11, 152, 159; Sayres at, 45, 63; schools at, 54, 166

Mount Zion Dots (baseball team), 159

Mulattoes: 10, 24, 36, 38, 59, 60, 63–64, 65, 69, 78, 80, 83, 84, 86, 88, 93, 103, 111, 113, 114, 115, 118, 120, 128, 151–52, 154, 181, 189, 190, 199; at Atlanta University, 174–75; as free people of color, 33, 105; as slaves, 113; social status of, 161, 179

Multiracial: use of term, 12

Municipal employees, 155

Murder, 35, 117

Murray, George, 91

Music, 77–80, 85, 86, 90, 109, 129, 158

Mustizo, 58

Myrick, S. P., 60–61

Nan (slave of the first Judkins Hunt), 39

Nancy (free woman of color), 45

Nancy (slave of Peter Ray), 74

Native Americans: diet, 145; and free people of color, 38, 118, 197; and the law, 36; pharmacology of, 31, 72; racial attitudes of, 28; removal of, 22, 26; and settlers, 19, 22–30; and slaves, 23; on Southern frontier, 8, 26; women among, 27–28. *See also* Cherokee Indians; Creek Indians

Negro: defined in Georgia, 100, 122, 152; use of term, 11. *See also* African-Americans; Mulattoes; Slaves

"Negro Life" conferences at Atlanta University, 4